Virtual Reality Therapy
for Anxiety Disorders

Virtual Reality Therapy
for Anxiety Disorders

ADVANCES IN EVALUATION AND TREATMENT

Brenda K. Wiederhold
and Mark D. Wiederhold

AMERICAN PSYCHOLOGICAL ASSOCIATION

WASHINGTON, DC

Published by
American Psychological Association
750 First Street, NE
Washington, DC 20002
www.apa.org

To order
APA Order Department
P.O. Box 92984
Washington, DC 20090-2984
Tel: (800) 374-2721; Direct: (202) 336-5510
Fax: (202) 336-5502; TDD/TTY: (202) 336-6123
Online: www.apa.org/books/
E-mail: order@apa.org

In the U.K., Europe, Africa, and the Middle East, copies may be ordered from
American Psychological Association
3 Henrietta Street
Covent Garden, London
WC2E 8LU England

Typeset in Meridien and Frutiger by World Composition Services, Inc., Sterling, VA

Printer: Sheridan Books, Ann Arbor, MI
Cover Designer: Berg Design, Albany, NY
Technical/Production Editor: Gail B. Munroe

The opinions and statements published are the responsibility of the authors, and such opinions and statements do not necessarily represent the policies of the American Psychological Association.

Library of Congress Cataloging-in-Publication Data

Wiederhold, B. K.
    Virtual reality therapy for anxiety disorders : advances in evaluation and treatment / by Brenda K. Wiederhold, and Mark D. Wiederhold.—1st ed.
        p. cm.
    Includes bibliographical references and index.
    ISBN 1-59147-031-5
    1. Anxiety—Treatment. 2. Virtual reality therapy. I. Wiederhold, Mark D. II. Title.

    RC531.W477 2004
    616.85'220651—dc22   2004005419

British Library Cataloguing-in-Publication Data
A CIP record is available from the British Library.

Printed in the United States of America
First Edition

Contents

PREFACE *vii*

I

OVERVIEW

1 Introduction: The Impact of Anxiety Disorders 3

2 A Brief History of Virtual Reality Technology 11

II

VIRTUAL REALITY AND ANXIETY DISORDERS: A USER'S GUIDE

3 Anxiety Disorders and Their Treatment 31

4 How Treatment Is Conducted at the Virtual Reality Medical Center 47

5 Side Effects and Contraindications 63

6 The Effect of Presence on Virtual Reality Treatment 77

7 Ethical Considerations 87

III

TREATMENT OF SPECIFIC ANXIETY DISORDERS

8 Panic Disorder and Agoraphobia 95

9 Obsessive–Compulsive Disorder 111

10 Posttraumatic Stress Disorder 117

11 Specific Phobias and Social Phobia 125

12 Aviophobia 139

13 Fear of Driving 147

14 Acrophobia 157

15 Claustrophobia   165

16 Arachnophobia   173

17 Fear of Medical Procedures   181

IV

CONCLUSION

18 Final Comments and Future Directions   191

REFERENCES   *197*

INDEX   *219*

ABOUT THE AUTHORS   *225*

Preface

nitial concepts for using virtual reality as an adjunct for mental health care treatment were apparently conceived over a decade ago. Its actual clinical use began in 1993. Since that time, those involved in the research and development of virtual environments have been very cautious not to "hype" the results and oversell the technology. What is clear, however, is that virtual reality and simulation work very well in the treatment of specific phobias. However, we must remember that virtual reality is only a tool. A therapist must first possess good clinical skills and an expertise in treating anxiety disorders and then learn to implement the virtual reality tool as part of established clinical practices.

We have been interested in using advanced technology for health care for the past two decades. Mark was a founding member of a group of explorers and entrepreneurs that started the Medicine Meets Virtual Reality annual conference. This conference was very instrumental in bringing together individuals who have significantly advanced the use of simulation for surgical training and operative procedural planning. In the mid-1990s the mental health interest group started by Brenda led to a specific section on mental health applications, which resulted in a spin-off conference, CyberTherapy. In 2004 it attracted 150 individuals from around the world, and it will be held internationally for the first time in June 2005 in Switzerland.

We began treating patients with virtual reality in the mid-1990s. The first systems were clunky and temperamental, and they always made the therapy session an adventure.

Our initial impressions that "this couldn't possibly work" very soon evolved into an appreciation for the utility of simulation technologies. We soon began trolling auto junkyards, flea markets, and airplane salvage yards as we began to construct "augmented reality environments" where a patient who is being treated for fear of flying would actually sit in a real airline seat, with seatbelt securely fastened. Our primary interest is using and developing low cost systems that have the potential for wide adoption by the healthcare community. Fortunately advances in computer technology have made this a reality.

The writing of this book has been an exciting journey that has allowed us to gaze back into the historical roots of virtual reality and ponder future directions. In our search to be as thorough and comprehensive as we could, we have uncovered new researchers and new studies of which we previously were unaware. Our goal has been to share the knowledge we have gleaned and help other clinicians make an informed decision on virtual reality's importance in their clinical practice or research setting. There are clearly still technical issues to be considered as well as cost concerns; in our practice, however, we have seen the benefits outweigh the costs.

We thank our editorial assistant, Ruth Kogen, for her help in keeping us going when the book was almost complete but needed a final push. We are particularly indebted to our patients who have provided invaluable feedback and taught us much about how to best use these tools. We also thank Judy Nemes at the American Psychological Association for being a pleasure to work with during this entire process. Our colleagues and those who share our vision are too numerous to name here. We would, however, like to give a special thanks to Alex Bullinger, Stéphane Bouchard, Walter Greenleaf, Hunter Hoffman, Sun Kim, Giuseppe Riva, and Skip Rizzo, who have provided invaluable feedback during the writing of this book and in our virtual reality research over the past eight years. The virtual reality community is a truly international group of talented and dedicated individuals. One of the most enjoyable aspects in writing this book has been the discovery of both important cultural differences in how virtual reality is used and how it affects patients. At the same time, we have gained an understanding of the universality of the successful applications of this technology. Although we have attempted to be thorough, we most likely have overlooked some important work. Please feel free to contact us, so that we may include your information in the second edition of this book.

We hope you will find the information contained in this book to be of value, and we hope this will translate into more effective treatments for those who suffer from anxiety disorders. We dedicate this book to our patients, who continue to teach us.

I
Overview

Introduction: The Impact of Anxiety Disorders

1

For many people, the sound of a seatbelt clicking into place feels as though the door has clanged shut on their jail cell. They feel strangled, as though they are trapped and death is imminent. Many people experience symptoms like these on a daily basis. Often, these feelings may seem unfounded and irrational, even to those who have these symptoms of anxiety. Family members might notice that one of their own is distressed or secretive. Anxious individuals may have trouble at work or school or withdraw from enjoyable activities. Conflicts often arise because of these changes or the anxious person's inability to complete tasks that he or she was able to formerly. All of these changes may be caused by an anxiety disorder.

One difficulty in treating anxiety disorders may arise because patients are too frightened to go through treatment. It might be too difficult for them to leave the house or even to talk to a stranger. Frequently these disorders worsen with time and lack of treatment. It is important for those who have an anxiety disorder to know that treatments are available and that they are not alone in their struggle.

Prevalence and Economic Costs of Anxiety Disorders

Anxiety disorders are the most common mental health disorders in America, the fifth most common diagnosis in primary care in America and the most common psychiatric diagnosis (DiBartolo, Hofmann, & Barlow, 1995). Twenty-three million Americans will experience an anxiety disorder in their lifetimes. Moreover, 33% of patients presenting with chest pain, abdominal pain, or insomnia actually have an anxiety disorder, as do 25% of those with fatigue, headache, or joint or limb pain (Sherman, 1997a). Specific phobias, one type of anxiety disorder, are more common than alcohol abuse, alcohol dependence, and major depression. The average person with an anxiety disorder has 10 encounters with the health care system before being correctly diagnosed, increasing health care costs and causing frustration on the part of both the patient and physician. Women, individuals under age 45, separated and divorced persons, and those in lower socioeconomic groups have the highest incidence of anxiety disorders. Unfortunately, these individuals are often least able to afford treatment (Regier, Narrow, & Rae, 1990).

With the advent of managed care and health care reform, clinicians are increasingly being pressured to become more efficient in treating their clients. Each year $113 billion is spent on mental health treatment in the United States (Rice & Miller, 1998). Of this amount, $47 billion is spent on the treatment of anxiety disorders, by far the largest chunk of mental health care dollars (DuPont et al., 1996).

In 1997, anxiety disorders accounted for an estimated $15 billion in direct costs, such as medical, administrative, and research costs, and $50 billion in indirect costs, including lost or reduced productivity, illness, and death (Sobel & Ornstein, 1997).

Treatment of Anxiety Disorders

A large-scale study by Goisman et al. (1993) compared different patterns for the treatment of anxiety disorders including the following methods: behavioral (relaxation, exposure, modeling and role-play), cognitive (thought stopping, mental distraction, thought recording), medication, psychodynamic, family therapy, and biofeedback. This study confirmed the findings of earlier studies, namely that behavioral treatments for anxiety disorders are underused even though research has proven their efficacy for treating these types of disorders (Goisman et al., 1993). Moreover, the most common behavioral techniques used, relaxation and imaginal exposure, are less effective than in vivo exposure. Furthermore, all behavioral techniques were used less frequently than psychodynamic psychotherapy, a modality that is of unproven efficacy in the treatment of anxiety disorders. Medications were also used more frequently than behavioral interventions and often in concert with other treatments despite evidence that medications may impair the effect of behavioral treatments.

Goisman et al.'s study confirms that wider dissemination of behavioral methods for the treatment of anxiety disorders is merited. It is possible that in vivo exposure is under-used because it is generally inconvenient and expensive. This technique often requires that therapists accompany patients into anxiety-provoking situations in the real world at great cost to the patient and with great time expenditure on the part of both therapist and patient. A further complication with in vivo exposure is that severely anxious or phobic patients may be unwilling or resistant to the intensity of in vivo exposure. Virtual reality (VR) technology offers a means by which therapists can provide in-office exposure therapy to anxiety patients, thus mitigating many of the complications of in vivo exposure. Given that in vivo exposure is one of the most powerful treatments available, VR-enhanced psychotherapy (also called *virtual reality graded exposure therapy* or VRGET) could offer practitioners an additional treatment tool.

Virtual Reality Treatment for Anxiety Disorders

VR is a new technology that alters the way individuals interact with computers. It can be defined as a set of computer technologies that, when combined, provide an interface to a computer-generated world. VR provides such a convincing interface that users believe they are actually present in a three-dimensional world. A virtual environment lets users navigate and interact with the three-dimensional computer-generated (and computer-maintained) world in real time where their actions and reactions are experienced in the present moment.

USE OF VIRTUAL REALITY IN CLINICAL SETTINGS

Virtual environments have begun to attract much attention in clinical medicine. Until recently, the application of VR in mental health was severely limited by the lack of inexpensive, easy-to-maintain, and easy-to-use personal computer (PC)-based systems. The high-powered and very expensive computational systems that had previously been required by VR technology were out of reach for most practicing mental health professionals. The development of user-friendly PC-based VR platforms is now helping to attract the interest of clinicians, and ongoing research projects are providing results that buttress the efficacy of VR in behavioral therapy.

Areas in which VR techniques have been successful include the treatment of specific phobias (such as fear of public speaking, fear of flying, fear of driving, fear of heights, and claustrophobia), neuropsychological evaluation and testing, distraction during painful medical procedures, and eating disorders. Well over 400 publications from at least 35 centers around the world are devoted to these areas. Early results seem to indicate that VR treatments are not only effective but have many advantages over conventional therapies, such as a lower cost and greater privacy (Wiederhold, Irving, Israel, et al., 2002). In general, this application makes intuitive sense in that it is another form of exposure therapy. Before a wider acceptance of this new technology occurs, however, it is crucial that clinical trials and comparison of outcomes are more widely published and evaluated by peer-review groups.

VIRTUAL REALITY IN THE TREATMENT OF ANXIETY DISORDERS

Three types of exposure therapy form the basic psychotherapeutic approach to treating specific phobias: systematic desensitization, in vivo, and imaginal exposure. Joseph Wolpe formally introduced systematic desensitization in 1958. This technique involves pairing relaxation with imagined situations that the patient has indicated cause anxious feelings. In vivo exposure involves having the patient confront the actual real-life phobic situation. Imaginal exposure involves having the patient visualize the phobic situation using mental imagery. One weakness found in some exposure therapies is that many patients using systematic desensitization and imaginal exposure appear to have difficulty imagining the prescribed anxiety-evoking scene (Kosslyn, Brunn, Cave, & Wallach, 1984). In addition, Marks and O'Sullivan (1988) found that approximately 25% of patients drop out of treatment because they are too afraid to face the threatening phobic object.

VRGET addresses some of the weaknesses of in vivo and imaginal exposure therapies. VRGET can provide stimuli for patients who have difficulty imagining scenes or are too phobic to experience real-life situations. Unlike in vivo exposure, VRGET can be performed within the privacy of a therapist's office, thus avoiding public embarrassment and violation of patient privacy. VRGET can generate stimuli of much greater magnitude than standard imaginal and in vivo techniques in situations such as car crashes or violent flight turbulence. Because VRGET is under the control of both patient and therapist, it appears to be safer than in vivo desensitization and has the merit of being more realistic than imaginal desensitization. Finally, VRGET has the further advantage of greater efficiency and economy. The ability to control an artificial environment and to introduce a predetermined set of stimuli or challenges can, in theory, parallel the standard model of office-based psychotherapy. The additional capabilities that are inherent in virtual worlds can lead to greater creativity and flexibility in exploring and understanding a patient's individual problems, concerns, and underlying health-related issues.

In terms of cost, traditional treatments of anxiety disorders often use physiological monitoring systems that are comparable to the cost of a VR system. One of the most commonly used physiological monitoring systems costs approximately $3,700 (J & J Engineering, Poulsbo, Washington). Another widely used system costs $8,400 (Thought Technology, Montreal, Canada). Given the typical monetary and time expenditure associated with treating anxiety disorders, investing between $5,000 and $20,000 in a VR system is not necessarily prohibitive.

Goals and Contents of This Book

The main goal of this book is to provide information on the applicability of VR to the treatment of anxiety disorders. We explain what VR is, what type of technology it involves, and how it is applied in clinical practice. We also describe practical, hands-on strategies and interventions designed to guide therapists through each step of the treatment process for each of the specific anxiety disorders.

The book begins with an overview of VR and its clinical applications for treating anxiety disorders. The remainder of the book is divided into three parts.

Part I, which includes this chapter and chapter 2, explains VR as a technology. In chapter 2, after providing a brief history of VR, its early development, and how it entered into clinical use, we introduce the concept of "presence" and describe the hardware and software involved and the different systems that are available.

Part II (chaps. 3–7) is intended as a user's guide to help clinicians understand how VR is implemented in the treatment of anxiety disorders. Chapter 3 discusses various kinds of anxiety disorders and discusses risk factors, medical morbidities, theories about anxiety, measurements of anxiety, and the various treatments of anxiety disorders. These treatments include VRGET, an alternative to traditional exposure therapy. Chapter 4 addresses the question of how to incorporate VR into clinical practice, delineating the steps of using VRGET to treat patients. This chapter also highlights the unique advantages that VR brings to the clinical arena. Chapter 5 focuses on guidelines for conducting VRGET and discusses cybersickness, side effects, and medical and psychological contraindications and other concerns about VR therapy. Chapter 6 addresses how to evaluate the effectiveness of VR systems and treatment outcomes. This chapter also includes a more in-depth discussion of presence and the effect of presence levels on the efficacy of treatment. Chapter 7 discusses some ethical issues relevant to using VR in clinical settings. As with any new form of treatment, issues arise about clinical competency and assessment of progress. Although many of the ethical issues concerning traditional forms of therapy apply to VR treatments, this chapter also discusses issues that are unique to VR therapy.

Part III (chaps. 8–17) is devoted to the treatment of specific anxiety disorders. After a brief introduction, the chapters are arranged from the more generalized disorders to the more specific phobias. Differences in the length of these chapters reflect the ease with which these disorders lend themselves to VRGET and the amount of research and clinical work that has been completed in these areas. Chapters 8 through 17 present treatment issues related to the following specific anxiety disorders: panic disorder and agoraphobia, social phobia, obsessive–compulsive disorder (OCD), posttraumatic stress disorder (PTSD), aviophobia (fear of flying), fear of driving, acrophobia (fear of heights), claustrophobia, arachnophobia, and fear of medical procedures.

The final chapter discusses the state of current research and future directions. It provides comments about the outlook for therapeutic VR applications in the future. An appendix provides a resource list as well as a listing of the various measurement tools used in the assessment of both general anxiety and the specific phobias.

A Brief History of Virtual Reality Technology 2

Virtual reality (VR) technology evolved through investments by the federal government, the U.S. Air Force, NASA, and more recently by the entertainment industry. VR was prefigured in a commercial version of a primitive immersive multimedia system developed by Morton Heilig in 1956. In Heilig's Sensorama simulation device, remarkable for its time, the user would be taken on a three-dimensional motorcycle ride complete with stereo sound, engine vibrations, smells (such as gasoline or food), and the sensation of motion augmented by air movement over the face (Heilig, 1962). Today this technique would be called "augmented" or "mixed" reality, because the combination of multiple stimuli with various sensory inputs greatly increases the experience of "presence" or immersion in the simulation.

Judith Maloney (1997) of the Rhode Island School of Design published a detailed history of the development of simulation environments. In this fascinating article, she traced the development of current entertainment complexes to public exhibits in the early 1800s. In the earliest forms of "simulation," viewers were seated in a room while circular painted walls of exotic locales were slowly turned, creating a sense of motion. Later music and sound effects were introduced, enhancing the experience. Simulator rides were first developed in the 1900s, combining movement of the viewers on platforms with movement of the panoramic scenes. These were later improved with "props," including sound, smell, and change of lighting to simulate the passage of time.

Later adopted by Disney, simulation rides have become immensely popular and diverse. Las Vegas has several locations that now advertise a group virtual experience. Several large media companies have been exploring the creation of VR theme parks. These commercial developments demonstrate how combinations of multiple stimuli increase the viewer's experience of realism and may help in the construction of virtual worlds for patients.

Up to this point, simulations occurred in groups, which probably helped in "inducing" the believability of these experiences. The ability to have a personalized virtual experience, however, came later with the development of head-mounted display technology. In 1968 Ivan Sutherland developed a head-mounted display that used two cathode ray tubes mounted on a simple headband and included a mechanical tracking system that allowed the user to view three-dimensional wire frame objects. A significant amount of time and investment was necessary to produce dependable, clear, and undistorted images. A high level of realism was approached when, in 1975, NASA contracted with Eric Howlett of LEEP Systems Inc. to produce an optical system that is used in most modern head-mounted displays today (Vince, 1995). The LEEP system produced wide angle three-dimensional stereoscopic images, which made a more immersive experience possible.

In the early 1980s, Myron Krueger became interested in understanding how people interacted with computers and computer-generated images. He developed computer-generated images and new electronic art forms and went on to develop a program (Videoplace; Krueger, 1983) that allowed people to interact and change computer-generated images through bodily movement. Krueger was one of the first to suggest a possible role for VR in the treatment of mental health disorders (Krueger, 1991).

The Media Laboratory at MIT has contributed many new ideas and technologies in the VR arena and was the first to create real-time high quality animation images. In 1985 the NASA Ames Research Center built the Virtual Interactive Environment Workstation, which produced a fully interactive virtual environment (Vince, 1995). The components included computer tracking, three-dimensional audio, stereoscopic digital liquid crystal displays, the data glove for gesture recognition and navigation, and a remote camera. More advanced work was continued at Wright Patterson Air Force Base where a Super Cockpit was built to manage the huge amount of data that a pilot needs to operate an increasingly complex aircraft (Vince, 1995). This was the first effort to understand how to integrate the full cognitive potential of a human operator in a virtual environment.

Until the mid-1980s, VR was available only to those who had large labs and contracts. This changed with the formation of VPL Research, Inc., started in 1984 by Jaron Lanier (Hamilton, 1993). This home garage start-up developed a series of relatively low-cost VR devices that were geared toward the consumer market. Some readers will remember the head-mounted displays and data glove that appeared on the covers of popular magazines. Both *Business Week* and *U.S. News and World Report* featured comprehensive coverage of VR (Hamilton, 1993; Sieder, 1996). VPL also developed Reality Built for Two, which for the first time allowed two users to interact with each other in a virtual world.

In the early 1990s, many smaller VR start-up companies appeared, offering a range of products, many of which were aimed at the consumer market. Several video game companies introduced inexpensive head-mounted displays and data gloves, but the success was short-lived. The consumer market for these devices did not materialize, and the majority of these companies went out of business or were acquired by larger companies. Today a smaller number of companies seem to have achieved a more stable business base and are primarily focused on a few industries and government contract work.

Virtual Reality in the Mental Health Care Setting

Although it is difficult to trace the origin of VR's application to mental health disorders, most people agree that Myron Krueger was one of the first to apply it. Krueger wrote many articles and books that evaluated the human–computer interaction in VR applications and a number of other simulation techniques. In *Artificial Reality II* (1991), Krueger discussed possible applications of VR in psychotherapy and suggested that patients may use the artificial experience in a positive way to overcome an inhibition normally present in "real life." Krueger also pointed out that in some cases patients are more comfortable "talking" or relating to computers, a finding that has been supported in a number of subsequent studies (Joinson, 1999, 2001; Richman, Kiesler, Weisband, & Drasgow, 1999). Krueger suggested that a virtual environment could be used to gradually introduce elements of change, such as human images or different surroundings, during a therapy session. This is probably the first suggestion for using VR for exposure therapy. Showing great foresight, he suggested that the patient and therapist could interact in virtual worlds through a telecommunication-type environment. These technologies are now under development but are not yet commercially available.

In a 1991 interview, Charles Tart recognized that even though the VR images were at that time primitive (animated and cartoonish), the user with a small leap of faith could become immersed in the virtual world and could have a meaningful experience (Bard, 1991). He also noted that some individuals are more apt to become deeply involved with watching television or reading a book and that a correlation between these activities might predict future success in VR. Tart suggested using virtual worlds to help patients recreate past traumas from childhood or other unpleasant experiences. By means of these recreations, the patient, under the therapist's guidance, could develop skills to cope with disturbing memories. He suggested recreating a "frame of mind" that could transform an adult into a child, at which point, underlying memories might become accessible. The vivid nature of VR suggests that this is possible. When experiencing a familiar situation in VR, one may notice memories beginning to resurface, as in other modalities like hypnosis. It seems to allow access to the subconscious. Tart also suggested that VR might be used for stress management, improving relations with others, and enhancing learning experiences.

Ralph Lamson (1997), a mental health researcher, stated that he was able to cure his acrophobia by using a VR system at a new technology exhibition held in 1990 in San Jose. The particular scenario showed a view from a number of tall buildings, similar to what one might encounter in a large metropolitan city. Lamson then used VR therapy to treat 36 students with acrophobia; by the end of therapy, only 10% of the students still met the criteria of the fourth edition of the *Diagnostic and Statistical Manual of Mental Disorders* (*DSM–IV*; American Psychiatric Association, 1994). The results were presented at the Medicine Meets Virtual Reality Conference in San Diego in 1996. Several interesting questions were raised at this conference, including what other phobias might be treated with VR, what possible side effects might ensue, and what special precautions might be required when introducing children to virtual worlds.

As ideas about the application of VR in the mental health care field evolved, Enrico Camara (1993) proposed using VR to treat specific phobias, such as social phobia and agoraphobia, projecting that a gradual desensitization could occur. He also suggested that the therapist accompany the patient into the virtual world to assist in the desensitization process. He queried whether the virtual world could be useful in understanding how schizophrenic individuals process information and see their environment.

In the same year, L. Casey Larijani (1993) suggested using virtual environments for role-playing during therapy. Using VR for role-playing could prove less threatening for some patients and could allow for more flexibility in the scenarios generated. He suggested that VR could be used for behavior modification and that shared virtual worlds could be used in group therapy. Shared environments could also prove useful for social skills training. He also pointed out that the virtual world allows the therapist to control the speed and intensity of the therapeutic process, thereby tailoring the virtual experience to each patient's specific needs.

In the early to mid-1990s, three groups of investigators—Ralph Lamson, Max and Sarah North, and Larry Hodges and Barbara Rothbaum—pioneered the first studies using VR to treat phobias. These efforts led to the formation of several small start-up companies and the publication of two books on VR therapy (Lamson, 1997; North, North, & Coble, 1996b). Two comprehensive reviews of the literature were published in 1996 (Glantz, Durlach, Barnett, & Aviles, 1996; Wiederhold & Wiederhold, 1996), helping to launch the journal *Cyberpsychology and Behavior*, which publishes the proceedings of the Medicine Meets Virtual Reality Conference, Virtual Reality and Mental Health Session, and its offshoot, CyberTherapy.

As the number of clinical trials increased, the sophistication of new virtual worlds, combined with decreasing costs of technology and migration to PC-based platforms, has propelled the field forward. A number of start-up companies now offer complete VR systems for the treatment of fear of flying, driving phobias, fear of heights, social phobia, agoraphobia, panic disorder, PTSD, fear of public speaking, and arachnophobia. These start-ups, together with several groups in Europe and Asia, make up the fledgling VR mental health care product marketplace.

Definitions

VR consists of a three-dimensional computer-generated world or environment where a human being can interface with the environment through a variety of computer peripheral devices, such as head-mounted displays and joysticks. The VR system has five major components: a computational device with a minimum 500 MHz Pentium chip, an advanced computer image graphics card, the virtual environment software program, a tracking device that tells the computer where the user is looking based on head movement (systems are being developed that are able to determine eye movement), and an image display system, such as a large high-resolution digital display or stereoscopic ("shutter") glasses. These systems are configured to display a three-dimensional computer-generated image—a virtual environment—that changes continuously depending on the orientation and gaze of the user. In this way, users "walk" through a building to explore different rooms, turn their heads to look around a virtual airplane cabin and out the window, or navigate in a virtual outdoor environment of streets, buildings, fields, and people.

Because the images must be updated quickly, especially if the user makes sudden head movements, the computing power required is significant. Until recently the only way to view VR images was to have access to a supercomputer and specialized support equipment, software, staff, and facilities associated with it. Virtual environments were initially limited to military and NASA flight simulations, mission training, and tele-presence scenarios. (*Tele-presence scenarios* refer to the ability to remotely or virtually control robotic rovers, such as the Mars lander.) Other VR groups, such as those in large government laboratories, major academic centers, and corporations (many of which were government contractors), were also involved in developing new applications based on supercomputers or powerful workstations. We are fortunate today to have desktop computers that are as powerful as the supercomputers of the early 1990s, making VR simulation available to anyone with at least a 500 MHz PC.

Virtual reality systems are differentiated by their cost and complexity and by how quickly and realistically the supporting computational engine can represent the environment. Immersion in the virtual world is most commonly accomplished by the use of head-mounted displays that project the computer image to the user through an optical system worn as a helmet or as a pair of glasses (see Figure 2.1). These displays also have speakers to channel sound directly from the computer to the wearer. Original VR viewing devices were heavy, expensive, and bulky, and almost all users experienced significant neck and back strain. These have subsequently been replaced with lightweight and relatively inexpensive head-mounted displays. These helmets are familiar to moviegoers from hits such as "The Matrix" and "Lawnmower Man."

Less fully interactive peripherals include large wraparound video screens, which give the viewer an almost 250° panorama or video input projected through a head-mounted display. Neither of these allows the user to manipulate the environment, but they do allow immersion in a scene through three-dimensional imagery.

FIGURE 2.1.

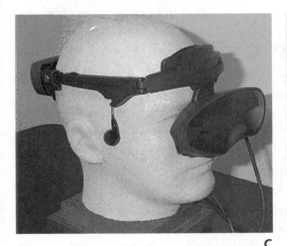

Head-mounted displays currently available for use with commercially available virtual reality software for mental health applications: A. I-glasses with Intertrax tracker. B. Liquid image. C. Sony Glasstron. D. VFX 3D.

PRESENCE

The quality of the user's immersion in the virtual environment, or *presence,* is directly related to the efficacy of the experience. *Presence* refers to a state of being in which the user becomes part of the virtual world. It is an experience wherein the user effectively leaves the "real" world for some period of time and is "present" in the virtual world.

The military had conducted most of the research on the quality of presence because training its personnel for dangerous or exacting work requires realistic images and experiences. One of the most expensive and realistic simulators is used to practice landing a jet on an aircraft carrier where the pilot can negotiate multiple approaches and landings in daylight and nighttime and under a variety of weather conditions. Much of the military research provides useful information on how to construct a high-quality virtual environment that induces high levels of presence in users. However, this research does not address the specific orientation and goals of mental health professionals who wish to use VR in treatment scenarios. Although presence is required for successful treatment, it seems to be achievable with lower definition environments at much lower cost. Presence is discussed in more detail in chapter 7.

VIRTUAL REALITY SYSTEMS

The price and complexity of VR systems vary greatly. High-end systems including the Cave Automatic Virtual Environment (CAVE) and the ImmersaDesk® cost in the $1 to $2 million range. Recently, systems have been designed to run on desktop personal computers; their costs run in the $5,000 to $10,000 range.

PC Systems

Until very recently, a distinction was made between PC-based system and computer "workstations." A workstation usually runs UNIX-based software and functions as a platform for display technology that falls between PC and supercomputer systems. With the advent of the 1.13 MHz Pentium chip, the PC has become powerful enough to handle complex three-dimensional simulations. Most workstation-based systems can now be run on PCs. In general PC-based computers need an upgraded graphics card to display most VR images. The total cost of the upgraded system is around $2,000. (A custom-designed computer can easily be ordered from most computer stores or from on-line suppliers.) Very recently, laptop computers have advanced sufficiently to run some available VR environments.

The VR software described in this book and designed for PC systems is becoming increasingly available, with at least 10 groups around the world developing programs on PC platforms for phobias and anxiety disorders, eating disorders, distraction techniques, and neuro-evaluative and neuro-rehabilitative tools. Available software programs are shown in Table 2.1.

The cost of software programs varies between $3,000 and $15,000. Researchers can use either the newer head-mounted displays from Sony, I-glasses, or the Kaiser Electro-Optics devices. Prices range from $1,000 to $20,000, with many other head-mounted displays available with varying options and prices. Today it is possible to obtain a complete VR system for around $5,000.

PC-based VR systems are still relatively new and have some minor problems. Newer software programs do contain "bugs," glitches in the program that can sometimes be a problem during therapy sessions. A typical bug may occasionally cause the program to "crash." However, the system is easily rebooted, and the user is returned to the environment within about 15 seconds. In our experience, this type of interruption does not impede the user's progress. Newer systems with better hardware and software design are being created every day and make such interruptions less likely. Problems can also be caused by new Windows operating systems or some other software programs that are unrelated to the VR system. For example, many users have Internet instant-messaging or anti-virus software that can and do crash many of the VR systems currently available because of the large amount of "virtual memory" required to run the VR program. *Virtual memory* refers to the amount of memory the VR program requires to make the calculations and perform the operations necessary to create the three-dimensional environment. To minimize problems, clinicians should try to have as little other software on the "clinic" computer as possible.

A common problem encountered in new application tools is the incompatibility of different software programs. Consumers use their favorite software programs, graphics and audio cards, and device drivers (the software code that makes peripheral computer devices work on your PC), but these products may not be compatible. The result is that to operate a number of VR environments and the associated peripheral devices the clinician may need to have different computers for each virtual environment. Clearly, this could be cost prohibitive for private clinicians. However, researchers world-wide are attempting to alleviate this difficulty. A related problem is that the programming of VR software has not been sequential, and as newer and easier VR software becomes available, older versions are discarded. Thus, certain commercial VR program upgrades may not run on earlier systems. Users of VR systems would benefit from universal standards for the creation of new environments, and users may be able to influence the VR developers and programmers to address such issues. Developers at MIT and at several

TABLE 2.1

Vendors With Commercially-Available Virtual Reality Equipment for Mental Health Applications

Vendor	Hardware/Software	Software programs	Location	Web site
Previ	Software	Flying Claustrophobia Eating Disorders Panic and Agoraphobia Public Speaking	Spain	www.previ.com
Virtually Better Inc.	Both	Flying Heights Public Speaking Thunderstorms Panic and Agoraphobia Virtual Vietnam	USA	www.virtuallybetter.com
VRHealth	Software	Eating Disorders Panic and Agoraphobia Claustrophobia Social Phobia Neurorehab	USA/Italy	www.vrhealth.com
Insight Instruments	Software	Flying	Austria	www.insight.com
Virtual Therapy Inc.	Both	Heights Flying Panic and Agoraphobia OCD ADHD	USA	www.science.kennesaw.edu
Imago Systems	Both	Driving	Canada	www.drivr.com
Hanyang University	Software	Driving Heights Public Speaking Panic and Agoraphobia ADHD Neurorehab	Korea	www.bme.hanyang.ac.kr.vr
5DT		Claustrophobia Heights Darkness	USA/South Africa	www.5DT.com

European VR development centers are currently attempting to address such problems by developing Internet-based environments that run on any computer or platform available (G. Riva, personal communication, January 2003).

Cave Automatic Virtual Environment

The Cave Automatic Virtual Environment (CAVE) was developed at the University of Illinois at Chicago Electronic Visualization Laboratory and is marketed by Fakespace Systems (www.fakespacesystems.com). It consists of a six-sided room with three walls and the floor used to display images from an Electrohome cathode ray tube projector. The wall displays are synchronized to a pair of liquid crystal display shutter glasses (stereoscopic glasses) worn by the user. This effect requires a Silicon Graphics Onyx2 computer (Silicon Graphics, Inc., Mountain View, California), which has the power to calculate the movement of three-dimensional models. A movement-tracking device worn by the user is attached to the shutter glasses, so that wherever the user looks the computer "creates" the correct view and orientation. Because of the size of the room, several individuals may occupy the "virtual world" at the same time, but the primary user is the only one "tracked" by the computer.

About 40 CAVE systems are in use worldwide in different applications. One of these applications is the visualization of complex data, such as macromolecules interacting with potential new drugs. In this system, scientists can "walk" around or through complex molecular structures. This process has provided insight into previously unknown aspects of such structures, in turn aiding in the design of new antibiotics (Rheingold, 1991). Another important use of CAVE systems is as part of computer-aided engineering systems used to design complex machinery or to explore the ergonomics of architectural spaces, automobiles, or other complex equipment. This allows "testing" of how humans operate or interact with complex machinery prior to spending millions of dollars to build prototypes.

The CAVE offers several advantages, including a totally immersive and surrounding field of view (298° horizontal × 226° vertical), high resolution (3,840 pixels horizontal × 2,560 pixels vertical), the ability to have more than one person in the room, the ability to manipulate virtual objects appearing in the room, and an apparently lower level of cybersickness. (Cybersickness is a potential side effect of VR usage and is discussed at length in chap. 6.) Disadvantages include cost, space requirements, and advanced technology systems, which require extensive maintenance and problem solving ability. Drs. Huang and Alessi, who have done most of the mental health research with the

CAVE system, have reported high levels of equipment maintenance and difficulty using physiological monitoring equipment caused by the interference of electrical fields produced by the monitoring sensors and by the VR projection devices (Milton Huang, personal communication, January 2001). The high cost of these systems also makes widespread use by psychologists and other mental health care professionals less practical. This cost is already dropping; Alex Bullinger in Switzerland is developing a new system that is expected to be on the market by spring 2005 and will be offered at a considerably reduced cost ($10,000 vs. $1 million). Another weakness inhibiting the use of CAVE systems for mental health applications is the lack of readily available software. Developing new programs is expensive and requires high-level computer experts. However, as prices of the system drop, more development will follow.

Despite these limitations, the totality of immersion combined with greatly enhanced freedom of motion make the CAVE environment an interesting tool for research. Moreover, as ideas are tested in these devices, successful ones can be transitioned to desktop systems. Advances in technology ultimately help reduce the cost and complexity of this system.

ImmersaDesk®

The ImmersaDesk®, also developed at the Electronic Visualization Laboratory in Chicago, consists of a 66-inch-wide projection-based immersive VR system (Figure 2.2). The projection screen is tilted upward to face the viewer, who can see three-dimensional holographic images of objects that appear to literally be floating in space above the screen. As with the CAVE, the user wears a pair of stereoscopic glasses containing a tracking device that allows the computer to correctly align and present a continuously changing view of objects or scenes. The display resolution of 1,280 pixels × 1,024 pixels is projected at a rate of 100 images/second. The fields of view are 95° vertical × 105° horizontal.

A newer version of the ImmersaDesk, the R2, is a mobile projection-display device that can be transported and set up in less than one hour. More than 50 ImmersaDesks are used today, primarily in the design and engineering fields. Some of the advantages of the R2 are its impressive holographic display of images and scenes, transportability with a self-contained system, and CAVE Library software, which can be accessed in real time from remote locations. The disadvantages include cost, weight (800 lbs), and general unavailability of mental health related software.

Rizzo at the University of Southern California is the leader in the use of the ImmersaDesk for mental health applications (Rizzo et al.,

FIGURE 2.2.

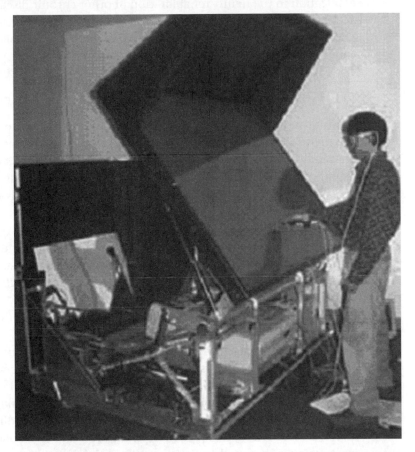

Example of an ImmersaDesk® System © 1997, Electronic Visualization Laboratory, University of Illinois at Chicago.

1999). He has developed a variety of neuro-cognitive testing tools, which project three-dimensional images to evaluate cognitive functions. These tools test spatial navigation, smooth pursuit, left-right discrimination, tracking, mental rotational skills, three-dimensional judgment, and hand–eye coordination. The patients can interact with the floating hologram through either a "wand," which is held in the hand like a stick but has a separate tracker, or a modified "tennis ball," which is ergonomically designed for elderly patients who have a decreased sense of grasp. The computer system matches the movement of the hand-held tracking devices with the preprogrammed computer-generated images. Rizzo's approach should revolutionize the perceptual and cognitive skills-testing methods currently in use. Rizzo has tested the apparatus on patients with Alzheimer's disease and is evaluating its application to the neuro-rehabilitation of other chronic diseases. Overall, patient acceptance has been high with low incidence of side effects. These same devices are now being tested in the treatment of obsessive–compulsive disorder.

OTHER TECHNOLOGICAL DEVELOPMENTS

Exciting new technologies are now allowing for the introduction of real digitized images into the virtual world. Using digital cameras, which are readily available and inexpensive (Microsoft sells an inexpensive digital camera for about $30), clinicians can easily add a digital photo of, say, a child's room or the child's classroom to a virtual world. The child could then be in the therapist's office but "virtually" at home or at school, thus making it possible to address problems triggered by these specific environments. Some of the more expensive and advanced digital cameras are able to provide a 360° view of the surrounding environment, adding tremendous flexibility in the construction of new worlds. As a result of advances in the entertainment and consumer products arenas, adding digitized representations of real-world environments is now within reach of individual users.

These techniques have the potential to help treat attention deficit disorder, social anxiety disorder, and public speaking anxiety, among other disorders. By including pictures of the child's actual classroom, the therapist can work with the child on concentration skills during tests and assignments. In addition, working with photographs of classmates, co-workers, or family members, children can develop social skills in the safety of a virtual environment before attempting interaction on the Internet and then the real world. (This is discussed later in this chapter and in chap. 9.) Incorporating photographs into virtual environments can also help to create a realistic audience for a patient who can practice giving a speech over and over, until the activity is no longer frightening.

Another therapeutic application of VR technology is in the treatment of eating disorders and body dysmorphia (Alcaniz et al., 2000; Perpiña et al., 1999; Riva, 1998a, 1998b; Riva, Bacchetta, Baruffi, Cirillo, & Molinari, 2000). In the treatment of eating disorders (anorexia nervosa, bulimia nervosa, and obesity; Riva, 1998b), the patient's "body experience" is central and VR technology allows the clinician to increase the patient's body awareness and address negative body images (Riva, 1998b; Riva et al., 2001). For example, one system allows users to match their current self-image and their ideal self-image with two-dimensional and three-dimensional figures of different sizes. The disparity between these images is an indicator of the user's body dissatisfaction. In another application, Alcaniz and colleagues (2000) have used VR technology that produces three-dimensional images of a body that can be "morphed" or modified by the user. Such technology is used to help patients increase awareness of how they see and relate to their various body parts. Although still in the developmental stage, these applications of VR to eating disorders and body dysmorphia have shown promising initial results.

Virtual technology also allows for tactile interactions, giving the user the ability to grasp and manipulate virtual objects. This technology can be used to help desensitize patients to painful or disturbing tactile stimuli. The manipulation of virtual objects is accomplished with a "data-glove," which is embedded with both tracking and movement sensors (Figure 2.3). This device is worn on the hand like a regular glove, connected to the computer, and used to pick up virtual objects.

FIGURE 2.3.

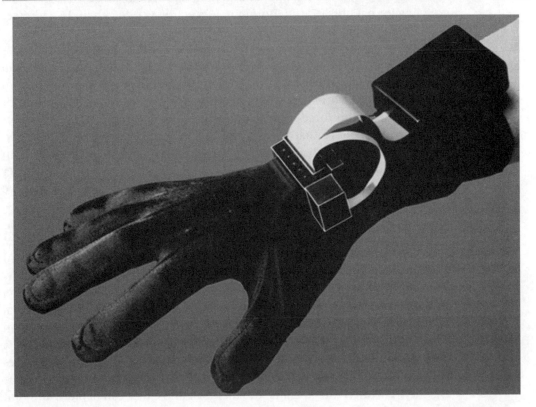

This glove is used to add realistic sensory stimulus to virtual environments. Image courtesy of www.5dt.com. Reprinted with permission.

Hunter Hoffman (1998) has pioneered the use of the data glove for mental health applications in a technique called "augmented reality" or "tactile augmentation." In augmented reality, the user can, for example, pick up a virtual plate in the virtual world, simultaneously holding a real plate in the gloved hand. This "mixed" reality, combining virtual and real world sensations, boosts the feeling of presence and immersion. Hoffman's augmented reality technique has been successfully used on patients who are undergoing painful medical procedures (e.g., burn and wound care) and physical therapy. It provides a high level of distraction and, in clinical studies, has actually reduced narcotic doses needed to control patients' pain (Hoffman, 1998). These results suggest widespread applicability in the field of health psychology.

The data-glove is also used in the treatment of arachnophobia. Here patients are allowed to touch a virtual spider, and, after desensitization, to touch a toy spider. Research in this field indicates that patients treated with tactile augmentation respond better than those receiving no such treatment (Hoffman, 1998). Tactile augmentation allows for a greater degree of sensory stimulation and appears to be more convincing for patients (Carlin, Hoffman, & Weghorst, 1997; chap. 16 addresses arachnophobia in detail).

Other promising peripheral devices exist, such as the "force-feedback" glove. Force-feedback is a much more complex device than the data glove; it is used to simulate surface features and textures in the virtual world. In picking up or pushing a heavy virtual object, for example, the force-feedback glove produces a resistance that makes the user believe that a heavy object has been encountered. These systems are expensive, and, thus far, no large clinical trials have been implemented using this technology. A number of applications are under active investigation, including rehabilitation therapy following a stroke and range of motion exercises for patients with injuries or disabilities. Applications for anxiety disorders might include the treatment of repetitive behaviors in OCD patients or treatment of PTSD in rape survivors. (OCD and PTSD are addressed at length in chaps. 9 and 10, respectively.)

Future developments in VR technology include systems that allow the therapist to accompany the patient into the virtual world. To a certain extent this can be accomplished now with Internet-based virtual worlds. In an Internet virtual world, both patient and therapist log on to a particular Web site and adopt a preferred "avatar." An avatar is a persona, a male or female head or some type of animal whose features and colors can be customized, which allows the user complete anonymity. Through their avatars, the therapist and client can explore different worlds offered on the Web site or interact with other visitors who have adopted their own avatars. One use of these Internet-based virtual worlds is in the treatment of social phobia. After practicing with the therapist in a closed system, the client can visit a virtual world populated by other avatars, initiate conversations, and obtain feedback from other avatars in real time audio through the use of a simple microphone. Internet-based virtual worlds are also currently being used in the treatment of agoraphobia to expose the patient to unfamiliar worlds other than those the clinician can provide in the office setting. (This application is discussed in more detail in chap. 8.)

In summary, the therapeutic benefits of VR are becoming increasingly well recognized as they are confirmed through controlled clinical trials. The use of VR in the treatment of anxiety disorders is the most advanced application in this exciting new area. By the end of 2002, there had been more than 50 controlled clinical trials using VR for anxiety disorders treatment. The number of investigators and studies continues to increase annually with many new studies and new applications appearing in the literature almost monthly. Although we have outlined many of the technical shortcomings of this technology, we should also point out that the technology is advancing at a logorhythmic rate. For example, we already mentioned that the current 2.8 Gigahertz computers soon to be made available solve many of the jerky movements and unnatural feel of earlier virtual environments. Moreover, a number of international meetings are being held annually where clinicians and researchers showcase their new work, compare notes, and suggest ways of improving applications in the mental health field. Some investigators are actively seeking ways to provide VR systems through the commonly found game boxes of Sony PS2, Nintendo Game Cube, and Microsoft's X-Box. Alternatively, methods for delivering virtual worlds over the Internet are developing at lightning speed. These applications promise to dramatically improve not only access to health care, but also delivery of health care in general.

II

Virtual Reality and Anxiety Disorders: A User's Guide

Anxiety Disorders and Their Treatment | 3

A nxiety disorders are categorized according to the type of stimuli that are feared, the etiology of the disorder, and the nature of the symptoms. Exhibit 3.1 shows the 12 codable anxiety disorders contained in the *Diagnostic and Statistical Manual of Mental Disorders* (4th ed., Text Revision; *DSM–IV–TR*; American Psychiatric Association, 2000).

In general, the majority of all anxiety disorders share two common symptoms. First, patients with these disorders usually experience more intense levels of apprehension and worry and for longer periods of time than the average person experiences in everyday life. Second, patients often develop ritual acts, repetitive thoughts, or avoidance mechanisms to protect themselves from the anxiety.

Risk Factors

Anxiety disorders are most likely due to a combination of factors including genetic predisposition and social, psychological, and environmental conditions (Sherman, 1997a). Phobias, for example, exhibit a strong familial pattern; first-degree relatives have a greater than average likelihood of

EXHIBIT 3.1.

Diagnostic and Statistical Manual of Mental Disorders (4th ed.) Codable Anxiety Disorders

Panic Disorder Without Agoraphobia

Panic Disorder With Agoraphobia

Agoraphobia Without a History of Panic Disorder

Specific Phobias

Social Phobia

Obsessive–Compulsive Disorder

Posttraumatic Stress Disorder

Acute Stress Disorder

Generalized Anxiety Disorder

Anxiety Disorder Due to a General Medical Condition

Substance-Induced Anxiety Disorder

Anxiety Disorder Not Otherwise Specified

Note. From *Diagnostic and Statistical Manual of Mental Disorders* (4th ed., Text Revision, pp. 429–484), by the American Psychiatric Association, 2000, Washington, DC: Author. Copyright 2000 by the American Psychiatric Association. Reprinted with permission.

also having a phobia of the same specific subtype. This resembles the strong genetic link observed in patients with obsessive–compulsive disorder (OCD). The strongest risk factor associated with phobias is the presence of another psychiatric disorder, and the most frequent co-occurrence is with panic disorder (Boyd et al., 1990).

Panic attack symptoms appear to be universal; they have been found in populations in Korea, New Zealand, Lebanon, Germany, Puerto Rico, and the United States (Weismann et al., 1995). There is some evidence of a single, dominant gene related to panic disorder (American Psychiatric Association, 2000; Crowe, Noyes, Wilson, Elston, & Ward, 1987). Panic attacks can be triggered in susceptible individuals by such factors as elevated amounts of carbon dioxide in the air, hyperventilation, and caffeine ingestion (Stein & Uhde, 1994). Further discussion of risk factors for panic attacks and other specific anxiety disorders can be found in their corresponding chapters.

Medical Consequences and Comorbidities Associated With Anxiety Disorders

Anxiety disorders are associated with a wide variety of somatic symptoms: fatigue, weakness, flushing, chills, insomnia, dizziness, paresthesias, restlessness, palpitations, chest pain, rapid heart rate, hyperventilation, choking, dry mouth, nausea, diarrhea, and urinary frequency. On average, a person with an anxiety disorder sees a primary care physician 10 times before being correctly diagnosed, thereby increasing health care costs (Seppa, 1996). Since the mid-1980s, surveys have shown a general improvement in primary care diagnosis of anxiety, but these disorders are correctly identified in only 66% of clinic visits.

In many serious and chronic medical conditions, high levels of anxiety cause increased morbidity and mortality. Studies have linked high levels of anxiety to sudden fatal heart attack, hypertension, risk of myocardial infarction, and coronary heart disease. A 32-year longitudinal study of 2,000 men found a significant correlation between high anxiety and sudden cardiac death. After correcting for several physical conditions, high anxiety did not raise the risk of fatal or non-fatal heart disease, but it did increase the chance of a sudden fatal heart attack (3–4 times as high as those without anxiety; Kowachi, Sparrow, Vokonas, & Weiss, 1994). The National Health and Nutrition Examination Survey I assessed 2,992 participants for anxiety and depression between 1971 and 1975 and conducted a follow-up study from 1982 to 1984 and again from 1986 to 1987. No patients had elevated blood pressure. The researchers found that high depression and anxiety scores were independent predictors for the development of hypertension (Jonas, Franks, & Ingram, 1997). In the Normative Aging Study, 1,759 men without coronary heart disease were followed from 1975 to 1995. As part of the study, the participants completed a Worries Scale (Tallis, Davey, & Bond, 1994) to assess levels of stress and anxiety. The researchers found that worry doubled myocardial infarction risk and coronary heart disease by 1.5 (Kubzansky, Kawachi, & Spiro, 1997).

Theories About Anxiety

Emotional processing theory provides a basis for understanding why exposure-based therapies lead to fear reduction in phobias. Emotional processing theory posits that fear memories are stored in neurological networks that include three types of data: knowledge regarding the feared stimulus, memory regarding the response to the stimulus, and data regarding the meaning of the stimulus and response. In order for emotional processing of fear and consequent fear reduction to occur, three components are necessary: activation of fear (physiologically and subjectively) during exposure, a decrease of fear within the exposure treatment session, and a reduction in fear across treatment sessions (Foa & Kozak, 1986; Foa, Steketee, & Rothbaum, 1989). In studies done by Borkovec and Sides (1979) and Lang, Melamed, and Hart (1970), phobic patients who showed greater cardiovascular responses when presented with the feared stimuli and greater declines in heart rate, both within and across desensitization sessions, benefited more from treatment than phobic patients who did not show such physiologic activation and habituation.

CONCORDANCE AND SYNCHRONY

Long considered related to the fear reduction process are the concepts of concordance and synchrony (Hodgson & Rachman, 1974). *Concordance* refers to the similarity between various measures (for instance, physiological and self-report) across a group of participants. *Synchrony* refers to the parallel, within-subject changes of various measures (self-report and physiological) as treatment proceeds (Beckham, Vrana, May, Gustafson, & Smith, 1990). According to a study done by Cook, Melamed, Cuthbert, McNeil, and Lang (1988), patients with specific phobia showed a higher rate of synchrony and concordance between physiological (heart rate and skin conductance) and affective self-report measures when presented with phobic stimuli than did patients with either social phobia or agoraphobia. This may be due to the high cue specificity of fear memories associated with specific phobias, which makes individuals more responsive to exposure-based treatments than those with phobias containing more complex fear structures.

Beckham et al. (1990) conducted a study on individuals with flight phobia assessing synchrony and concordance as measures of fear. Stress inoculation training was conducted with minimal therapist involvement, and participants were invited to participate in a 60-minute post-treatment flight. During the post-treatment flight, heart rate and self-reported anxiety (subjective units of distress ratings) were measured at five points in time: during a preflight assessment, on the plane prior to take-off, after take-off, 5 minutes before landing, and after landing. Eight weeks later participants were contacted and asked to report on the number of flight opportunities and number of flights taken and avoided during the two months since the posttreatment flight. Data analysis showed those who had flown during the 2 months had the highest level of fear activation (measured by heart rate prior to take-off) and fear decrement (measured by heart rate during flight) during the posttreatment flight. Self-report measures were not related to subsequent flying. Synchrony was evident between self-report and physiological measures only for in-flight measures (after take-off and 5 minutes prior to landing). This substantiates the theory put forth by Hodgson and Rachman (1974) that synchrony occurs most often when participants are placed in highly arousing situations. Synchrony proved to be a predictor of successful treatment outcome with individuals with agoraphobia and with specific phobias in a study done by Vermilyea, Boice, and Barlow (1984).

Measurement of Anxiety

Measurements of anxiety are best completed using multiple assessments that show both subjective and objective arousal. We have found it useful at the Virtual Reality Medical Center (VRMC) to use four levels of assessment, including both objective and subjective measures. The tools we use are physiological measures, questionnaires (self-report), subjective units of distress reports, and behavioral observations.

PHYSIOLOGICAL MEASURES

Physiological measurements are the most objective indicators of an individual's level of anxiety. Such measurements include skin resistance, heart-rate variability, peripheral skin temperature, and respiration rate. Changes in skin resistance, which decreases as sweat gland activity increases, reflect the patient's level of sympathetic arousal (Schwartz & Associates, 1995). Heart rate, peripheral skin temperature, and respiration rate can also directly reflect the patient's level of distress. Physiological data may be obtained noninvasively using such in-office equipment as the popular I-330 C2 computerized biofeedback system with PDS Physiological Programming Software (manufactured by J & J

Enterprises, Poulsbo, Washington) or the Biograph and CardioPro software (manufactured by Thought Technology, Inc., Montreal, Canada). These systems allow the patient to receive visual and audio feedback, which can be useful in educating patients about their responses and teaching them how to monitor and control these responses.

By studying the physiological reactions of nonphobic individuals using virtual environments, a baseline or "normal" response is determined. This can then be used to compare phobic individuals' reactions and to determine when physiological desensitization is occurring. The majority of nonphobic individuals do get some arousal when placed into a virtual environment, but as one study of 23 participants showed, they are able to stabilize their physiology after a 20-minute exposure (Wiederhold, Gronskya-Palesh, Miller, del Poso, & Wiederhold, 2000). Another study of 75 computer exposition attendees revealed that nonphobic individuals' overall physiology does not fully stabilize after a 6-minute exposure (Wiederhold, Jang, et al., 2001). However, the nonphobic individuals do not show the dramatic physiological arousal that phobic individuals show when placed for the first time in the novel environment.

QUESTIONNAIRES

For each anxiety disorder patient treated with VR therapy, a number of questionnaires are commonly used to assess the patient's condition both before and after treatment. With all treatments given at the VRMC, we use a set of questionnaires related to the patient's overall condition and experience. Pretreatment questionnaires include the Beck Depression Inventory (2nd ed.; Beck, Steer, & Brown, 1996), the Self-Evaluation Questionnaire (Forms Y-1 and Y-2 of the State–Trait Anxiety Inventory; Spielberger, Gorsuch, Lushene, Vagg, & Jacobs, 1983), the Tellegen Absorption Scale (Tellegen & Atkinson, 1974), and the Dissociative Experience Scale (Carlson & Putnam, 1992). Post-treatment questionnaires include the Beck Depression Inventory (2nd ed.), the State–Trait Anxiety Inventory, the Simulator Sickness Questionnaire (Kennedy, Lane, Berbaum, & Lilienthal, 1993), and the Questionnaire on Presence and Realism (Stanney, 2002). Coupled with these general questionnaires is a set of questionnaires specific to each disorder. (For an exhaustive list of self-report questionnaires used in the treatment of panic and phobic disorders, listed by disorder, see Antony & Swinson's [2000] excellent review in their book, *Phobic Disorders and Panic in Adults: A Guide to Assessment and Treatment.*)

One test that can be particularly useful with virtual reality graded exposure therapy (VRGET) is a Behavioral Avoidance Test. This type of test measures the degree of anxiety and avoidance both before and after treatment and assesses treatment effectiveness by gauging the patient's ability and willingness to perform an anxiety-inducing act both before and after treatment. Performing an in vivo Behavioral Avoidance Test before treating phobic individuals is not always possible, depending on the presenting phobia, because of the difficulties involved in arranging the exposure situation. To have the flexibility to do this test in the virtual world would allow for an objective measurement of anxiety level and treatment outcome success (P. Renaud, personal communication, September 1, 2000; Renaud & Bouchard, 2001). Studies have shown the Behavioral Avoidance Test to be a sensitive, objective measure of treatment effectiveness when performed after treatment (Craske, Rapee, & Barlow, 1988; Steketee, Chambless, Tran, Worden, & Gillis, 1996). When performed before treatment, the Behavioral Avoidance Test can help to determine the degree of phobic avoidance by measuring behaviors not measurable in vivo. A group at Quebec University at Hull is researching the visual tracking of virtual objects as a measure of behavioral avoidance (Renaud & Bouchard, 2001). Participants perform a visual tracking task of a neutral target and a virtual spider with using a head-mounted display and tracker. Twelve of the participants had arachnophobia and 12 did not. The initial analyses indicate very distinct patterns of tracking performance between the two groups, with the phobic individuals being less accurate and slower in their tracking patterns than the others. Their tracking pattern also varies depending on whether the target is neutral or is the virtual spider and whether the target travels in a predictable path or an unpredictable one. Such studies help in the development of objective means to rate the efficacy of VRGET.

SUBJECTIVE RATINGS OF ANXIETY

Subjective units of distress ratings (from 0 = no anxiety to 100 = maximal anxiety) is a self-report measure that allows the therapist to monitor the patient's subjective reaction to the session (Wolpe & Lang, 1964). Although it is important to note the patient's subjective reactions to anxiety provoking stimuli, many studies have shown these not to be an indication of treatment success or failure because social desirability and denial do influence patients' self-reports (Paulhus, 2002).

BEHAVIORAL OBSERVATION

Therapists also use their clinical skills of observation during the session to complement the other tools (subjective units of distress ratings, questionnaires, and physiological measures). Observations of patients' behavior, their reactions to treatment, how they interact with the virtual world, and so on can all provide material that may help guide the treatment. It is important to note if the patient is relaxed, gripping the arms of the chair, exploring and interacting with the virtual world (leading to more immersion), or sitting back passively. Other observations include noting whether the patient is practicing cognitive coping skills and slow abdominal breathing to manage anxiety. Behavioral observations are used to evaluate patient baselines and responses to treatment, and such observations need not be limited to direct expressions of anxiety (Barlow, 1988).

Treatment of Anxiety

Research has shown that anxiety disorders are most effectively treated with medication, cognitive therapy, behavioral therapy, or a combination of these modalities (Barlow, 1988).

MEDICATIONS

Pharmacological treatments of anxiety disorders are common and should be familiar to all therapists who treat these disorders. Many patients are treated with medications in primary care environments and may present for psychotherapy already using one or more medications (Antony & Swinson, 2000). Commonly prescribed medications include serotonin reuptake inhibitors, beta-blockers, tricyclic antidepressants, monoamine oxidase inhibitors, and benzodiazapines. Generally, serotonin reuptake inhibitors (such as Prozac) are the drug of choice because they are associated with few side effects and are nonaddictive. However, studies have shown that some anxiety disorders respond more specifically to other drugs (Barlow, 1988; Heimberg, Liebowitz, Hope, & Schneier, 1995). It is well known that beta-blockers (propranolol is the most commonly used) are highly effective in treating the physical symptoms associated with performance anxiety. Beta-blockers have the advantage of being usable on an "as-needed" basis. A tricyclic antidepressant, clomipramine, is commonly given to patients with OCD and has been successful in reducing symptoms. Another tricyclic antidepressant, impramine, has been used to treat panic disorder, agoraphobia, and general anxiety disorder with varying degrees of success. Some of the benefits associated with impramine may be due to its effects on comorbid depression. High potency benzodiazepines have been used to treat panic disorder, but they are associated with side effects, addiction, and a high relapse rate. It is also suggested that benzodiazapines may inhibit the neurochemical desensitization that exposure therapy aims to effect. According to Westra and Stewart (1998; Westra, Stewart, & Conrad, 2002), taking benzodiazepine as needed to cope with anxiety and panic is associated with poorer cognitive–behavioral therapy (CBT) outcome in panic disorder patients. Buffett-Jerrott and Stewart (2002) have found that benzodiazepine-induced memory impairments do not appear to lessen with drug tolerance and that benzodiazepines may not only impair explicit memory (conscious, effortful memory), but also hamper implicit memory processes (unconscious, automatic memory) necessary for CBT. Monoamine oxidase inhibitors may be effective in treating a variety of anxiety disorders; however, the side effects and dietary restrictions often reduce patient compliance.

Thus, pharmacotherapy is a powerful tool in the treatment of many disorders, but it has a number of disadvantages, including side effects, high dropout rates, high relapse rates, long-term dependence, and interference with non-drug treatments (because of state-dependent learning and attributing improvements to the drug; Barlow, 1988; Carlson, 1999). It is widely agreed that treatment of anxiety disorders calls for at least some behavioral or cognitive–behavioral component (Barlow, 1988; Carlson, 1999). Medications are more effective when used in combination with these treatments.

COGNITIVE THERAPY

Cognitive therapy is often used as an adjunct to exposure therapy when treating anxiety disorders. Cognitive therapy addresses the distorted thoughts that exacerbate dysfunctional behaviors (Antony & Swinson, 2000; Leahy & Holland, 2000). By identifying and treating thought distortions, therapists can often help patients to effect positive changes in their behaviors. Cognitive approaches are diverse, but most involve some educational component where therapists help the patients to learn more about their fears. Another common approach is cognitive restructuring, which entails helping patients to recognize and turn irrational (automatic) thoughts into rational responses. Often this takes the form of challenging catastrophic thinking and guiding the patient into more realistic assessments of situations and their consequences. Challenging the assumptions behind the patient's distortions allows the patient and therapist to address the patient's belief system on a deeper level.

Although cognitive therapy is often incorporated into exposure treatments, some studies have indicated that cognitive therapy does not increase treatment success rates (Emmelkamp & Mersch, 1982;

Williams & Rappoport, 1983). Some patients may become distracted by cognitive intervention techniques, thus reducing the efficacy of the exposure therapy. In one study, a cognitive approach was, in fact, shown to be detrimental, by delaying symptom improvement (Michelson, Mavissakalian, & Marchione, 1985). Cognitive interventions may be appropriate in the treatment of some anxiety disorders but may not be helpful with others.

BEHAVIORAL TECHNIQUES

Behavioral interventions are used with success in treating anxiety disorders (Barlow, 1988; Leahy & Holland, 2000). Behavioral techniques include assertiveness training, behavioral activation, communication and social skills training, distraction, modeling, problem solving, thought stopping, visualization, exposure, relaxation, and breathing retraining. For the purposes of this book, we limit our discussion to relaxation, breathing retraining, and exposure techniques.

Relaxation procedures can take a variety of forms, all focusing on providing the patient with the means to counteract physiological anxiety responses. Relaxation is often used as a coping mechanism during exposure therapy (Ost, 1987). Relaxation can be as simple as teaching progressive muscle relaxation where the therapist guides the patient through awareness of various muscle groups in the body to identify and relieve areas of tension. Deep breathing and visualization can then be used to relax these areas. Often such procedures are accompanied with a therapist-dictated audiotape, which is given to the patient as homework. Alternatively, therapists may use noninvasive sensors to measure, record, and show the patient's physiology to them in real-time visual or auditory signals. This helps increase patient awareness and has been found to increase patient response when taught prior to exposure therapy. Sensors can measure muscle tension using EMG or electromyography recording. By feeding back the electrical signal produced by the muscles, the therapist can guide the patient through exercises that allow him or her to feel the difference between a tense muscle and a relaxed one.

Often used in conjunction with relaxation training, breathing retraining helps patients become aware of their breathing patterns and allows them to differentiate between slow, deep diaphragmatic breathing and fast, shallow chest breathing. During panic attacks, there is a tendency to hyperventilate, which can increase symptoms and panic. Breath awareness is often a useful adjunct to treatment (Schwartz et al., 1995). Patients have reported that using the visual feedback provided by a biofeedback system allows them to become aware of subtle anxiety symptoms and enables them to use their breathing and coping skills at a much earlier stage, thereby averting a panic attack. They also report gaining a sense of empowerment at knowing they can "control" their symptoms (Wiederhold, 1999).

Exposure therapy is considered indispensable in the treatment of many phobic disorders (Antony & Swinson, 2000; Davey, 1997). The various forms of exposure therapy include systematic desensitization, imaginal exposure, or in vivo exposure. Systematic desensitization consists of a hierarchy of more and more anxiety-provoking scenes represented visually and sometimes auditorally to the patient. Relaxation techniques are paired with the imagined scenes to reduce the physiological stress response. The patient moves through the hierarchy of anxiety-inducing items, often with the aid of the therapist, and approaches new items only when previous ones can be visualized with little or no anxiety. Imaginal exposure without relaxation involves having the patient close his or her eyes and visualize the anxiety-provoking scene, staying with that scene until the patient becomes desensitized to it. In vivo exposure involves exposing the patient to the actual real-life phobic situation. This is often done after first teaching the patient anxiety management techniques, such as thought stopping, relaxation, diaphragmatic breathing, and distraction. Alternatively, these techniques may be introduced concurrently with the in vivo experience. Exposure techniques are usually found to be effective, with a report of some improvement in 70% of phobic individuals (Masters, Burish, Hollon, & Rimm, 1987).

Exposure therapies, although effective in treating anxiety and phobias, do have some deficiencies. One problem with imaginal exposure is that many people are unable to effectively visualize the situations that cause them anxiety. It is estimated that only 20% of patients can visualize well (Kosslyn et al., 1984). Such patients are unable to feel present in the phobic situation in order to re-experience the fear stimuli. Because the fear structure is not activated, disconfirming information cannot be introduced to change the fear structure. In the case of in vivo exposure, loss of confidentiality, lack of controllability, added time, and added expense all make this treatment less desirable. With aviophobia, for example, the paucity of controlled studies may in part be due to the expense of using actual airplanes to effect the exposure therapy. In vivo exposure is also "too real" for some individuals to ever consider. For example, some patients with an intractable fear of flying might consider in vivo exposure therapy so undesirable that they may never seek treatment for their phobia. Studies have shown that less than 15% of those with phobias seek treatment (Agras, Sylvester, & Oliveau, 1969; Boyd et al., 1990).

VIRTUAL REALITY GRADED EXPOSURE THERAPY

VRGET can be thought of as a highly specialized exposure technique that can enhance and accelerate treatment. VRGET offers several advantages over both imaginal and in vivo exposure therapies. Virtual exposure is safer than in vivo exposure because it is entirely under the patient's and therapist's control and can be "switched off" any time it becomes intolerable. With VR therapy, there is also the added benefit of being able to expose a patient repeatedly to the specific part of a scenario that causes fear. For example, a patient who only fears airplane landings but is comfortable with all other aspects of air travel would be able to practice landings as many times as necessary in the virtual world with several landings possible during the 45–50 minute session. When performing treatment in vivo, the patient would have to take an entire flight each time to get exposure to just one landing. Estimating a 30-minute drive each way to the airport, arrival 1 hour prior to the flight (at each end of the trip), and a 30-minute flight, the time investment is a minimum of 3½ hours (assuming the flight is on time) for the patient and therapist just to gain exposure to two landings. Using VRGET, at 45 minutes per session, with three landings accomplished in two sessions, the patient is exposed to six landings in three sessions or 1½ hours. The military has realized the value of simulated flights in training its pilots. It currently uses simulator training for skill building in pilots so that they may be allowed to practice difficult maneuvers ad infinitum before attempting them in a real airplane.

When the locus of fear is unknown, VR therapy is used to pinpoint the precise stimuli that are causing the patient's fear and has the advantage of allowing the therapist to monitor and control the stimuli being presented to the patient. The flexibility of the virtual environment allows the therapist to tailor sessions to meet the needs of individual clients. The intensity of the threatening stimuli can also be controlled in the virtual environment as the client becomes desensitized (Glantz et al., 1996). The virtual environment also allows the patient to "overpractice" in situations often much worse, more "exaggerated," than those that are likely to be encountered in real life. This allows patients to develop a sense of mastery and the confidence to carry out the task successfully.

In comparison to imaginal exposure, VR therapy may be more realistic in that it can engage several different sensory modalities, such as sight and sound. Vestibular cues, such as motion and vibration, can also be included to help the patient to feel more present in the experience. VR therapy is interactive and provides constant stimuli, which makes it less likely that the patient can "drift" from the imaginal scene.

VR therapy offers the advantage of allowing the therapist to see exactly what the client is seeing so that therapy can be tailored to what is activating the fear structure for the client. This flexibility should allow therapy to proceed more efficiently (Glantz et al., 1996). In summary, the advantages of VR exposure therapy include interactivity, flexibility, controllability, confidentiality, safety, timesaving, cost savings, and repeatability.

In a recent controlled study, VRGET proved more effective at promoting behavioral change than did imaginal exposure therapy (Wiederhold, 1999). VRGET provides both interaction and immersion, which result in a user feeling "present" in the scenario. This allows participants to feel as though they were in the passenger cabin of an airplane rather than seated in a chair in the therapist's office. For the time they are in the virtual world, their reality is altered and they become a part of the scenario. This active participation seems to allow patients to become more anxious and then to become more habituated as treatment continues. In terms of emotional processing theory, it might be said that the fear structure changes as competing information regarding the feared stimulus is received and as responses to the once feared stimuli are changed. This is in contrast to the experience of participants in imaginal exposure therapy who often cannot hold the mental image or elicit the anxiety appropriate to the real life cause of fear. Because of this inability to elicit anxiety, a change in the fear structure may not occur (Wiederhold, Gevirtz, & Spira, 2001).

The possibilities offered by VR technology in this context are numerous and extremely advantageous. The feeling of actual presence that patients experience in these environments, involving all the sensorimotor channels, enables them to really "live" the experience in a more vivid and realistic manner than they could through their own imagination (Vincelli & Molinari, 1998). The ability to structure and control stimuli and, at the same time, objectively monitor user responses to the stimuli offers a considerable increase in the likelihood of therapeutic success as compared to traditional procedures.

The advantages of VR therapy as compared with imaginal exposure include the following:

1. VR therapy is highly immersive. It stimulates several sensory modalities, and patients report being able to become "present" or "immersed" in the computer-generated world. For patients who cannot easily visualize, this may be a better alternative for allowing some anxiety to occur and then reducing anxiety with repeated exposures.
2. The therapist sees what the patient sees. Emotional processing theory states that in order for a phobia to be successfully

treated, a patient's fear structure must be activated and modified (Foa & Kozak, 1986). With VR therapy, the therapist can see the exact stimuli that are activating the patient's fear structure and can then repeat exposure to those stimuli to reduce the fear and modify the fear structure. With imaginal exposure the patient may at times drift "off task," and it is difficult for the therapist to know when this is happening. With VR therapy, the exposure is continuous.

3. VR therapy is more realistic than imaginal exposure for most people. This should translate into fewer treatment sessions, and, therefore, less cost for treatment (Wiederhold, Gevirtz, & Wiederhold, 1998; Wiederhold & Wiederhold, 1998).

4. Patients seem more receptive to VR treatment than imaginal. VR therapy appears to have more face validity for them, increasing the likelihood that patients will complete the entire treatment regimen. In addition, therapists may have a stronger belief in the abilities of VR therapy versus systematic desensitization, and this may also boost success rates in patients.

Although VR exposure therapy has been mainly used in combination with CBT, there does exist a place for psychodynamic therapy also. Kahan (2000) discussed the case of a patient who had developed a fear of flying 33 years prior to therapy. Using VR exposure therapy in conjunction with the psychodynamic treatment, this patient was able to elicit the affect and memories of the circumstances surrounding her fear and saw how her fear was a representation of other feelings—of leaving a place of safety to go to a place of "turbulence" and confusion. This awareness, which allowed her to dismiss the cognitive distortions she had held onto for so long, was accomplished in only six sessions with VRGET; she had been in therapy for much longer and been unable to really elicit those emotion-laden memories. Perhaps a melding of psychodynamic therapy and CBT, in combination with VRGET, may prove beneficial to some patients. In some patients who have difficulty in becoming immersed or present, we have been using hypnosis to assist in making the transition from the real to the virtual world.

This new and innovative tool, VR treatment, does produce a change in the traditional client–therapist relationship. On the one hand, the patient develops the sense of being more skilled in operating effectively in difficult situations and can test these skills more effectively than through the imagination. On the other hand, in the safety of the therapist office, patients can "test" their limits and recreate and use a real experiential world, with one part of themselves drawn into the world, and the other remaining grounded in the knowledge that "this is not real—I can try new things and test my new powers." The therapist also feels empowered, knowing he or she has a powerful new tool that can be used as an adjunct to his or her own solid clinical skills to intervene quickly and effectively in helping overcome the distress of the client (Vincelli, 1999; Vincelli, Choi, Molinari, Wiederhold, & Riva, 2000; Vincelli & Riva, 2000).

How Treatment Is Conducted at the Virtual Reality Medical Center

4

W
e began using virtual reality (VR) therapy at the Virtual Reality Medical Center (VRMC) in 1997. Before that, we had been using exposure therapy with our patients who presented with anxiety, panic, or phobias either as visualization, systematic desensitization, or in the real world (in vivo, described in chap. 3). Our initial program combined real time physiological monitoring with VR software to treat fear of flying.

The first system consisted of a rather heavy and bulky head-mounted display manufactured by Liquid Image (Canada), with a tracker that was very finicky and did not allow other metal objects or electric devices near it. When this occurred, the image flickered and sometimes caused the VR world to spin continuously. To counteract the front heavy head-mounted display, a bungee cord was attached to it to lighten the weight from the patient's neck. The beauty of the software, however, was that it was made specifically for the techno-phobic therapist population. Knowing that therapists would rather spend time relating to their patients than tending to computers, simple keystrokes allowed the therapist to change the scenarios from taxi to turbulence to landing. The virtual world initially seemed quite cartoonish when we first began training therapists, and we wondered whether it really would work. When we used the system on a research assistant with a subclinical phobia of flying, we found that it indeed did elicit anxiety both subjectively and objectively (heart rate increase and sweat gland activity increase). We then started work on developing a clinical protocol that would help us decide whether VR exposure was superior to imaginal exposure (a method used by many San Diego area clinicians to treat fear of flying). The study results showed that VR treatment was indeed a better and more effective method, and in fact in that small study (10 participants in each of 3 groups), there was a 90% success rate for VR therapy versus a 20% success rate for imaginal exposure (Wiederhold, 1999). (Success was determined by the participant no longer meeting criteria for specific phobia according to the *Diagnostic and Statistical Manual of Mental Disorders* [4th ed., Text Revision; *DSM–IV–TR*; American Psychiatric Association, 2000].)

Since 1997, VRMC has expanded the offering of VR systems and protocols, and now we treat a wider range of disorders using advanced technologies, such as the Internet, videoconferencing, VR, robots, and advanced physiological monitoring systems. We currently treat fear of flying, fear of driving, claustrophobia, agoraphobia and panic, generalized social phobia, fear of public speaking, fear of heights, PTSD resulting from motor vehicle accidents, eating disorders, body dysmorphic disorder, and attention deficit disorder. We are also investigating the use of VR treatment as an adjunctive therapy to medication for distraction and pain mitigation for unpleasant or painful medical procedures.

VRMC serves as a clinical research facility, a beta test site for testing and validating new technologies, a training center for individuals pursuing doctorate degrees in a variety of disciplines, and a clinical site offering services to the community, with a sliding fee scale based on income level. The non-profit 501(c)(3) affiliate, the Interactive Media Institute, also sponsors public education, research studies, and an international conference with presentations by clinicians, researchers, and funding agencies.

Though treatment at the VRMC includes new technologies, therapy performed here is grounded in traditional cognitive–behavioral therapy (CBT) techniques. CBT is based on the idea that emotions are interconnected with thoughts. The key to this type of therapy is the examination of how thoughts and feelings interact to drive behavior. CBT teaches patients to gain control over behaviors and cognitions to affect emotions. The cognitive part of treatment involves working with automatic thought patterns and investigating how they tie into emotions. The behavioral part of treatment includes looking at actions and determining what reactions are most common in specific situations. For example, for a flying phobic, a behavior (buckling the airline seatbelt) may be immediately followed by a thought (the plane is going to crash if I stay here), which in turn affects emotions (panic!). By changing the initial thought through education, relaxation and coping techniques, and repeated exposure, the emotion no longer automatically takes hold. VR enhances the essential exposure component of treatment.

What has technology allowed us to do now that was not possible before? It has allowed us to treat our patients more effectively, without the difficulties of imaginal exposure, and efficiently, without the safety, cost, and confidentiality concerns that arise with in vivo exposure (Rothbaum, Hodges, Anderson, Price, & Smith, 2002; Wiederhold, Jang, Gervitz, et al., 2002). It has allowed us to appeal to a group of individuals who had previously tried imaginal therapy without success because they lacked visualization skills. It has allowed us also to reach out to a group of individuals who were too overwhelmed by the thought of being stuck on a real freeway or on a 30-minute airplane flight that are part of the in vivo treatment. We can slowly and systematically advance our patients through therapy and the fear hierarchy as physiology stabilizes and as a sense of mastery is reached in various scenarios. Patients can become empowered and increase their level of self-efficacy. The system allows continued physiological monitoring during exposure, which helps the therapist identify precisely the cues that trigger anxiety and fear.

Technology also allows interoceptive exposure to be conducted in "near real world settings." Patients can breathe rapidly to bring on sensations of hyperventilation while standing in an open field (virtually) or driving on a virtual freeway. By allowing patients to recreate panicky feelings in a setting similar to the one they encounter in the real world, they can begin to understand that those feelings are "dangerous" only because of the cognitions associated with them. They are not really going to have a heart attack or go crazy when those feelings occur. By practicing skills in a virtual driving or flying scenario, they appear to gain more understanding of their cognitive distortion of real world experiences. They can also practice conventional coping skills such as breathing and relaxation in a setting similar to what they experience in the real world. It is important to remember that VR therapy is used only as a tool, an adjunct, to traditional CBT.

Will the virtual experience eventually replace in vivo, real life exposure? Certainly not today, and proof of therapeutic success still requires performance in real world settings. The goal of therapy remains what it always has been: We want patients to be able to overcome their avoidance and discomfort in real world settings. What we find with virtual reality is that skills learned in the virtual world do in fact generalize and transfer to the real world. There is much discussion in the VR community about the appropriate level of fidelity to realism required during therapy (see chap. 6). Some of the more technical and adventurous members try to achieve better and better resolution and realism. We have found, however, that for phobia treatment, animated images are sufficient to elicit anxiety. Some patients have actually said the animated image might be preferable. For instance, we have found that in the fear of flying scenario, because the scene is not an exact replica of a plane, the patient does not get caught up in minor discrepancies that distract from the task. Rather, as therapy progresses, the patient begins to "fill in the blanks" and makes the experience very personal. One patient said she could imagine the flight attendant asking her if she wanted the "chicken" or "beef" dinner. Another reported smelling "jet fuel" though no such smell was present in the VR treatment session. Patients shape and create their own virtual experience, and as they become more present and immersed in the virtual world, therapeutic benefit occurs. As Baños and her colleagues (1999) described it, patients exhibit a "willing suspension of disbelief," which allows them to become present in the virtual world (p. 147). They give themselves permission to become immersed, to relinquish control, and to allow the stimuli to become real. As one patient told us, "VR is in your face—you can't escape it!" It is difficult to drift off task because numerous senses are stimulated during the experience. Soon after we set up the clinic, the computer malfunctioned once during the exposure session. One of our patients said, in effect, "Wow, I was on the plane flying and then when the computer stopped it was like, oh yeah, I'm just in the office. But until then, I was there on that plane."

Patients often report experiences previously forgotten and out of their conscious memory. Often these are pleasant memories of such things as how they used to love to travel by air or drive long distances. Some patients do, however, disassociate during the experience. Therefore, caution must be exercised not to progress these patients too quickly through the virtual experience. Clinicians should look for a lack of physiological or subjective arousal as a sign of dissociation, because therapy is not successful if a patient does not stay present. Patients may have used dissociation as a defense mechanism in the past, and only by providing a safe and trusting environment and by progressing at a slow pace can they stay on task. This is necessary so that continuous exposure occurs and leads to desensitization and habituation. By monitoring the patient's physiology and by observing his or her outward demeanor, it is possible to see whether the pace is too fast for that patient. In addition, because the therapist can communicate with the patient by microphone, direct contact can be maintained if necessary.

Patients who seek therapy at VRMC undergo initial intake and evaluation as part of their first visit. In general, the best candidates for VR therapy are those who (a) do not have medical contraindications, (b) do not have a history of cybersickness, and (c) are easily able to become immersed or present in the virtual world. (Medical contraindications to VR treatment are discussed in detail in chap. 5.) The type of clinical disorder encountered during the initial intake can often determine whether VR therapy is an appropriate choice. The selection criteria are the same as those used in treating any other patient with an anxiety disorder when the presence of other co-morbid conditions can have a significant impact on therapeutic success. Additional factors are those that apply to any patient seeking mental healthcare services, namely, commitment to therapy, willingness to undergo the therapeutic process, and faithful completion of "homework assignments" between therapy sessions.

Before participants in our initial fear of flying controlled study began therapy, we administered a Tellagen Absorption Scale to determine absorption ability and the Stanford Hypnotizability Profile to determine hypnotizability. The Tellagen Absorption Scale and Hypnotic Induction Profile have been found to correlate highly with each other, and now patients are given only the Tellagen Absorption Scale. On the basis of studies by Baños et al. (1999) and our clinical observations we also administer the Dissociative Experience Scale. If they score low on the Tellagen Absorption Scale, however, it may take several sessions to become immersed, whereas those who score high on the Tellagen Absorption Scale may find themselves a part of the world on the first exposure. Those who have a strong need to stay in control and not let go must also be encouraged to give themselves permission to become immersed. We have also found that for the most resistant among patients, it is sometimes effective to put them into a light hypnotic state prior to exposure, so that their conscious, vigilant mind may give way to a more relaxed way of processing.

All patients are encouraged to enter into a relaxed state prior to exposure, performing five or more minutes of slow, diaphragmatic breathing with visual feedback. This serves both to increase their skill set by developing coping mechanisms in the real and virtual worlds and to develop a sense of mastery. Our extensive clinical experience with more than 4,000 patients has led us to conclude that treatment is more effective when the patients are relaxed.

A brief review of session structure follows. This is provided as a template; it can vary from individual to individual depending on the particular circumstances and needs.

Intake Session

During the intake session, the therapist takes a thorough history of the patient's presenting problem. Some patients come in knowing what has caused their phobia, whereas others do not remember its beginnings. This session is very much like the initial intake session of a conventional therapy, involving discussion with the therapist. At this point, education about the nature of CBT is important. We want patients to actively participate in their own recovery and to understand the therapeutic process. Patients are given homework assignments, usually from commonly found patient workbooks. A typical assignment for this session may be to read a chapter about anxiety. Patients are given self-report questionnaires to take home, complete, and bring back to the next session.

Treatment Session 1

The first treatment session begins with a Psychophysiological Stress Profile (Diaz, Vallejo, & Comeche, 2003), which is a simple procedure designed to record baseline heart rate, breathing, and other noninvasive physiological measures. This helps the therapist determine how the patient's body would react to and recover from stress, and it allows the patient to become familiar with the physiological monitoring devices at the clinic. When the profile is completed, the therapist discusses the basic physical and mental reactions to stress and anxiety with the patient. The therapist teaches the patient some breathing skills and gives the patient a relaxation tape to take home. We feel it is important for patients to leave with a tool and to make a commitment to practice their breathing 4–5 days per week. An additional assignment is also given from the patient workbook.

Session 2

During session 2, the patient again practices breathing skills with visual feedback on a computer screen. The patient and therapist review questionnaires that were completed. The therapist teaches thought stopping and rationale refutation techniques and answers any questions the patient may have about the workbook assignment. (All therapists at VRMC are required to read the patient workbooks before beginning to treat patients so that they are familiar with the material and techniques the patients are learning.) Next, the therapist introduces the VR hardware and allows the patient to become familiar with navigating in a neutral virtual environment. This session does not involve exposure to anxiety-inducing simulations, because it is important for a patient to understand the methods behind the treatment and to be able to practice the traditional therapeutic cognitive techniques that they were taught before becoming involved in the VR phase of their treatment. A hierarchy of feared situations is then constructed and is used to determine how VR therapy will proceed, as well as to schedule in vivo exercises between sessions.

Sessions 3–8

During session 3, and in all subsequent sessions, the therapist reviews homework with the patient and discusses any difficulties or questions on worksheets in the workbook. Then, the therapist records a baseline of the patient's diaphragmatic breathing. At this point, most patients are ready to begin exposure in the VR world. The head-mounted display is placed on the patient, and he or she is given a little time to become oriented and comfortable with how to move about and interact in this world. Lights are turned off in the therapy room to block external stimuli. Exposure to the least anxiety provoking scenarios then begins. The therapist monitors the patient's physiological reactions during the VR exposure and records them for review with the patient after exposure concludes. After a 20-minute exposure, the therapist switches on the lights and removes the head-mounted display from the patient. The patient is asked to estimate his or her subjective units of distress levels. Although the estimate is based on patient memory of anxiety and is not done in real time, it was found during the first 6 months of using the virtual worlds that asking the patient for anxiety ratings during virtual exposure actually decreased presence and immersion levels, thereby reducing treatment efficacy. Patients actually said it was "popping" them out of the experience.

Next, the patient's physiological reactions to the world are reviewed and discussed. As with imaginal and in vivo therapy, as the patient becomes more aware of his or her own reactions, the cognitive distortions seem to diminish as treatment proceeds. The therapist then reviews any clinical observations with the patient. Patient comments about the VR world, including suggestions for improvements in future iterations, are also noted. The patient spends only 20 minutes of each therapy session immersed in VR. In fact, most of the session is spent in traditional therapist–patient interaction.

To understand more fully how patients progress through therapy, we are developing a model that compares both objective and subjective responses to the virtual world. The model described below examines the role of synchrony and compares various patterns of objective and subjective arousal.

Most of the hundreds of patients treated at the VRMC who presented with a specific phobia but no trauma required on average of 8–10 sessions of VR exposure. There is a range of individual responses that can be easily addressed by the VR sessions. Those presenting with, PTSD resulting from a motor vehicle accident may require 12–15 sessions to resolve their anxiety. Probably our shortest treatment time was with a male in his 70s who came to us more than 2 years ago because he was afraid to drive on freeways. He came for an intake session, a breathing retraining session, and one exposure session. He called prior to the next scheduled appointment to say he did not require our services any longer because he was fine. Since then, he has returned all completed posttreatment follow-up questionnaires reporting continuing lowered anxiety scores and a return to normal driving on the freeway.

As mentioned above, we use a variety of evaluative measures to help patients progress through therapy. These range from subjective to objective as shown in Figure 4.1. Subjective units of distress are recorded before and after treatment and are used to determine the level of anxiety the patient feels during the presentation of virtual

FIGURE 4.1.

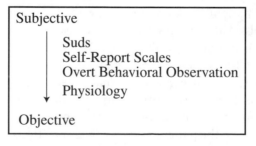

Evaluative measures used during virtual reality treatment sessions. SUDS = subjective units of distress.

stimuli. Also before and after treatment, patients are given self-report questionnaires to help determine the amplitude of fear as well as the specific parts of a situation that elicits anxiety—such as take-offs versus turbulence versus purchasing a ticket for individuals with flying phobia—and to see how these fears are affected by treatment. *Overt clinical observation* refers to the therapist's observation during the VR exposure. Is the patient sitting passively, gripping the arms of the chair, or is the patient interacting with the world but in a more relaxed manner? These observations should be discussed with the patient after the exposure is completed. Physiology is measured noninvasively as part of the session to provide an objective measurement of patient anxiety and to see how patient physiology reacts as sessions progress and desensitization occurs.

After more than 3,000 sessions with patients at the VRMC, we have also been able to classify patients into four groups based on a framework that uses both subjective and objective (physiology) measures of anxiety. The framework can be seen in Figure 4.2. Current physiological classification is based on skin resistance; an updated version of this framework includes heart rate variability (Wiederhold, Jang, & Wiederhold, 2002). Patients in Group 1 of the framework exhibit high objective and subjective anxiety when placed in the virtual world. These patients tend to become highly immersed, or present, in the virtual world and quickly become a part of it. Their fear structure is activated and open to change, and they tend to progress through treatment rapidly (Foa & Kozak, 1986).

An example: We had a patient who had been fearful of flying for 27 years. Her specific fear was of crashing during the flight. When

FIGURE 4.2.

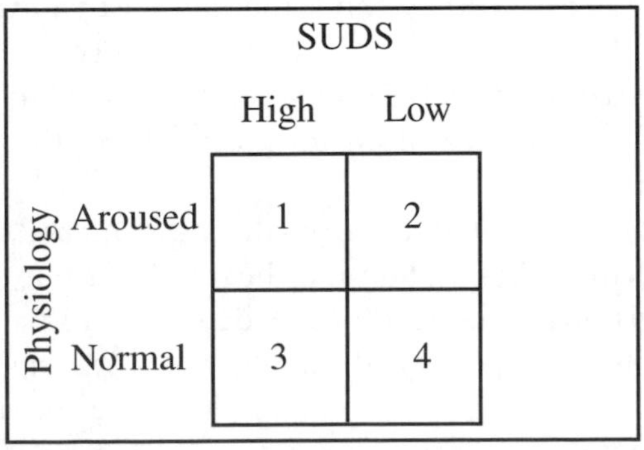

		SUDS	
		High	Low
Physiology	Aroused	1	2
	Normal	3	4

Subjective units of distress (SUDS) versus skin resistance.

given the Hypnotic Induction Profile and Tellegen Absorption Scale, she scored high on both, indicating that she had the ability to become quickly absorbed into activities. This was true also of the VR exposure. During the first session she reported subjective units of distress levels that increased to 95 (out of a possible 100). Her skin resistance also showed dramatic decrease during the VR flight, indicating arousal—at one point it was 40% below baseline levels. This patient was exposed to the VR a total of 6 times, each for 20 minutes in duration, and has been flying successfully since. At 3-year follow-up, her fear had not returned.

Patients in Group 2 show high levels of physiological arousal when exposed to the VR world, but they report low levels of subjective anxiety. This may be due to an inability to admit their fears to the therapist or it could be a sort of emotional numbing or a disconnect between what their minds are experiencing and what the body is feeling. An example of a patient we saw who fit into this category was a young man who feared having a panic attack on the airplane and being unable to find an escape. Prior to coming to treatment, he had been teased about having to "go play with video games" to overcome his fear. When he was placed in the VR flying situation, his skin resistance decreased by 45%, a clear indication of anxiety. He rated his own distress levels as 1 (out of 100), indicating that he had felt no fear. He was encouraged to try and relinquish control and to allow himself to become a part of the world. He did continue treatment, and in subsequent sessions he was able to report anxiety, as well as show physiological arousal. He admitted later that he was initially embarrassed that a "cartoon" could generate so much anxiety. We would say that he was "transformed" into a "Group 1-like" individual. He was able to fly, but he required more sessions because of his initial resistance.

Group 3 individuals report high levels of arousal subjectively but show relatively little physiologically. Individuals in this group may be reporting what they think the therapist wants to hear, and they may score high on social desirability scales. They may also have some sort of "disconnect" between mind and body. If an individual is coming for treatment as part of an insurance claim, there clearly is the issue of secondary gain.

One patient in this group had tried many "quick fixes" to overcome her fear of flying. She had heard about our successes with VR on a television program and traveled from out of state to be seen. She quickly established rapport with the therapist. When she was placed in the VR flying situation, she reported moderate anxiety (30) although little physiological arousal was detected (skin resistance decreased by only 5%). After she reported her distress levels to the therapist, the therapist showed her her skin resistance level. At this time the patient "confessed" that she had not really been able to become immersed or feel anxious but that she did not want the therapist to be displeased with her. The therapist explained that it was normal for some people to experience no anxiety at first exposure to the VR situation. In subsequent sessions, the patient, who had scored low on hypnotizability and absorption, was able to become immersed in the VR world, become aroused physiologically and subjectively, and then become desensitized. She had traveled to our center by train, but she was able to fly home.

Patients in Group 4 show no subjective or objective arousal. They either have no phobias at all, or they have phobias but are unable to become immersed or present in the virtual world. These individuals report subjectively what their bodies are also objectively telling us. In fact, we find that many nonphobic individuals actually become more relaxed during the passive VR environments, such as flying! One individual who participated in an early study at our center reported liking to fly and gave a subjective distress rating of 0. Physiologically, she actually had an increase in skin resistance during the flying experience, showing that she had actually became more relaxed than at baseline.

We have found that patients must become both subjectively and objectively aroused when moving through the VR experience if they are to become desensitized to their fears. This statement is based on what others have reported for more than 30 years (Foa & Kozak, 1986; Hodgson & Rachman, 1974; Lang, Melamed, & Hart, 1970; Rachman, 1978). Their research has shown that the phobic individual's fear must be activated both subjectively and objectively in order for that anxiety to decrease. Without the use of physiological parameters, it is difficult to tell whether the fear structure has been accessed and is open to change.

The patient is viewed as an integral part of the treatment team at VRMC and is encouraged to always take an active part in recovery. Therapist, developer, and patient form a powerful triad with a shared goal of effecting recovery. With the patient's permission, system developers often sit in on therapy sessions to see exactly how the patient interacts with their system. This leads to more user-friendly systems and allows the developer to see exactly what difficulties the patient might experience with the system and what improvements can be made. This also allows the patient to discuss firsthand what additions to the virtual world might be beneficial. The therapist can also express his or her assessment to the developer of what changes might be desirable. By having the patient as part of the team, software can be tweaked as development continues, rather than building a "pretty" but nonfunctional system. Although the cost of improvement of these systems may be high in this initial development stage, actual clinical practice using these perfected systems is cost effective.

After using this system for more than 5 years, the lessons we learned have allowed us to continue to develop new applications for the evaluation and treatment of mental health disorders. We try to maintain contact with all our patients after treatment ends, sending post-treatment follow-up questionnaires every 6 months. Our success rate as determined by improved patient scores in relation to *DSM–IV–TR* criteria currently stands at 91.6% overall, and we are striving to improve that rate.

Many of our newer VR systems now incorporate real-time digital video into the VR world. This allows patients with a fear of public speaking to bring in a PowerPoint presentation, port it directly into the virtual world, and practice a speech over and over before they deliver it at a conference or meeting. Videoconferencing capabilities also allow us to begin therapy with patients who are, at first, too agoraphobic to leave their home for treatment. Internet worlds and videoconferencing allow those with social phobia to practice their social skills and conversational abilities prior to going into the world. The Internet allows audio and videoconferencing, creating real time visual and audio contact. Feedback, whether positive or negative, is also real time. By seeing the patient interact with others in a realistic way, the therapist can spot any remaining deficits and work to ameliorate them prior to real world interactions outside the therapist's office.

Some believe that technology creates a barrier between patient and therapist. We have not found this to be the case. For the entire time the patient is in the office, we watch, monitor, and interact with them. The technology only provides a medium by which we can more effectively help our patients help themselves.

Whether to include physiology during the treatment session will vary depending on clinician. Our experience shows that the use of physiological feedback and training does add to treatment efficacy. In our controlled study completed in 1999 (Wiederhold, Gervitz, & Spira, 2001) we treated 30 subjects with fear of flying. Those who received VR therapy without physiological feedback had an 80% treatment success rate, whereas those who received VR therapy with physiological feedback for six exposure sessions had a 100% treatment success rate. Patients report to us that the use of physiological feedback allows them to become aware of anxiety when it is at a much lower level, so that they can then begin practicing coping mechanisms such as positive self-talk and diaphragmatic breathing. It also allows those who feel the need to be in control to know that they can control their thoughts and bodily reactions. In a subsequent 3-year follow-up of these patients no one in the physiological feedback group had experienced a relapse, but recidivism did occur in the group receiving VR therapy with no feedback.

When we first began treating patients, we attached a subwoofer to the bottom of a regular office chair so that the patient could feel vibrations during takeoff, turbulence, and landing in the virtual flight scenarios. Since that time, we have created rooms dedicated to different phobias with tactile augmentation. For instance, for patients with a fear of driving, the virtual experience now includes sitting in a real car seat, fastening a seat belt, driving with a steering wheel, brake, and gas pedal, and sitting with a vibrating platform to simulate motor vibrations, and the driving experience becomes even more real. For patients with a fear of flying, the virtual experience is augmented by making them sit in real airline seats, on the back row of a coach section of the plane, and with their seat belts fastened before takeoff. When patients do baseline breathing, they are facing the back of an airline seat. Then, when they go into the virtual world, they are also looking at the back of an airline seat (although they can turn their head and look around the plane or out the window). This seems to help "ground" them in the virtual world and appears to add to their sense of immersiveness. For patients with a fear of heights, they hold on to a cold, metal railing in the real world, and in the virtual world, they are standing on a scaffolding elevator with a steel railing. As they ascend higher and higher the sound of wind can be heard in the virtual world, and in the real world a fan is aimed toward them, and vibrations under their feet are generated by the audio amplifier mounted under the vibrating platform. (Platforms are shown in Figures 4.3, 4.4, and 4.5.) We try to make the experience as realistic as possible, and all the while the patients know that at any point they can escape the experience should they choose. In 5 years, however, we have only had one patient feel the need to do this, and this was because a flashback had occurred

For those patients who require continued exposure or who cannot tolerate the virtual world because of a vestibular abnormality, we do continue treatment in the real world. We also offer patient education such as airport tours and tours of the local aerospace museum. VR treatment is only one piece of a full multimodal therapy; it is not seen as replacing the other useful components of traditional anxiety treatments.

FIGURE 4.3.

Vibrating platform with actual automobile seat, steering wheel, and gas and break pedals to augment virtual reality while driving.

FIGURE 4.4.

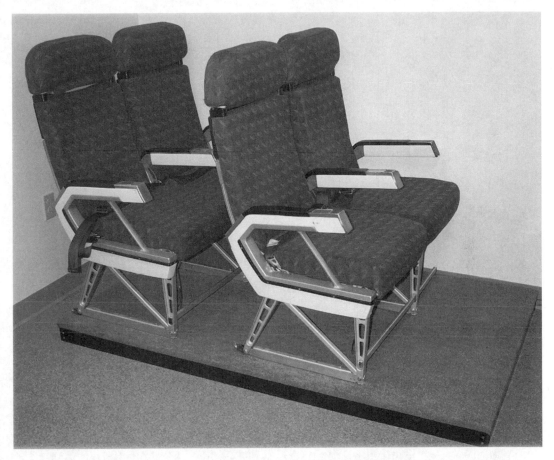

These are actual airline seats placed on a vibrating platform that the patient sits in while undergoing exposure therapy for aviophobia. The legroom reproduces the actual dimensions in a typical coach cabin. Be sure to fasten your seatbelt.

FIGURE 4.5.

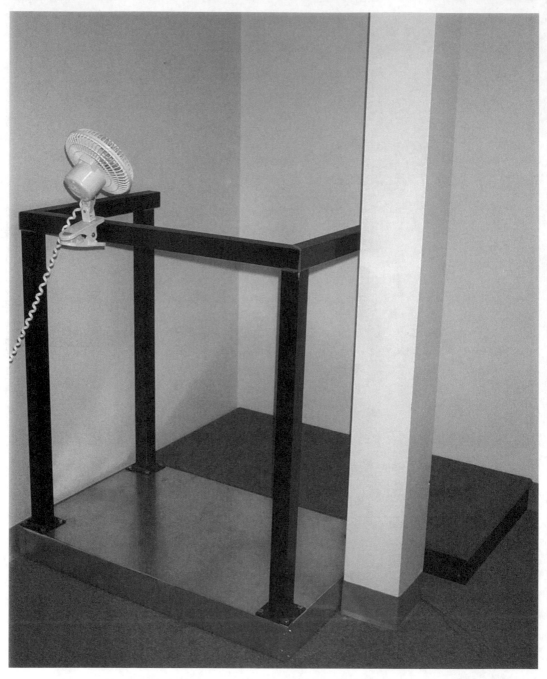

This vibrating steel platform is used for treatment of fear of heights. The fan, which is augmented by the sound, is used to simulate wind.

Side Effects and Contraindications

5

A ny patient who comes for virtual reality (VR) therapy requires the same type of comprehensive intake and evaluation as any other patient seeking mental healthcare services. Because VR therapy is still new, and content of virtual reality environments is limited, VR cannot treat all phobic presentations or clinical conditions. However, new environments are being created every year. In principle, there is no reason that VR technology cannot be applied for the treatment of all anxiety disorders. In fact, many practitioners are beginning to use VR to treat generalized anxiety disorders (C. Botella, personal communication, January 2004). However, patients need to learn how to interact with the virtual environment (among other things), and this can be accomplished through the skills of the therapist. Most patients require screening for a small number of medical conditions, such as migraine headache, seizure disorder, and vestibular abnormalities, which are contraindications for VR therapy. Patients who have higher levels of hypnotizability or are able to become immersed in movies, hobbies, or other tasks may become immersed or present in the virtual environments more quickly. However, patients who are not highly hypnotizable or those who score lower on the Tellegen Absorption Scale can still be successfully treated.

There has only recently been a concerted effort to understand potential negative effects of using VR in clinical populations. As VR therapy gains wider use and acceptance, this understanding is likely to increase. At a Medicine Meets Virtual Reality Conference, Virtual Reality and Mental Health, held in Newport Beach in January 2000, conference attendees voiced agreement that a task force was needed to collect data from clinical sessions and assemble a central database for further study and analysis. An informal poll of clinical users attending the meeting confirmed a relatively low incidence of side effects from clinical studies; however, it was generally agreed that the effects on a more diverse (outside of the laboratory) population of patients were not known.

The wider application of virtual environments in the clinical setting should take into account that particular groups of patients, or those with specific medical conditions, may require certain modifications of the VR system. (See the section Contraindications for the Use of Virtual Reality Graded Exposure Therapy.) Other ergonomic requirements may preclude some patients from interfacing with VR environments.

Medical and psychological concerns can best be addressed in clinical practice by the following: understanding the basic physiological changes that may occur during VR therapy; carefully screening patients; understanding the side effects and contraindications for the use of VR; understanding the needs of special groups, such as elderly populations; taking standard precautions prior to treatment; and considering what the potential long-term effects of VR use might be.

Physiological Effects of Virtual Reality Therapy

A number of physiological changes are shown to occur while individuals are engaged in virtual environments or while playing video games. This topic is extensively reviewed elsewhere (Gwyinup, Haw, & Elias, 1983), and only the information germane to the topic of medical consequences of immersive environments is discussed here.

Gwyinup et al. (1983) observed changes in both blood pressure and heart rate while participants played video games and suggested caution when these tools are used with patients with cardiovascular disease. Segal and Dietz (1991) also noted increased heart rate, increased systolic and diastolic blood pressure, and increased oxygen consumption while playing video games. The increase was similar in magnitude to mild intensity exercise. The mental workload is not insignificant during these tasks. In fact the psycho-physiological literature is full of studies using video games as a stress-inducing tool.

Denot-Ledunois, Vardon, Perruchet, and Gallego (1998) studied breathing patterns in children involved in video game playing. They reported an increase in breath duration, but no change in cortisol levels, heart rate, or thoracic expansion, suggesting that focused attentional tasks were associated with inhibition of breathing. Emes (1997) reviewed the video game literature in children and found associations between them and increased metabolic rate, heart rate, seizures, and tendonitis. No correlation has been found between video game use and psychopathology or academic performance. Kelley et al. (1992) found increased global cerebral blood flow during the playing of a commercial video game. A selective activation was noted in the right middle cerebral artery. Whether patients with cerebral ischemia are at increased risk is an open question. These findings are important in light of potential negative effects for patients with underlying medical conditions. Considerations of such physiological effects should be included in the clinician's judgment concerning the appropriateness of VR therapy for specific individuals.

In a study by Mager (2001), event-related potentials were recorded for claustrophobic participants who were undergoing desensitization through VR therapy. Thirty-two channels of electroencephalogram (EEG) were recorded by placing an electrode cap on the person's head under the head-mounted display. It was observed that EEG and event-related potential changes were highly correlated with levels of subjective anxiety in the virtual world. Thus, obtaining physiological feedback facilitates several tasks, including the ability to adjust the speed and course of therapy as necessary; immediate, objective feedback on patient's responses to particular virtual scenes and situations; and an objective record of the session that can be compared to subsequent sessions, giving a clear record of the response and progression of therapy (Mager, 2001).

Screening Tools

Some preexisting conditions, such as migraine and epilepsy, are contraindications to VR therapy. Clinicians are advised to use a quick medical pre-screening tool to conduct a pre-session evaluation to rule out such conditions as well as alcohol and substance abuse, and to take a medication history with attention to current medications. Patients should also read and sign an informed consent form that clearly and fully explains therapy and its potential risks. A step-by-step explanation of the treatment hierarchy should be offered and advancement along the hierarchy mutually agreed upon. Risks and benefits must be clearly and carefully explained to patients, and any discussion or questions must be documented in the patient chart. Patients should be told that they are free to withdraw from VR therapy at any time and that they can complete non-VR therapy or be referred to others for additional options. Finally, appropriate post-VR session observation should be routine.

The Virtual Reality Medical Center has developed a Medical Pre-screening Protocol that can be easily adapted to any clinical program. The four major components of the protocol include obtaining a thorough medical history from the patient, asking specific questions to rule out serious medical conditions, completing an abbreviated cybersickness questionnaire, and continuing observation throughout the session and after its completion for the appearance of symptoms. Several existing questionnaires can be administered to assess for the risk of cybersickness. The most commonly used, the Simulator Sickness Questionnaire has been shown to be a reliable indicator for predicting cybersickness in military pilots and in undergraduate populations (Stanney & Kennedy, 1997). This questionnaire is a reasonable starting point for the assessment of discomfort in patients. Asking directly for any history of motion sickness can also be helpful.

If patients score highly on the Simulator Sickness Questionnaire or report symptoms while immersed, several options are available for the continuation of therapy. Withdrawal from the environment and substitution of a less immersive system, such as two-dimensional computer display, can be attempted. Shorter, more frequent sessions may be tried, and, if necessary, patients can be pretreated before the VR session. Options for pretreatment include oral anti-motion sickness medication or a dermal patch. As with any medication, potential drug interactions or adverse drug effects should be considered. It is a good idea to rule out pregnancy; glaucoma; gastrointestinal disease; or liver, kidney, or metabolic abnormality, as well as urinary obstruction and drug allergy, before use of anti-motion sickness medication. Patients should likewise avoid alcohol, antihistamines, and anti-depressants before the use of anti-motion sickness medicine.

Cybersickness

Cybersickness is a cluster of symptoms that can be caused by exposure to virtual environments. McCauley (McCauley & Cook, 1986; McCauley &

Sharkey, 1992) first used the term *cybersickness* to describe symptoms of disorientation, nausea, dizziness, headache, blurred vision, and *vection* (the feeling of moving through space) that can accompany exposure to a simulated world. To a large extent, the syndrome is similar to the motion sickness experienced during automobile or airplane travel; however, important distinctions are explored below.

Various studies have placed the incidence of cybersickness in virtual environments at between 2% and 60%, depending on length of exposure, type of simulation, and sophistication of the equipment (Wiederhold, Rizzo, & Wiederhold, 1999). The three most frequent symptoms involve the vestibular system, the ocular system, and the gastrointestinal system. The vestibular system may be involved when miscues occur between perceived motion and actual motion in the virtual world. The resulting symptoms may include dizziness, light-headedness, and vection. The most common form of vection is when viewers experience motion on a screen but are themselves seated or standing still. It is similar to the experience of watching a roller-coaster ride on television. Ocular symptoms, such as visual blurring, headache, and eyestrain are most often due to poorly aligned optical systems or to optical paths that are not adjusted to the individual user. In particular, mismatch of the optical paths to the intrapupillary distance is the most common cause of eye discomfort. This same mismatch and discomfort may occur to users of binoculars or microscopes. Disturbances in vestibular function in combination with visual distortions can induce nausea, vomiting, and eructation (belching).

Three less commonly seen symptoms include "simulator sleepiness," postural abnormalities, and musculoskeletal discomfort. The sleepiness induced by virtual worlds is not a new finding, but it is incompletely understood. The incidence of sleepiness (sometimes called *sopite syndrome*), which can be accompanied by generalized fatigue, is generally below 5% (Lawson & Mead, 1997). One possible explanation could be over-stimulation of the visual and auditory centers, with reflex withdrawal from the offending stimulus. Postural instability occurs within a wide range of severity, including frank ataxia. The symptoms of disorientation can persist even after finishing the VR task, with a real potential for serious injury. (Some individuals may fall down or walk into walls.)

Older, heavier models of head-mounted display often caused neck, back, and shoulder strain and were also associated with headaches. Complaints of carpal tunnel syndrome (also known as *Nintendo wrist*) may occur with users who navigate the virtual world for long periods of time. Table 5.1 lists the symptoms associated with cybersickness.

The great majority of studies of cybersickness have been performed on military populations whose use of simulators is an important and

TABLE 5.1	
Symptoms of Cybersickness	
Target area	**Symptom**
Visual	Visual blurring
	Double vision
	Tearing
	Irritation
	Redness
Auditory	Tinnitus
	Decreased hearing
Vestibular	Dizziness
	Nausea
	Vomiting
	Sweating
Central nervous system	Headache
	Seizures
	Flashbacks
	Disorientation
	Instability
Musculoskeletal	Neck strain
	Wrist strain
	Back pain

integral part of training and in whom cybersickness has posed significant problems. For those with significant simulator exposure, symptoms could interrupt the training session or persist for several hours after the session ends. In some reports, symptoms occurred days or weeks after exposure. In studies of flight simulators, "flashbacks" have also been seen in a small number of participants. These symptoms are particularly troublesome, especially when they occur during real-life driving or flying activities.

In 1989, Kennedy, Lilenthal, Berbaum, Baltzley, and McCauley reviewed more than 1,000 training sessions on Navy flight simulators and found that trainees exhibited symptoms including difficulty concentrating, nausea, ocular blurring, sweating, headache, eyestrain, and fatigue. The incidence of symptoms during the simulation session ranged from 10% to 26%, depending on the task and situation. In addition, 45% of users experienced symptoms after the session, with 25% having symptoms persisting for more than 1 hour, and 8% of participants complaining of symptoms lasting for more than 6 hours.

The figures cited above are significant, and cybersickness must be considered seriously as a potential problem for patients using VR therapy. However, in the military studies participants spent a much longer time (several hours) in simulators than do typical patients in a VR therapy session (45 minutes). In addition, the military studies involved the performance of very stressful and demanding tasks, with the added stress that the outcome of the performance would have a direct effect on the participants' careers as potential pilots. Another important difference is that the pilots are literally flying a virtual airplane and must focus on the minute detail of meters, gauges, and warning lights. Patients, in contrast, have a more relaxed experience, knowing that they will not suffer major negative consequences.

In general, symptoms and levels of distress typically decrease over time, suggesting an adaptation to the virtual environment. A review of clinical studies using patients with mental health disorders shows that on average about 2% to 4% of patients experience some mild forms of cybersickness (Wiederhold et al., 1999). The majority of these symptoms include mild transitory dizziness and, more rarely, visual blurring and mild transitory nausea. The geriatric population, at least in initial studies, does not seem to have an increased incidence of side effects. Overall, using virtual worlds in clinical practice does not seem to cause significant cybersickness-related symptoms. These conclusions are only preliminary; much larger samples of patients, with a much broader range of underlying medical conditions, must be studied. In addition, observations must include longer follow-up. If symptoms do occur, pretreatment with anti-motion sickness medicine would alleviate almost all symptoms. In a study of 150 individuals, Regan and Ramsey (1996) found that a 40-minute pretreatment with 300 micrograms of hyoscine hydrobromide significantly reduced symptoms of simulator sickness. Many types of anti-motion sickness medications are available over the counter and are effective in alleviating symptoms. Other methods that can help prevent symptoms include gradual introduction to virtual worlds and shorter exposure times (20 minutes rather than 45 minutes). Costello (1997) provided a comprehensive summary of much of the cybersickness data.

Contraindications for the Use of Virtual Reality Graded Exposure Therapy

Contraindications to VR therapy include migraine headache, seizure disorder (from multiple causes), and history of serious vestibular abnormalities. Musculoskeletal disorders may make VR therapy diffi-cult or impossible, whereas visual disturbances and deafness do not necessarily rule out treatment but do require modifications of the stan-dard procedure. Cardiovascular disease, hypertension, and severe chronic obstructive pulmonary disease may rule out VR treatment depending on the severity of the disorder. Serious psychiatric disease is an additional contraindication, as the effects of VR on such popula-tions are not yet known. As with any clinical practice, emergencies can occur; standard procedures should be in place and clinicians and staff should be trained to deal with such events.

Although rare, photic over-stimulation can, in some patients, cause migraine headache, as is the case with the use of simulators (Viirre & Bush, 2002). A number of studies have evaluated the incidence of seizures in children and adults exposed to video games (Fylan, Harding, Edson, & Webb, 1999; Harding & Harding, 1999; Inoue et al., 1999; Kasteleijn-Nolst Trenite et al., 1999; Millet, Fish, Thompson, & Johnson, 1999; Pellouchoud, Smith, McEvoy, & Gevins, 1999; Ricci & Vigevano, 1999). A 1998 report in *Nature Medicine* chronicled seizures in more than 300 children who watched a particular animation on television in Japan (Harding, 1998). It is relatively easy to inquire about seizure history from patients or parents; however, identification of those pa-tients who may be at increased risk for seizures, but who have no seizure history, is more problematic. It may be useful to rule out patients with conditions involving a high risk for seizures, paying particular attention to any history of head trauma, history of brain mass, or past history of encephalitis.

Vestibular abnormalities are another class of disorders that require special attention. Many of the symptoms of cybersickness are due to physiological vertigo, where the vestibular system and the visual system are miscued. Patients with pathological vertigo should probably be excluded from VR environments. Because many elderly individuals have difficulty with otosclerosis (calcification in the inner ear leading to balance problems), it is important to ask about any history of dizziness.

Other contraindications for VR therapy include musculoskeletal disorders, which may hinder the use of equipment or cause injury or discomfort in patients. Musculoskeletal abnormalities or severe injuries may preclude the patient from wearing the head-mounted display. Any type of neck injury or cervical degenerative disease may make a heavy head-mounted display difficult to wear. Decreased mobility at the neck may adversely affect how the patient interacts with the virtual world. Patients with arthritis may be unable to turn or move in the environ-ment and may not be able to operate a joystick or a data-glove.

Visual disturbances and deafness are not contraindications for VR therapy but may require modification of the virtual environment. One investigator has used three-dimensional sound as a means for a blind child to navigate a three-dimensional virtual maze (Sanchez & Lumbreras, 1999). Any difficulty with gait or balance could pose a risk for patients, especially in those applications where locomotion is an important part of the virtual task.

A few case reports have documented ataxia following exposure to virtual environments. The ataxia was temporary and resolved spontaneously, but patients with baseline gait abnormalities may be at increased risk. Kennedy et al. (1989) found a correlation between high scores on the Disorientation subscale of the Simulator Sickness Questionnaire, and the incidence of postural instability following VR exposure in military personnel. However, in a sample of 40 undergraduates, Kennedy et al. found no symptoms of postural instability following VR exposure. The difference in these results is explained by the length of exposure, with the undergraduates having spent much less time in the simulator. Cobb (1999) observed that postural instability is a rare occurrence that is both transitory and mild in most users.

A number of other conditions could, in theory, pose increased risks to individuals, but no known adverse effects have been reported in the literature. Severe cardiovascular disease, such as congestive heart failure, advanced coronary artery disease, and cardiac arrythmia, could pose risks for treatment of panic disorder or PTSD, where the visual stimuli can cause marked emotional change. However, this concern is based on physical response to stimuli, not on the emotional implications. In fact, a panel of experts recently published a finding that the most appropriate therapy for PTSD is exposure therapy, with no concerns of "retraumatizing" the individual (Ballenger et al., 2000). Patients with hypertension or severe chronic obstructive pulmonary disease might also be at risk of stress. We had a case of one patient who experienced a panic attack during VR therapy at our institution (Wiederhold, 1999).

VR treatment of serious psychiatric disease is currently regarded as relatively risky; however, many investigators are now exploring the use of VR to treat and evaluate schizophrenia and multiple personality disorder. The potential effects of VR therapy on patients with serious mental health disorders are not known. Therefore, extensive evaluation of these patients is necessary before proceeding.

Precautions

Simple steps can be taken to maximize patients' positive experience and to minimize their negative experience during the VR session. The patient and therapist should establish a clear signal that allows the patient to terminate the session at any time. Allowing the patient to maintain a locus of control is helpful in this circumstance where VR therapy may be a totally new experience. In particular, this feeling of control may increase the level of comfort and decrease the side effects (Stanney & Hash, 1998). It is important for the therapist to be observant of signs of discomfort, because some patients are uncomfortable or embarrassed to voice negative comments. Physiological monitoring during the session can be used to objectively measure some aspects of discomfort and may be a useful adjunct to therapy. Obvious rapid changes in vital signs, such as heart rate, skin resistance, and respiratory pattern, could indicate distress. Finally, gradual introduction of the patient to the environment can greatly facilitate acceptance and reduce side effects.

Following the VR session, it is important to allow time for questions, discussion, and relaxation. Patients who are driving should sit in the waiting room and relax after the VR session especially if they experience dizziness during treatment; most mild and transitory symptoms of cybersickness dissipate during a short amount of time. Some therapists may want to include a release form for those who wish to drive themselves. In rare instances, patients experience dizziness or instability while driving following a VR session. Patients should be encouraged to contact the therapist if they experience any postsession discomfort. Any adverse events should be reported so that they are included in the Adverse Effects Database referred to in the introduction to this chapter.

When using VR systems to treat an elderly population, clinicians should allow extra time for introductory explanations and VR system set up. In our experience the elderly adapt easily to VR systems, and most find the experience enjoyable. It is very important that the VR systems be introduced gradually and that ample time is allowed for questions. In general, many elderly patients have baseline problems with the vestibular system and balance in general. Although not seen in our clinic, careful attention to possible symptoms of dizziness and vertigo can prevent falls. It would be advisable in any case to have an assistant near the patient to prevent any sudden movements and to assist in preventing falls. Of particular concern are the numbers and length of cables used in VR systems because patients might become entangled in or trip on them.

Long-Term Effects of Virtual Reality Exposure

Very little information is available concerning long-term effects of VR exposure. Ungs (1989) reported the results from a questionnaire given to 196 pilots who had experienced VR side effects for longer than 24 hours. In this study, 4.6% of respondents experienced negative effects for more than 24 hours after the conclusion of the session. These symptoms included visual flashbacks, balance disorder, and lack of hand-eye coordination. Of note, 1.5% reported difficulty flying an aircraft. Exactly how the VR experience produces changes that linger over time is not known.

An important area of concern in the use and application of virtual tools involves possible psychological and psychiatric side effects of virtual environments. Although there are no existing data on this subject, several investigators have voiced concerns and raised potential issues. Mantovani (1995) suggested that as VR becomes more real and believable, the ability to differentiate VR from "real" reality may become difficult for some individuals and patients. In this context, the effect of virtual environments approaches that of drugs, such as hallucinogens. It is possible that some individuals may prefer the virtual world to the real world and completely withdraw from society. There is also some concern that an individual's sense of reality may become blurred or incorporated into the virtual world and that the patient may be unable to distinguish safe from dangerous or high-risk practices and behaviors. Taken further, this scenario could lead to addiction to the virtual environment. We have already witnessed the growth of Internet addiction to Internet chat rooms, gambling, pornography, shopping, day trading, and on-line relationships.

Cartwright (1994) questioned how VR might interfere with normal psychological processes, and he suggested that careful observation is necessary when using VR with drug users and individuals with schizophrenia, obsessive-compulsive disorder, and mild "neurosis." He wondered (as have many mental health professionals) whether schizophrenic individuals will become confused by real versus virtual worlds. Because identity and gender swapping are possible in multiuser domains, he questioned whether such patients' individual identities will become fused with the "group world." Cartwright is not alone in voicing concern that use of virtual worlds might lead to an increase in alienation and isolation by individuals with social phobia.

Mukaetova-Ladinska and Lawton (1999) describe a case report of an elderly gentleman who exhibited a brief psychotic episode secondary to computer game playing. A recent report from the Japanese news media reported an excessive video game user actually hijacked a commercial airplane over Japan (Ischimura, Nakajima, & Juzoji, 2001). Rheingold muses in the popular book *Virtual Reality* (1991) that humans may prefer the speed and efficiency of machines and, over time, may lose sight of the benefits of being human. Gupta, Klein, Barker, Franken, and Banis (1995) describe potential problems with claustrophobia, acrophobia, and other anxiety, and in our experience, a subset of patients do become mildly claustrophobic when donning the head-mounted-display. The discomfort can, in most cases, be treated, but in a few patients other methods of visual display needed to be used. Woodbury, a psychoanalyst, suggests dangers in treating patients with acute psychotic panic (1998). Such patients who are already confused, have abnormal cognitive function, are disoriented as to place, person, and time, feel that their mind is being invaded, and fear that their personal thoughts are being read by others will not be a good candidates for VR.

Another potential issue involves a VR-induced hypnotic-like state, whereby false memories might be introduced in susceptible individuals or where the individual might become suggestible to certain thoughts and actions. This is at present a theoretical concern; however, the recent concern with false memory syndrome leads one to be cautious. It is clear that much more information needs to be collected and analyzed before VR is used routinely in other areas of medicine and mental health.

There are particular concerns in using VR with children and adolescents. Two studies, one by Plusquellec (2000) and the other by Shimauchi (1999) evaluate the mental health of adolescents, and both offer concerns of social isolation and addiction. They both suggest that appropriate education and periodic discussions are effective means to combat these negative effects. Tazawa, Soukalo, Okada, and Takada (1997) note excessive video game playing in Japanese children who present with vague symptoms and poor school performance. There are many concerns in Japan at this time about the excessive use of video games by children. Griffiths and Hunt (1998) performed a study of 387 adolescents who routinely played video games. Using a modified scale from the *DSM–III–R* criteria for "pathological gambling," the data revealed that 20% of the adolescents met the criteria for dependency on video games.

Being male and playing games at an earlier age were positively correlated with addictive tendencies. The 20% figure suggests that millions of adolescents are addicted to video games. There are certainly signs of a dedicated cadre of video game enthusiasts. One only needs to visit the Sega, Nintendo, and Sony Web sites to see the extent of involvement. Many video game enthusiasts have established intricate networks of users over the Internet, with thousands of Web sites devoted to individual games or characters. Greenberg, Lewis, and Dodd (1999) studied a variety of addictive behaviors in college students and found that overlap exists between addictions to alcohol, cigarettes, caffeine, and chocolate, and activities such as gambling, television, Internet use, and exercise. As interactive entertainment becomes more widely available, it will be interesting to see if a new generation of VR addicts emerges.

Summary

When used appropriately, VR therapy can be a very effective treatment option. A basic understanding of the physiological changes that result from immersion in virtual environments, along with careful screening of patients, can help the clinician understand which patients might experience side-effects or might be poor candidates for VR treatment. The incidence of negative effects is very low. The great majority of patients enjoy the experience, and some return periodically for "booster" sessions. Consideration of the needs of specific populations, such as the elderly or those with disabilities, can increase user comfort and benefit. As with any new technology being applied to treating psychological conditions, careful consideration of any long-term effects is essential. Application of standard tools used in clinical research combined with the oversight of clinical trials by institutional review boards and evaluation by the scientific community should continue to evaluate and assess the role and effect of VR in clinical settings.

The Effect of Presence on Virtual Reality Treatment

6

The efficacy of virtual reality (VR) systems is directly related to the quality of *presence*, the sense of being a part of the virtual world, generated in the user (Wiederhold & Wiederhold, 2000). Virtual worlds can be evaluated with respect to their potential to engender a high degree of presence in the user for each specific application. In this chapter we further define *presence*, examine the elements that contribute to developing presence in virtual systems, and consider the questions surrounding the quantification of presence as a measure for evaluating the virtual experience.

Definition of Presence and Research Findings

Presence refers to how immersed the user feels in a virtual environment. If you are driving a virtual car and you are fully immersed, you are present in that environment. In the clinician's office, if you are being treated for fear of flying and think you are on a real airplane as opposed to being in the office setting, you are described as being immersed. Although much has been published about presence from a human factors point of view, little research has been done on the psychological or "emotional" aspects of presence.

Many researchers have explored the perceptual and the philosophical aspects of presence. Although the findings are occasionally difficult to translate to the clinical realm, several important constructs have emerged. Jack Loomis (1993) extensively studied the phenomenon of presence and described continuity between the synthetic experience and the actual experience of everyday life. He pointed out that all of our sensory experience is *mediated,* that is, our sense of reality is constructed through sensory input processed by the nervous system (p. 54). It is in this way that virtual worlds become simply an extension of our sense of reality; they are sensory experiences processed in the same manner as "real" experiences. The difference between the virtual experience and the "real" experience lies in the degree to which individuals can distance themselves from conscious awareness of the extra component of mediation involved in the experience of VR therapy, that of interfacing with a machine. The extent to which individuals can experience the full range of sensory stimuli as real depends on the extent of their experience of presence.

Another conceptualization of presence is as a triad consisting of immersion, interaction, and intuition (Witmer & Singer, 1998). *Immersion* refers to being totally inside the virtual scene, as in the Cave Automatic Virtual Environment environment. *Interaction* relates to the ability of the user to affect the virtual environment and how the virtual environment affects the user (e.g., would the user duck when a baseball is rapidly projected at his nose?). *Intuition* refers to how users, especially new users, communicate with their surroundings in "natural" or intuitive ways. In this sense, a novice user of VR technology should intuitively be able to move, interact, and communicate in the virtual world without instruction simply on the basis of their knowledge of how to do these things in the "real" world.

Mantovani and Riva (1999) have explored the concept of presence in relation to how the user interacts socially in an environment. In their conceptualization, the user would be expected to produce socially appropriate responses to particular social situations (e.g., responding to a store clerk, ordering food). This application draws on the previously discussed idea of intuition and how the novice can easily interact with the virtual environment. Riva put these two concepts of social interaction and intuition together to produce an environment for the evaluation and treatment of social phobia (Riva, 1999; Wiederhold & Wiederhold, 2000). Though present, an individual may not be interacting in the virtual world because of social phobia. It might be possible to track a user's movements and number and type of social interactions as an indication of successful socialization.

Wiederhold, Davis, and Wiederhold (1998) examined responses to simulations using head-mounted displays in three-dimensions versus responses to two-dimensional computer images to assess whether there were differences in the experience of immersion. This study measured the responses of four nonphobic and one phobic individual to a 10-minute virtual flight viewed through a head-mounted displays and the same flight viewed on a flat two-dimensional computer screen. A repeated measures design was used to include level of immersion (head-mounted displays vs. computer screen), order of pairing (computer screen first, head-mounted displays second, or vice versa), and eyes-open baseline and flight sequence (engines on, taxi, takeoff, flying in good weather at altitude, and landing). Physiological parameters measured were skin resistance, heart rate, peripheral skin temperature, respiration rate, and brain wave activity. Nonphobic participants showed an average increase in skin resistance of 24% above baseline levels during a 10-minute computer screen flight, indicating physiological relaxation. At the end of a 10-minute head-mounted displays flight, physiological stabilization had not yet been achieved, with a decrease of skin resistance from a baseline of 21% still indicated. This physiological arousal was also indicated in subjective reports of the participants' abilities to become "present" in the scenarios much more easily in the head-mounted displays condition. The phobic participant showed a decrease in skin resistance of only 9% between baseline and end of flight on the computer screen, whereas in the head-mounted displays condition, the participant had a decrease of 48%. The participant also reported subjectively feeling more anxious (i.e., immersed) in the head-mounted displays condition than in the computer screen condition. Self-report scores of ability to become immersed (Tellegen Absorption Scale) did not differ significantly between phobic and nonphobic individuals, nor did Hypnotic Induction Profile scores (Spiegel & Spiegel, 1987).

More advanced virtual simulations may involve manipulation and navigation to enhance the experience. Manipulation of objects is possible with the data glove or other haptic responsive devices. Manipulation is very important in those applications where tele-presence is involved. This is seen today where law-enforcement or military personnel operate a robotic device, such as those used by bomb squads. A similar application is seen with the operation of the Space Shuttle robotic arm. Accurate and precise movements and feedback are important for obvious reasons in these applications. The information gained from these uses can be carried over into clinical applications. Navigational skills in virtual environments depend on the ability of users to accurately remember scenes and cues that allow them to find their way. These skills are especially important in new applications for testing neuro-cognitive functions in patients.

More recently, researchers have looked at presence during simulated driving tasks and found that pictorial representation was the least important factor in providing a sense of realism (Huang, Himle, & Alessi, 2000; Welch, Blackmon, Liu, Mellers, & Stark, 1996). In the driving scenario, the sense of motion through the scene seemed to be the most important factor. This information is important because it suggests that less expensive simulation tools may still evoke a sense of presence and may be effective for therapeutic uses. This is the general consensus of clinical VR investigators.

Emotional Aspects of Presence

Huang and Alessi (1999a, 1999b) first coined the term *emotional presence* at the Medicine Meets Virtual Reality (MMVR) conference in Newport Beach. Their model, based on cognitive-relational emotion theory, allows for the emotional state of the user to be incorporated into the concept of presence. Because emotional responses are fairly well understood in terms of physiology, understanding emotions during presence might provide a method which links physiological state to levels of immersion and presence. Introduction of a fearful stimulus should result, for example, in an increase in heart rate and a decrease in skin conductance.

In a special issue of *CyberPsychology and Behavior* on presence, Huang et al. proposed that VR researchers move beyond the simple concept of existing in a virtual environment and move to an in-depth evaluation of how humans react to the total experience of a virtual world. In addition, they emphasized the importance of looking at the response of each individual to a virtual environment. When patients are exposed to a virtual world, differences in or deficits in "attention, kinesthetic perception, spatial recognition, reality testing and other mental faculties" (Huang et al., 2000, p. 323) affect the quality of the experience. Clinically this is an important statement, because not all environments are appropriate for all patients. Some patients are unable to drive even a simulator, for example, if they have severe posttraumatic stress disorder following an automobile accident. Some intermediate method may be necessary with such patients.

Baños et al. (1999) explored psychological factors of presence and found that absorption was positively correlated with presence in virtual environments. Absorption ability may be an important indicator and should be assessed before the session to determine whether it is predictive of patient acceptance of or compliance with therapy. Baños et al. (1999) found that individuals able to experience high levels of presence generally had more emotional feelings as measured by high scores on anxiety scales. This suggests an interesting direction for research: Can VR treatment be used to provide an alternative technique for treating depression?

In another study, Baños et al. (2000) found that both reality judgment (the impression that what occurs in VR is real) and presence are equally important in the effectiveness of treatment in virtual environments. Reality judgment could be helpful insofar as patients who can successfully immerse themselves may be more effective at achieving resolution of underlying psychological problems and hence may be more able to achieve therapeutic success. These views need further testing before any recommendations can be made concerning the type of patients who can benefit from VR therapy.

Virtual Reality Research on Presence

VR research on presence was undertaken using an acrophobic environment (Schuemie et al., 2000). The study involved 37 participants and measured sense of presence with a self-report questionnaire. Fear increased with higher presence. The aim of the study was to elicit both physiological and psychological reactions to virtual stimuli that were modeled to resemble anxiety-provoking real world stimuli. To do this, nonphobic participants were placed where they faced elevations. It was predicted that because the participants had no fear of heights, they would be able to adjust to the virtual world without the avoidance that might have been shown by phobic participants.

The virtual environment used was an 8-meter-high virtual cliff. A 14-item questionnaire for presence was used, with 5-point Likert type scales ranging from −2 to +2. The state scale of the State–Trait Anxiety Inventory was used to measure the state anxiety. The trait anxiety was measured using Cohen (1977) scales concerning heights. Hardware consisted of a Silicon Graphics Workstation, a VR4 head-mounted displays and Polhemus tracking device. Participants stood on a platform that was approximately 4 meters in diameter. They were asked to explore the virtual world, were shown different text messages during the 20-minute exposure, and were asked to respond to the text instructions. After 2 minutes, parts of the virtual world were lowered, and participants could see that they were standing on a cliff with the ground approximately 8 meters below them. Participants could fulfill instructions by walking across one of two small bridges or by simply walking across the virtual depth. Even though they were not phobic, they tapped their feet on the real floor before crossing the bridges; they appeared to experience some mild level of anxiety about being on a virtual cliff.

Elements That Contribute to Presence

Creating an artificial environment is a complex task that requires a computer to create, in real time, an experience that allows the user to be present in an artificial space. Because computers do not process imagery as fast as the human brain, the recreation of images during the session lacks the fidelity of real life imagery. Technical issues, such as field of view, image update rate, color and contrast, and texture quality, greatly affect the virtual scene. Despite the potential for improvements in the fidelity of images, the user's sense of presence can be increased in other ways. Introducing movement into the scene focuses attention on the action and away from the background. Adding different sensory stimuli to the virtual scene is another way to increase the realism of the experience. The senses of sight, sound, touch, and smell can be added to virtual experiences, and many studies have examined the influence of these elements.

At the Virtual Reality Medical Center (VRMC), virtual environments are enhanced with some cues to increase presence. Vibrations simulating those experienced while driving, flying, and riding in an elevator are produced in the platforms for these environments. Breeze is simulated with a fan to enhance the experience of height while treating acrophobia. Toy spiders are used as tactile stimulation in environments to treat arachnophobia. All of these features of augmented reality improve the sense of presence and thus improve the efficacy of treatment.

Studies on Presence in Virtual Reality

In a large study, researchers examined 322 individuals' responses to multisensory cues in a virtual world (Dinh, Walker, Song, Kobayashi,

& Hodges, 1999). The results showed that tactile, olfactory, and auditory cues were actually more effective than visual stimuli in increasing the sense of presence. The content and context of the virtual experience most likely affect the quality of presence and immersion. Different cues are likely to be more important in some environments than others, and findings that are based on one type of environment may not be generalizable to other environments.

In another study using three-dimensional visual images, the addition of fragrances added to the sense of realism (Davide, Holmberg, & Lundstrom, 1999). Olfactory cues also may increase the sense of presence at telerobotic sites, assist training in navigation and escape from dangerous environments, and enhance the experience of video games or movies. Olfactory cues may find potential application in the treatment of PTSD in wartime combatants where the virtual experience might be enhanced by smells, such as sulfur (explosions) or gasoline (military transport). Olfactory enhancements are currently being used in conjunction with VR applications as distractions from medical procedures (Wiederhold & Wiederhold, 1999).

Thermal variations of the environment can also add to the sense of realism. For example, a heat lamp can be used to recreate the sensation of the sun on the patient's head and back, or a cold metal bar can be held by a patient during a virtual height simulation to enhance the experience of standing in front of a precipice.

Whatever the cues are, the correct coordination of sensory inputs is crucial in virtual worlds. Lapses in coordination or mismatches in the virtual world are easily detected and detract from the experience in a manner similar to the experience of a minor miscue between voice and image, such as on television or in a badly dubbed movie. The distraction of miscues was examined in an interesting study where the movement of objects in a virtual world was linked to sounds (Hahn, Fouad, Gritz, & Lee, 1998). Miscues were shown to have a negative impact on the user's sense of realism in the virtual world. The authors reported that the technique could be broken down into three parts: sound modeling, sound synchronization, and sound rendering. The miscues send a strong signal of something wrong and make it impossible for the patient to focus on the therapy session.

Comfort during the session is essential. In older VR systems, the most common causes of negative experiences included fatigue, neck pain from heavy head-mounted displays, eyestrain, and problems with video display technology that led to unnatural movements and lag time. Many of these concerns have been ameliorated by improved technology, such as lighter weight head-mounted displays and improved video resolution. Another concern for researchers and clinicians using physiological monitoring devices is to ensure that the user is accustomed to the research environment and to the monitoring devices prior to running tests or expecting valid feedback. Discomfort with sensors or unfamiliarity with the equipment may cause stress responses that are not related to the virtual environment itself. All attempts to provide a distraction-free environment should be made to establish and maintain a sense of presence.

In summary, sensory stimuli can greatly enhance the user's sense of presence in the virtual world. Visual, auditory, tactile, and olfactory inputs are under continued examination by various research groups. Coordination of these inputs with the video display is important in maintaining the synchrony of the experience. User comfort with the equipment and the absence of distractions during the session are the final components to consider in creating a strong virtual experience. Interruptions of the session may lead to an ineffective intervention. There seems to be a "learned" quality about the sense of presence that can be harnessed in the therapeutic process. Some patients may take several sessions to become immersed in the virtual world. However, as found by Hoffman, presence seems to increase over the first three sessions and then stabilizes (Hoffman, Patterson, Carrougher, & Sharar, 2001). After they are immersed, they can fully participate in the session. Ongoing research is being conducted to try to understand why some patients adapt to virtual environments more easily than others do.

Quantifying Presence

There is much interest in quantifying presence, because the degree of presence is important to how effective the VR therapy session can be. Sheridan (1992) reviewed the concept of presence in the late 1990s and found no reliable and objective measurement of presence. For the most part, this statement remains true today. Because presence is believed by many authors to be important in establishing a therapeutic experience with patients, some method of quantification is necessary.

Many studies of presence involve nonphobic individuals focusing on specific tasks. This task performance is done to measure performance success, which, in theory, indicates presence. The question of whether successful task performance is an accurate indicator of presence has not yet been answered. In the context of psychotherapeutic treatment, one way of quantifying presence might be whether the patient had a successful therapeutic outcome.

The use of questionnaires and scales to evaluate an individual's potential for hypnotizability and absorption are under investigation. Several questionnaires have been developed that give some indication of involvement during the virtual experience, but the exact physiological metric is currently not known and is the subject of intense investigation and speculation. Suggestions for possible means of testing for presence include heart rate, blood pressure, respiratory rate, eye blink, pupil size, evoked potential, and electroencephalogram (EEG). Most researchers agree that more work is necessary to understand the physiological changes that accompany the sense of presence (Mager, 2001; Mager, Bullinger, Roessler, Mueller-Spahn, & Stoermer, 2000; Meehan et al., 2000; Pugnetti, Meehan, & Mendozzi, 2001; Wiederhold, Gevirtz, & Wiederhold, 1998; Wiederhold, Jang, & Wiederhold, 2002; Wiederhold & Wiederhold, 1998, 2000, 2001). Witmer and Singer (1998) developed a presence questionnaire that is in wide use today. At VRMC, for example, we have found that skin conductance is a good indicator of presence when used during the therapy session. Heart rate appears not to be sensitive enough, but analysis of heart rate variability shows promise. We are in the process of evaluating the heart rate variability data from 3,000 VR sessions from our database. Preliminary studies show that the low frequency/high frequency (LF/HF) ratio correlates well with skin conductance levels and is another measure that responds in near real time. We have also shown that levels of EEG brain waves (alpha, beta, delta, theta, and sensory motor rhythm [SMR]) show correlation with the degree of immersion. We have found a correlation between the level of presence and task performance and an inverse relationship between presence and simulator sickness (side effects experienced during a VR tour; Wiederhold, Gevirtz, & Wiederhold, 1998; Wiederhold, Jang, & Wiederhold, 2002; Wiederhold & Wiederhold, 1998, 2000, 2001).

At VRMC, we use a comprehensive method to evaluate patients in virtual worlds. The method has five components, combining subjective and objective information. The first component involves the therapist asking the patient for feedback on his or her level of discomfort (such as a subjective units of distress level). Careful observations, the second component, are made of patient verbal and nonverbal behavior (e.g., hand clenching, foot tapping). Third, physiological data are obtained, including heart rate, heart rate variability, blood pressure, skin resistance, respiratory rate and mechanics, EEG (if appropriate), and skin temperature. Fourth, patients complete questionnaires both before and after the session. Finally, the therapist asks the patient for feedback after the session, allowing plenty of time for questions. This method provides a wealth of useful data that begin to address issues related to treatment successes. Patients continue to provide the most important feedback concerning the virtual experience. Attention to charting and allowing the patient to comment after the session are crucial.

Summary

After reviewing the literature on presence, we are convinced that presence is an important consideration in the clinical use of VR therapy, but the degree and quality of presence required for success are not known. Research focused on the physiological monitoring of presence seems most promising, and future developments include studies using brain imaging of individuals who are in virtual environments as a logical next step. These will offer some clues to the underlying neuro-anatomic and neurophysiologic features that operate during presence in a virtual environment. Initial work using both PET scans and MRI have been carried out while volunteers navigate video game worlds. To date, no large clinical study of brain imaging has been performed with humans in immersive virtual environments, and, before these studies can be performed, certain technical issues must be solved, such as how to introduce a field emitting head-mounted displays into the MRI device. Current methods of evaluating the client's experience and degree of immersion include asking the patient for feedback, clinical observation, monitoring physiological data, and asking the patient to fill out questionnaires before and after the session.

Ethical Considerations   7

E thical considerations in the application of virtual reality (VR) treatment to psychotherapy should follow the general guidelines provided by the American Psychological Association in its *Ethical Principles of Psychologists and Code of Conduct* (2002; see also http://www.apa.org/ethics/code.html). The American Psychological Association does not at present provide specific guidelines for electronically mediated therapeutic interventions, but it does recommend that practitioners refer to the following guidelines in particular when using new media: Boundaries of Competence (Standard 2.01), Confidentiality (Standard 4), Assessment (Standard 9), Therapy (Standard 10), Basis for Scientific and Professional Judgments (Standard 2.04), Human Relations (Standard 3), Bases for Assessment (9.01), and Fees and Financial Arrangements (Standard 6.04). The following discussion addresses these standards as they relate to the practice of VR therapy. Issues that pose ethical concerns unique to the practice of VR therapy are also examined.

Competence
(Standard 2)

In the Boundaries of Competence (Standard 2.01), the guidelines urge that psychotherapists provide only services for which they have appropriate education, training, or experience. VR therapy, like other "emerging areas in which generally recognized standards for preparatory training do not yet exist," requires that therapists make every effort to "ensure the competence of their work and to protect clients/patients, students, supervisees, research participants, organizational clients, and others from harm" (p. 1064). Therapists practicing VR therapy must be competent in the use of the technology, in the application of the technology to specific disorders, and in the treatment of these disorders. New technological developments affect the delivery of services, and maintaining competence is crucial. As research progresses on VR therapy as a treatment modality, keeping current on its application to clinical practice is vital.

According to Standard 2.04, Bases for Scientific and Professional Judgments, psychologists must ensure that the work they perform is based on current professional information. To stay current on the use of new technology in clinical practice, psychologists must consult with colleagues, attend continuing education courses and meetings where VR technology is discussed, and stay abreast of published literature.

Human Relations
(Standard 3)

The Human Relations standard includes Multiple Relationships (3.05). Psychologists in small towns know very well that such relationships may be unavoidable. One psychologist may have to treat several members of the same family or their child's teacher. This is especially true in the field of VR therapy, because very few clinicians in the United States use this technology in their private practice. Therefore, patients seeking VR treatment have few choices when it comes to clinicians, making multiple relationships even more likely. The code specifically

states that "multiple relationships that would not reasonably be expected to cause impairment or risk exploitation or harm are not unethi-
cal" (p. 1065).

Confidentiality

According to the standards under Privacy and Confidentiality (Standard 4), the limits of confidentiality should be discussed with patients.
Of particular concern to VR therapists is the potential for breaches
of confidentiality when using Internet-based virtual worlds. This
practice is a relatively new and exciting area of growth in virtual
reality technology and therapy. In Internet-based worlds, users adopt
an avatar (such as a male or female face or an animal face) and
navigate in three dimensions in various "constructed worlds," which
vary from landscapes to different types of rooms, to a world that
is modeled after a bar with live music. In these environments, it is
possible to approach (navigate) individuals or groups of individuals
and, through a microphone (similar to Internet telephony), have
real time conversations. In these worlds there can be as many as
100 avatars. The interaction is anything but predicable, and visitors
are required to use many of the same social skills that are used in
everyday life. Because visitors are anonymous, some avatar characters
can choose to be antisocial or just plain weird. Although it is possible
to enter these shared worlds anonymously, visitors might accidentally
or through deception reveal their true identity. This is an area where
the therapist and the patient can enter the virtual world together
and where ethical issues related to confidentiality are a major concern.
As with any electronic media, risks to privacy and limitations to
confidentiality may be beyond the therapist's control.

Therapists and researchers using Internet-based programs must
decide how to use data from cyberspace. Can information from chat
rooms be used in publications? Should researchers monitor on-line
discussion groups? Is it ethical to give psychological advice online? The
American Association for the Advancement of Science has set up a
Web page featuring discussion on these topics and information on
"human subjects' research in cyberspace" (www.aaas.org/spp/dspp/
sfrl/projects/intres/main.htm) and is evaluating these and other important questions. Another more general online source for ethical issues
in science and engineering is www.onlineethics.org.

Fees and Financial Arrangements (Standard 6.04)

As with all therapy services, billing arrangements, compensation, and fees should be discussed with the patient as early in the therapeutic process as possible. In a survey of current therapists providing VR therapy for anxiety disorders in the United States, additional fees are not assessed to the patient for use of the technology. Instead, fees are based on a traditional therapy fee structure.

Assessment (Standard 9)

The standards concerning Assessment (9.01–9.11) in therapy sessions are of central concern to practitioners of VR therapy. Some specific measures have been developed in clinical practice, and, in many cases, these may be successfully adapted for use in VR settings. Objective assessment tools, such as physiological monitoring, are currently being used and show great promise for the standardization of measurements. We have found that including both subjective assessment tools, such as paper-and-pencil self-report questionnaires and subjective units of distress measures, in combination with real-time physiological monitoring has been extremely useful in gauging the patient's response to VR. By ascertaining whether the patient is becoming anxious as part of the VR exposure, we can determine how slowly or quickly to proceed. We want the patient to experience some level of anxiety, but not to become overwhelmed. Tools for pretreatment assessment such as the Tellegen Absorption Scale, can help the clinician determine how easily a particular patient will become "immersed" in the VR world, and allow therapy to proceed accordingly. Clinicians must be qualified to score and interpret the assessment tools, they must use reliable and valid questionnaires, and they must ensure that assessment results are reviewed and explained to the patient.

As with any therapy encounter, treatment should begin with an initial intake session where a thorough clinical history and evaluation are undertaken to determine the proper diagnosis and the course of treatment.

Therapy (Standard 10)

In the guidelines for Therapy, the issue of informed consent is of particular importance. Informed consent requires therapists to make every reasonable effort to inform patients of the procedures, limits to confidentiality, risks, and costs involved. Like other exposure therapy clinicians, VR therapists must describe how the exposure will unfold, the sequence of the sessions, and the potential for patient discomfort as the feared stimuli are introduced. In addition, as in real-life exposure, patients must be told that results often take time and that setbacks are a part of the therapy process. Many patients when beginning treatment for their phobias experience increased fatigue or report increased tension or irritability. Informing patients of these possibilities may help alleviate their anxiety when these symptoms do appear (Antony & Swinson, 2000).

Unlike traditional real-life exposure, VR therapy offers patients a higher level of control. It is important to discuss this with patients at the beginning of treatment, so that they understand that therapy can progress at the pace they set and that they can terminate the exposure should it become overwhelming. This level of increased control actually seems to allow patients to remain in therapy and "push the envelope" when confronting fears, knowing that they can stop at any time. Previous research has shown that patients who perceive control over the exposure session show a greater treatment response (McGlynn, Rose, & Lazarte, 1994; Rose, McGlynn, & Lazarte, 1995).

Of particular concern for patients engaged in VR therapy is the possibility of side effects, such as cybersickness. In the intake session, patients should be assessed for health problems that might make them more vulnerable to cybersickness, such as an inner ear difficulty, vestibular abnormalities, or a prior history of motion sickness. Pretreatment with anti-motion sickness medications may alleviate some symptoms and this option should be discussed with patients. In addition, if patients are prone to migraine headaches, they may be more likely to experience headache symptoms from exposure to the virtual world. Although not all patients with migraines experience headaches, the possibility that they might should be discussed. As Whalley (1993) pointed out, "The broad aims of psychotherapists are to encourage personal development and fulfillment, to allow individual responsibilities to be defined and accepted and, potentially to assist individuals to move to full independence, integrated within societies expectations and norms" (p. 283). Therapists using VR technology must use it within such a framework.

Cultural Considerations

Not all patients experience VR scenarios in the same way, and therapists should be aware that individual differences may lead to a decrease in the effectiveness of treatment. For example, the environment created in Italy for agoraphobia features a large plaza with a fountain in the center and residences around the perimeter (Vincelli & Riva, 2000). This environment looks distinctly European, and although it may still be effective for treating European patients, patients from non-European cultures may not be able to generalize their simulations to their real life surroundings.

Furthermore, a social phobia treatment developed in London may involve a virtual underground subway as one exposure environment (James, Lin, Steed, Swapp, & Slater, 2003). Patients who live in parts of the world where there is no subway may have difficulty engaging with this environment. Though no research has been completed in this area, it is important that therapists be aware of cultural differences and modify treatment accordingly.

Summary

The American Psychological Association Ethical Guidelines should be used to guide practitioners of VR. Many of the ethical issues relevant to VR therapy are similar or identical to those applicable to traditional therapies in general and to exposure therapies in particular. Concerns specific to VR therapy include the disclosure of possible side effects and the possible limits to confidentiality when using Internet-based virtual worlds during therapy. VR therapy is a powerful new tool that, if applied wisely and with due consideration of existing and future ethical guidelines, it should find wide application. Craig Childress (1998) made the following important distinction: "We must guard against projecting onto this new communication medium fear regarding change and the unknown which might cause us to withhold appropriate interventions. The challenge is to neither undervalue nor over inflate either the potential risks or the potential benefits available from interactive text-based therapeutic interventions" (p. 1).

III

Treatment of Specific Anxiety Disorders

Panic Disorder and Agoraphobia 8

Panic Disorder With or Without Agoraphobia

As listed in the *Diagnostic and Statistical Manual of Mental Disorders* (4th ed., Text Revision; *DSM–IV–TR*; American Psychiatric Association, 2000), the essential features of panic disorder are "the presence of recurrent, unexpected Panic Attacks, followed by at least 1 month of persistent concern about having another Panic Attack, worry about the possible implications or consequences of Panic Attacks, or a significant behavioral change related to the attacks" (p. 433).

PREVALENCE

Each year, panic disorder afflicts more individuals than AIDS, stroke, or epilepsy (http://www.nimh.nih.gov). The one-year prevalence rate (the likelihood one will be diagnosed with panic disorder in a given year) is estimated at 1% to 2%, with a lifetime prevalence of panic disorder (with or without agoraphobia) at 1.5% to 3.5% (American Psychiatric Association, 2000, p. 436). In community samples, about one third to one half of those who have panic disorder also have agoraphobia. The typical age of onset is either in late adolescence or the mid-30s. Twice as many women as men have panic disorder with or without agoraphobia. In the Epidemiological Catchment Area (ECA) study carried out with National Institute of Mental Health sponsorship, 2.8% to 5.7% of the population sample met *DSM–IV* criteria for agoraphobia, with an additional 1% meeting *DSM–IV* criteria for panic disorder (Myers et al., 1983). Panic disorder is chronic and is associated with high morbidity. Panic disorders may adversely affect an individual's normal functioning and quality of life and lead to financial problems, family stress, and less social support (DiBartolo et al., 1995). Rates of suicide attempts by patients with panic disorder are high (20%), particularly when other psychiatric disorders are present. Anywhere from 30% to 50% of patients with panic disorder may develop depression (Gorman & Coplan, 1996). All patients presenting with panic disorder should be screened for comorbidities and for suicidal ideation (American Psychiatric Association, 2000). Panic disorder can be accompanied by a variety of physical symptoms and may be misdiagnosed or overlooked in assessments of a general medical condition by physicians or emergency room attendants (American Psychiatric Association, 2000; Hales, Hilty, & Wise, 1997). Careful screening is important in this area to differentiate between physical and psychological factors.

RISK FACTORS

Panic attack symptoms appear to be universal; they have been observed and studied in populations in Korea, New Zealand, Lebanon, Germany, Puerto Rico, and the United States (Weismann et al., 1995). Evidence of a single, dominant gene related to panic disorder has also been found (American Psychiatric Association, 2000; Crowe et al., 1987).

Panic attacks can be triggered in susceptible individuals by such factors as elevated amounts of carbon dioxide in the air, hyperventilation, and caffeine ingestion (Stein & Uhde, 1994). In one study, 21 patients and 17 nonpatients were given 10 mg/kg of caffeine; 71% of patients versus 25% of nonpatients reported subjective and somatic signs of increased anxiety. Patients also reported that these symptoms were similar to those felt during a panic attack (Uhde et al., 1985). Hyperventilation involves overbreathing, which removes CO_2 from the body, and produces respiratory alkalosis. In hyperventilation studies, patients report symptoms mimicking panic symptoms much sooner than the control participants. This may be due to a continuous pattern of rapid breathing, which accounts for lower resting CO_2 levels (McNally, 1987). In studies where CO_2 was administered to study participants, no significant differences in physiological measures were observed between patients and control participants, but subjective anxiety was marked in patients. It may be that with lower CO_2 levels, or higher induced CO_2 levels, patients experience a sense of loss of control that accounts for panic symptoms (Barlow, 2002).

CONVENTIONAL TREATMENTS

Treatment of panic disorder and panic disorder with agoraphobia usually involves medication, cognitive–behavioral therapy (CBT), or a combination of the two. Medications used include selective serotonin reuptake inhibitors, tricyclic antidepressants, benzodiazepines, and monoamine oxidase inhibitors (American Psychiatric Association, 2000; Saeed & Bruce, 1998). (For a detailed discussion of medications used with anxiety disorders, see chap. 3.) CBTs may include relaxation, breathing retraining with or without the use of physiological monitoring and feedback, exposure therapy, and cognitive restructuring. It is generally understood that CBT is the most effective psychotherapeutic treatment modality for panic disorder and panic disorder with agoraphobia and can be used effectively in combination with pharmacologic therapy (American Psychiatric Association, 2000).

Nonpharmacologic treatments for panic disorder with agoraphobia, as outlined by Barlow and others (American Psychiatric Association, 2000; Barlow, 1988; Barlow & Mavissakalian, 1981; Chambless & Goldstein, 1983; D. Clark et al., 1988; D. M. Clark, Salkovskis, & Chalkley, 1985; D. M. Clark et al., 1994; DiBartolo et al., 1995), use a mixture of cognitive and behavioral techniques. These techniques allow patients, with the therapist's assistance, to identify and modify their dysfunctional thought processes and behaviors. Treatment normally includes exposure to the feared situations, as well as interoceptive exposure, which involve having the patient perform such activities as purposefully overbreathing (hyperventilating) to simulate the same symptoms they experience with panic attacks. Such interoceptive exposure allows patients to realize that they have control over their symptoms and to understand that the symptoms are not dangerous. Performance of in vivo or imaginal exposure and interoceptive exercises should take place after the patient and therapist have established a trusting alliance, and after cognitive restructuring, breathing retraining, and relaxation techniques have first been learned. This allows patients to feel safe during the exposure and brings greater awareness of the cognitions associated with their physical responses to panic.

In one study, Craske, Street, and Barlow (1989) examined the use of distraction techniques during exposure. One group of participants ($n = 16$) was taught to use thought stopping and self-statements intended to focus their attention during in vivo exposure. A second group ($n = 16$) was taught to use distraction techniques (such as word rhymes) during exposure. The two groups did not differ at posttreatment; however, at follow-up the group using distraction had experienced a slight deterioration in treatment gains. Although it may be assumed that using distraction is an avoidance strategy, other researchers have not examined this in panic disorder with agoraphobia patients. Researchers who have examined this technique in treatment of specific phobias achieved mixed results; some found distraction to be effective (Antony, McCabe, Leeuw, Sano, & Swinson, 2001) and others found that distraction interferes with fear reduction during exposure (Weir & Marshall, 1980). Most protocols for panic disorder with agoraphobia involve 12 to 15 sessions. A very detailed description of CBT for panic disorder and agoraphobia can be found in Salkovskis, Clark, and Hackmann (1991); Mathews, Gelder, and Johnston (1981); and Barlow (1988).

EXPERIENTIAL–COGNITIVE THERAPY

A virtual reality(VR) treatment protocol for panic disorder and agoraphobia, called experiential–cognitive therapy (ECT), has been developed at the Applied Technology for Neuro-Psychology Lab of Istituto Auxologico Italiano, in Verbania, Italy, in collaboration with the Catholic University of Milan, Italy (Vincelli & Riva, 2000). The protocol has been expanded and is now being tested in an ongoing multinational research study, combining the efforts of researchers from the above-named institutions with three new institutions: The Virtual Reality Medical Center (VRMC) in San Diego, California; Hanyang University and Seoul Paik Hospital at the Inje University in Seoul, Korea; and the University of Quebec at Hull in Canada (Vincelli et al., 2000). We describe this protocol in some detail to provide those unfamiliar with VR therapy with some insight into the process and its procedures.

The goal of ECT is to modify dysfunctional cognitions and to desensitize patients to the fear and anxiety associated with certain situations. In initial pilot studies in Italy combining virtual reality graded exposure therapy (VRGET) and traditional CBT techniques (Vincelli & Riva, 2000), treatment has been successful using an average of seven treatment sessions in combination with posttreatment "booster" sessions. For the ECT protocol, a program called the Virtual Environments for Panic Disorders (VEPD) VR system was created. VEPD was developed using a Thunder 600/C VR system by Virtual Engineering, using a Pentium III computer, an inexpensive head-mounted display, a head-tracking device, and a joystick motion input device (Dolocek, 1994). VEPD is a four-zone virtual environment. The four zones represent potentially frightening situations: a supermarket, a subway, an elevator, and a large open plaza area that intersects with an empty highway (see Figure 8.1).

The therapist can manipulate the characteristics of the different zones. For example, the elevator may be made smaller, or more virtual people may be added to make it seem more crowded. In the supermarket, the patient walks around the aisles of a supermarket (in which more "customers" can be added), picks up groceries, and must stop at the cash register to pay for them. The subway ride includes the experience of riding a subway that moves between different subway stations. The open plaza area includes buildings, a church, and a pub.

Participants are being recruited at the institutions in Italy, Korea, Canada, and the United States, and they must meet the *DSM–IV* (American Psychiatric Association, 1994) criteria for panic disorder with agoraphobia. Actively suicidal, psychotic, or medically ill patients

FIGURE 8.1.

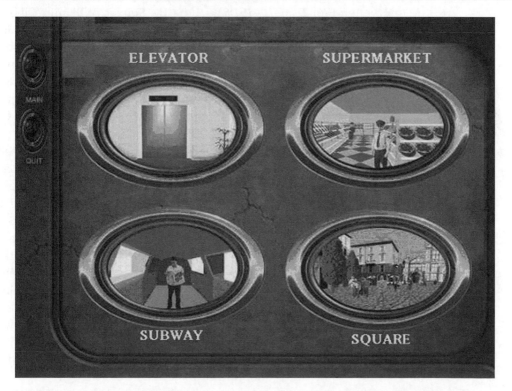

The four zones in the Virtual Environments for Panic Disorder program developed by Dr. Giuseppe Riva, Milan, Italy, to treat patients with panic disorder and agoraphobia.

are excluded from the study. After the nature of the study is explained and participants have signed an informed consent, they are randomly assigned to one of three groups: the ECT group, which will experience the VR treatment; a traditional CBT approach; and a wait-list control group. Participants who are taking medication must be stabilized for 2 months prior to participation and must agree to remain on this dosage while in the study. Participants are given self-report questionnaires at pre-treatment, after the completion of the clinical trial, and at post-treatment follow-up periods of 3 months, 6 months, 12 months, and 24 months. The following questionnaires are being used: (a) the Beck Depression Inventory II; (b) the State–Trait Anxiety Inventory (Spielberger, Gorsuch, Lushene, Vagg, & Jacobs, 1983); (c) the Agoraphobic Cognitions Questionnaire (Chambless, Caputo, Bright, & Gallagher, 1984); and (d) the Fear Questionnaire (Marks & Mathews, 1979). During the assessment period, subjective measurements (patient self-report and patient diaries) are used and during exposure periods subjective units of distress are measured.

Prior to treatment, the clinician performs an intake and history of the patient, along with a measure such as the Structured Clinical Intervention for *DSM–III–R/DSM–IV* (SCID; Spitzer, Williams, Gibbon, & First, 1992). The first treatment session consists of patient education concerning the cognitive–behavioral treatment approach and an introduction and brief exposure to virtual environments. Patient education is necessary to involve the patient as an active participant in the therapy process. Many patients interpret their panic attacks as an indication of some physical illness. Information and psycho-education about the nature of anxiety can be helpful, especially when tailored to the patient's specific concerns. The therapist and patient discuss in vivo self-exposure as a homework assignment, and they construct a hierarchy of self-exposure situations. In vivo practice may include a support person if necessary at the beginning (Marks, 1987). According to Barlow, Craske, Cerny, and Klosko (1989) and D. M. Clark et al. (1988), self-exposure reduces avoidance as well as improves catastrophic thoughts, physiological arousal and panic symptoms, and cognitive distortions. Long-term follow-up studies show that improvements through the introduction of self-exposure are sustained over time (Marks, 1987). This technique results in an increase in patients' self-efficacy and allows them to attribute treatment success to their own efforts and abilities. By performing these tasks on their own in the real world, patients prove the generalizability of the skills they learned in VR, and this demonstration increases confidence. Therapist's belief in homework determines in large part if patients will do homework (Beck, Emery, & Greenberg, 1985). Therapists participating in the study will be trained on the importance of homework.

Session 2 begins with breathing retraining and relaxation. Before beginning the graded exposure, it is important to provide the patient with a tool to stop the exposure should anxiety symptoms occur. A large percentage of panickers describe hyperventilation as one of their panic attack symptoms (P. Holt & Andrews, 1989). This observation lends support to the idea that hyperventilation may play a causal role in panic attacks. This theory posits that panic attacks are the product of stress-induced respiratory changes that then provoke fear because they are perceived as dangerous. The physiological results of hyperventilation can lead people to fear that they are having a heart attack or that they are losing the ability to regulate their bodies. Many researchers have found that training patients in slow, diaphragmatic breathing techniques is helpful with this group (Ley, 1991). D. Clark et al. (1985) showed a marked reduction in panic attacks in panickers who received two weekly sessions of breathing retraining and cognitive restructuring training.

During Session 3, cognitive restructuring and graded exposure begin (Wells, 1997). The cognitive treatment focuses on correcting misappraisal of bodily sensations as dangerous. The cognitive strategies work on reducing attentional vigilance to physiological symptoms of arousal and anticipation of panic attack recurrence. Helping patients to recognize that the panic attacks involve an interaction between bodily sensations and negative thoughts about these sensations is the first step in teaching them to challenge their misinterpretations of symptoms. The patient is guided toward an objective awareness of his or her cognitive distortions and how easily they can occur during periods of heightened anxiety. The cognitive strategies are conducted in conjunction with the behavioral technique of graded exposure in VR.

In Session 4 (like Session 3), both graded exposure and cognitive therapy are performed. Session 5 introduces interoceptive exposure (Barlow, 1988; Barlow et al., 1989). According to the cognitive model, panic disorder is a "phobia of internal bodily cues," with panic attacks serving as conditioned alarm reactions to particular bodily cues. The purpose of interoceptive exposure, therefore, is to modify associations between specific bodily sensations and panic reactions. D. M. Clark (1989) and Barlow et al. (1989) have discussed interoceptive exposure as a three-step process involving first the induction of paniclike sensations by such things as voluntary hyperventilation and spinning in a chair; second, demonstrating the patient's mistaken beliefs about the catastrophic results of these symptoms; and, third, encouraging the patient to practice behaviors that "test" previous beliefs about the symptoms along with reinforcing more realistic thoughts related to the symptoms. This technique can also be used during the exposure to the virtual environments. The VEPD environments involve effects that mimic the physical symptoms of panic attacks including tunnel vision, blurry vision (as happens with dizziness), and increased heartbeat and breathing sounds mimicking palpitations and hyperventilation. The therapist is able to introduce these stimuli with a simple keystroke, causing the patient to experience symptoms similar to those of a panic attack in a much simpler manner than described above. After the induction of paniclike sensations, the patient uses breathing retraining and relaxation to control symptoms.

Session 6, similar to sessions three and four, consists of cognitive restructuring and graded exposure with breathing exercises. Session 7 involves discussion of relapse prevention, a homework schedule for continued self-exposure, a planned booster session schedule, and reinforcement of the patient's ability to maintain treatment gains after treatment has ended. The number of booster sessions scheduled depends on the need of the patients, but three sessions should be planned 1, 3, and 6 months after treatment has ended. The goal of these sessions is to work with the patient to identify difficulties that may emerge and to provide positive reinforcement to the patients for the tasks that have been carried out.

In initial sessions in using driving scenarios (situations such as traffic and freeways that people encounter while driving) created in Korea and the Italian four-zone scenario shown in Figure 8.1, patients have been able to experience some anxiety and have been willing to stay with this anxiety while using cognitive and breathing techniques to lessen the anxiety. Because the virtual environment provides a safe place for this practice to occur, patients are willing to try this. When the techniques work in resolving the anxiety, their sense of efficacy and self-control increase, and they become more willing to "test" these skills again in the world; they know that they have the power to effectively manage their anxiety.

Agoraphobia Without a History of Panic Disorder (AWOPD)

Those who have agoraphobia experience anxiety that centers "on the occurrence of incapacitating or extremely embarrassing paniclike symptoms or limited-symptom attacks rather than full Panic Attacks" (American Psychiatric Association, 2000, p. 441). The patient fears being in places where escape would be difficult or embarrassing or where help might not be available (p. 432). Unfortunately, very little is known about the course of this disorder; however, evidence suggests that considerable impairment persists for long periods of time if treatment is not undertaken. For those who have panic disorder, agoraphobic avoidance may first occur in situations associated with the first panic attack (Faravelli, Pallanti, Biondi, Paterniti, & Scarpato, 1992).

PREVALENCE

The lifetime prevalence rate for agoraphobia has been reported at 6.7% (Magee, Eaton, Wittchen, McGonagle, & Kessler, 1996). AWOPD has been somewhat of a controversial diagnosis; some researchers have reported that almost all those who seek treatment for agoraphobia also have a history of panic disorder (M. G. Craske, Miller, Rotunda, & Barlow, 1990). However, other community studies find that a large percentage of those meeting diagnostic criteria for agoraphobia do not have a history of panic attacks (Eaton, Dryman, & Weissman, 1991). Perhaps those who have panic, or both panic and agoraphobia, are the ones who tend to seek treatment (Boyd, 1986).

VIRTUAL REALITY TREATMENT APPROACHES

New technologies may prove very enabling for AWOPD patients. One study used a computer-aided system to administer anxiety questionnaires, self-exposure techniques, and anxiety management techniques to 15 patients with agoraphobia (Shaw, Marks, & Toole, 1999). Most patients showed moderate to marked improvement, although they reported that they would have preferred some contact with a clinician. In another study, patients with panic disorder used a palm pilot to record hourly data for 7 days resulting in a reduction of anxiety symptoms (Taylor, Fried, & Kenardy, 1990). Another report discusses how the availability of information on the Internet is allowing patients to learn skills and obtain information prior to seeking professional help (Huang, Rajarethinam, Abelson, & Alessi, 1998).

As described in chapter 4, exposure therapy, sometimes in combination with medication, breathing retraining, biofeedback, and relaxation techniques, is the traditional treatment for agoraphobia (Barlow, 1988). However, current exposure treatments have not been found to be effective for all those seeking treatment. Some individuals may also not be able (or willing) to tolerate the side effects of the medications used (Barlow, 1988). In an effort to provide help for individuals who have not responded to treatment, several groups have begun to experiment with VRGET to treat agoraphobia. These include the groups listed as working on panic disorder with agoraphobia multicenter studies, as well as another group in Georgia, led by Max North. North's work with agoraphobic patients is described below.

Nonimmersive Computer Techniques

One study used a nonimmersive two-dimensional computer simulation to assess 18 patients with agoraphobia. In a preliminary finding the computer program showed improvement of agoraphobic symptoms (Hutchinson, 1992). In a second study, participants with agoraphobia acted as therapists and guided a computer figure into an elevator. A thermometer on the screen measured the computer figure's anxiety level from "comfortable" to "panic" and gave a total score for the figure. Points were given on the basis of the number of exposure routines accomplished. The anxiety level was based on what situation the computer figure was in (approaching the elevator, entering the elevator, remaining inside the elevator, or riding to various floors on the elevator). The exposure lasted for 45 minutes, and participants completed three sessions.

The study found that different personality factors appear to impact performance on computer-simulation treatment. In particular, lower-agreeableness individuals outperformed those who scored higher on agreeableness as measured by the NEO Personality Inventory (NEO–PI–R; Costa & McCrae, 1992). Individuals with higher openness scores on the NEO–PI–R also performed worse than those who scored low on openness. The authors did not expect these findings; they had thought that individuals who scored high on agreeableness would have performed better because they wanted to please the therapist. They speculated that lower openness scorers might have performed better because they conformed to demand characteristics of the computer simulation (Harcourt, Kirkby, Daniels, & Montgomery, 1998).

Kirkby, Daniels, Harcourt, and Romano (1999) used these same simulations with 18 individuals who completed three exposure sessions, one per week for 3 weeks. The following measures were given before and after treatment: the Fear Questionnaire, Agoraphobic Cognitions Questionnaire (Chambless et al., 1984), Body Sensations Questionnaire, and the Revised NEO Personality Inventory (NEO–PI–R). Results showed that the longer the exposure, the more likely participants were to guide the computer figure into the elevator and the less likely they were to use the "stairs," an avoidance technique. Questionnaire scores decreased over treatment, showing a lessening of anxiety.

Virtual Reality Graded Exposure Therapy

One of the criteria for agoraphobia is anxiety about being in places or situations where escape might be difficult or embarrassing, and fears usually involve a cluster of situations rather than just one. To study this, North, North, and Coble (1995a) used several virtual scenarios. Virtual scenes included a series of bridges suspended at various heights over a canyon, hot-air balloons that could be positioned at different heights, an empty room, a dark barn, a dark barn with a black cat, a covered bridge, an elevator, and a series of balconies. The participants were 30 undergraduate students who were diagnosed with agoraphobia. They were treated individually for eight 15-minute sessions (one per week for eight consecutive weeks) using VR exposure. At the end of treatment, 24 of the participants (80%) experienced at least a 50% decrease in discomfort levels in the virtual situations (North, North, & Coble, 1995a, 1995b, 1996a, 1996b, 1996c; Riva, 1997).

The advantages of VRGET when compared to in vivo (real life) exposure include the following:

1. There is no loss of patient confidentiality. Because the treatment sessions can be performed in the therapist's office, there is no need for patient and therapist to venture out into public, risking exposure of the patient to possible embarrassment and loss of confidentiality.
2. There are no safety issues. The patient is in the safety of the therapist's office, where the VRGET can be terminated and the VR system turned off on request. When using in vivo exposure, there is less control of the exposure scenario.
3. There is more flexibility in the session. If a patient is only scared of one aspect of exposure (e.g., the actual experience of standing in a grocery checkout line), then this can be practiced over and over in the virtual world. In the real world, a patient may feel conspicuous by repeatedly standing in the checkout line at the grocery store.
4. The experience is just "unreal" enough that many patients who have resisted in vivo exposure are willing to try VRGET. Patients know they can stop the virtual experience versus feeling "trapped" in real-life scenarios (Wiederhold, Gevirtz, & Wiederhold, 1998; Wiederhold & Wiederhold, 1998).
5. VRGET consumes less time; it eliminates the need to drive the patient to the shopping mall or grocery store, go through the paces with them, and so on. Because the treatment can be conducted more easily within the session, it is cost effective (Wiederhold, Gevirtz, & Wiederhold, 1998; Wiederhold & Wiederhold, 1998).

In a study using a driving simulation with tunnel scenes, seven participants with panic with agoraphobia were treated. Before beginning treatment, participants were given the following self-report measures: Attitude Towards Agoraphobia Questionnaire (Jang, Ku, Shin, Choi, & Kim, 2000), the Anxiety Sensitivity Index (Peterson & Reiss, 1992), the Agoraphobic Cognition Questionnaire (Chambless et al., 1984), the Body Sensation Questionnaire, the agoraphobia checklist, and the Fear Questionnaire. Physiological measures included blood pressure, sweat gland activity, pulse, respiration, and heart rate. Subjective distress measurements were assessed during VRGET, and the psychiatrist present had the participant do relaxation exercises if he or she experiences excessive anxiety. Patients filled out a Simulator Sickness Questionnaire following exposure to determine whether any symptoms such as headache or nausea occurred during the exposure (Jang et al., 2000).

For the VRGET a tunnel scene with a traffic jam was used (Figure 8.2). The road was modeled after one in Seoul, Korea, and included a segment with high buildings and trees, a section of secluded road that

FIGURE 8.2.

Tunnel scene with a traffic jam.

winds past a mountain, an empty tunnel, a tunnel that can be driven through, and finally a tunnel in which one enters and which is subsequently filled with cars crowded behind the participant's car.

Patients were asked for their subjective distress level ratings every 2 to 5 minutes. They reported not being able to become immersed in the VR world and after two exposure sessions, the protocol was ended. The authors identified extraneous light sources, discomfort associated with the head-mounted display, the location of the therapist and computer operator in relation to patients, and discomfort related to the physiological sensors placed on patients as factors that contributed to an unsuccessful virtual experience (Jang et al., 2000). Although the experiment was terminated, the study provided highly useful information on how crucial it is to block extraneous light during VR sessions, on the best location of therapist in reference to patient (which was out of view), and on the need to orient patients to the physiologic sensors prior to collecting data. The protocol used was modified to account for these shortcomings and is currently being used at the VRMC with a 90% degree of success (defined as ability to successfully perform the real world task following treatment).

VRGET Case Study

We (Wiederhold & Wiederhold, 2000) reported a case study involving an 18-year-old male patient referred to us by his physician for treatment after finding no organic causes for the symptoms he was experiencing. The patient lived at home, held a job, and had been attending a local university for several weeks before becoming unable to attend class without his mother present. Later, he became unable to attend classes at all and finally discontinued working because he could not remain at his workplace without a close friend or one of his parents being present. The patient was experiencing panic attacks several times a day without provocation, and by the time he went for treatment he was unable to venture farther than two blocks from his home.

Treatment began with patient education, cognitive coping techniques, and breathing retraining. The patient practiced cognitive techniques and diaphragmatic breathing between sessions, and these techniques remained an integral part of subsequent therapy sessions. We devised a hierarchy of situations that progressively provoked higher levels of anxiety, and he was encouraged to practice exposure in real life after undergoing the virtual exposure during the therapy sessions. Anxiety management techniques were used both during VRGET and real-life exposure. The virtual exposure began with a beach scene that the patient thought would cause no anxiety (Figure 8.3). However, when he was allowed to navigate through the environment using the

FIGURE 8.3.

Those who have panic disorder with agoraphobia can practice skills in open areas such as this beach.

head-mounted display and joystick, he reached the edge of the sand, gazed out over the ocean, and realized that this caused him much anxiety. He had forgotten a panic attack he had on a sailboat several years earlier in which he had to be brought back to shore. The cues in the scene brought up past memories, which, despite a thorough intake, had not been revealed. The anxiety elicited by this scene allowed for processing of these memories to occur and provided another goal of therapy—the ability to go sailing again.

When placed in the virtual scene depicting an open plaza area (Figure 8.4), he "walked" behind the buildings and saw an open highway that made him very anxious. His comments were, "This is a long

FIGURE 8.4.

This plaza environment where patients encounter other individuals is used to treat social phobia and panic with agoraphobia. Software developed by Dr. Giuseppe Riva, Milan, Italy.

way from my home; I've never been here before." In subsequent sessions, he was guided through a beach scene, restaurant scene, office scene, grocery store, and open plaza. Homework tasks mimicked these scenarios to enforce his sense of mastery and self-efficacy. At this writing, he has been successfully employed for 6 months at a new job, is able to drive to Los Angeles with little or no anxiety, has enrolled in college again, and is able to go sailing. Therapy is now focusing on overcoming his fear of flying.

The system used in this study was developed by Giuseppe Riva at Istituto Auxologico Italiano in Verbania, Italy. The environments run on a personal computer and use an inexpensive head-mounted display and joystick to allow for both head tracking and movement with a joystick to explore and interact with the virtual worlds.

Summary

Panic disorder is widespread, and many people who have it also suffer from agoraphobia. Current treatments focus on pharmacologic remedies and cognitive and behavioral interventions. VRGET is a new approach to nonpharmacologic intervention that may reach patients unwilling or unable to use in vivo techniques. It is a more efficient and cost-effective form of exposure therapy. Initial results from clinical use of virtual environments for the treatment of panic disorder are promising.

Obsessive–Compulsive Disorder

9

Obsessive–compulsive disorder (OCD) is characterized by obsessions, recurrent, intrusive ideas, images, impulses and compulsions, and repetitive behaviors that are performed to decrease the discomfort. For example, people with this disorder may be obsessed with disturbing images or thoughts of germs and may then feel the need to wash their hands over and over in an effort to prevent thoughts of germs and to decrease the discomfort of the thoughts (American Psychiatric Association, 1994).

Prevalence

OCD affects 1 in every 50 people, or approximately 5 million Americans; men and women are equally likely to have this condition (Kent, 1996). OCD appears to run in families and generally begins when people are teenagers or young adults. As many as 80% of patients with OCD may also meet the diagnosis for concurrent depression (Barlow, DiNardo, Vermilyea, Vermilyea, & Blanchard, 1986).

The symptoms of OCD are similar in different ethnic and racial groups, as shown by several cross-cultural studies

(Akhtar, Wig, Verma, Pershad, & Verma, 1975; Hinjo et al., 1989; Khanna & Channabasavanna, 1987). The symptoms seem to manifest themselves as a gross exaggeration of natural human activities or rituals found in different cultures (Fiske & Haslam, 1997). Persons with OCD normally show an increase in activity in the cingulated gyrus and frontal lobes. In studies in which OCD patients were told they were holding "contaminated" objects, functional MRI showed an increase in activity in the basal ganglia, amygdala, prefrontal cortex, and anterior cingulated cortex; the increase did not occur when they were told that they were holding "clean" objects (Breiter et al., 1996). PET scans have shown decreases in prefrontal cortex activity after both behavior therapy and pharmacotherapy, correlating with a decrease in patient symptoms (Rubin, Ananth, Villanueva-Meyer, Trajmar, & Mena, 1995).

Risk Factors

Although there is no clear genetic indicator for the disease, OCD tends to run in families. A person with OCD has a 25% chance of having a blood relative who has it. Like other mental illnesses, it is more prevalent among identical (70%) than fraternal (50%) twins (Moe, 2001). Researchers do not currently understand OCD's genetic mechanisms, although they suspect that multiple genes are involved.

Children having a parent with OCD are more likely than others to have social, emotional, and behavioral disorders. In addition, child-rearing practices such as overprotection may be a risk factor in the development of anxiety disorders. Several studies have found a familial component in the expression of some forms of OCD. Patients with familial OCD are not characterized by peculiar clinical features, but they do appear to have a lower threshold for events that may trigger OCD. Women with OCD may experience a worsening of symptoms during premenstrual syndrome and pregnancy and postpartum. A recent study suggests that fluctuating hormones may trigger symptoms during pregnancy.

Several psychological theories about the cause of OCD have been proposed, but none has been confirmed. Some reports associate OCD with head trauma or streptococcal infections. Although several studies show brain abnormalities in patients with OCD (decreased caudate size, decreased white matter) the results are inconsistent and still under investigation. It is interesting that 20% of patients with OCD also have motor tics, suggesting that it may be related to Tourette's syndrome, but this link has not been proven or explained.

Treatments

The most effective behavioral treatment for OCD is exposure combined with response prevention. In this treatment, the patient is exposed to situations that normally cause compulsive behavior. The patient is then prevented from responding with the usual associated ritual. Results from 18 studies indicate that 51% of patients are free of symptoms following this type of treatment; an additional 39% show moderate improvement (Foa, Steketee, & Ozarow, 1985). Two medications used to treat OCD are clomipramine and fluoxetine. Studies on the medications' effectiveness have shown somewhat mixed results, but relapse does occur when medications are discontinued (Mavissakalian, Turner, & Michelson, 1985).

SIMULATED-BEHAVIOR THERAPY

In the early 1990s, Baer, Greist, and Marks began to explore a telephone interface for simulated behavior therapy of OCD. The study used a telephone interface to make treatment accessible. This interface is an interactive voice response system that asks the patient several questions and uses the answers to determine how to help the patient. The system, called BT Steps, appears to be helpful in reducing OCD symptoms (Greist, 1995). The program has nine steps—four that prepare patients, two that set them on a therapeutic course, and three that continue through therapy. The steps involve education, behavioral assessment, a treatment plan, treatment, and relapse prevention. The phone system "remembers" a patient's previous responses and aids the patient in building an exposure and ritual prevention hierarchy. Step 7 in the program is the first exposure and ritual prevention session, in which the patient is asked to expose the on-screen figure to dirt in the back garden. This action may be repeated again and again to maintain the gains achieved. During the first controlled study that systematically tested this system, 17 patients completed at least two sessions using the system. Those completing the sessions reported a 50% decrease in discomfort. Eighty-five percent of patients subjectively rated themselves as much or very much improved (Greist, 1995).

VIRTUAL REALITY THERAPY

In a pilot study exploring the use of computer-aided vicarious exposure with ritual prevention, a desktop VR system that displayed two-dimensional images was used to run 13 OCD and 10 non-OCD participants. Patients performed three 45-minute sessions once a week for 3 weeks without therapist guidance (A. Clark, Kirkby, Daniels, & Marks, 1998). The following scales were administered 1 week prior to treatment and 1 week after treatment ended: Yale–Brown Obsessive–Compulsive Scale (Goodman et al., 1989), the Padua Inventory (Burns et al., 1996), and the Beck Depression Inventory (Beck et al., 1996). A real-world Behavioral Avoidance Test consisting of planting an actual daffodil bulb was done both before and after treatment.

The participants were given computer-delivered instructions on using the program. The instructions stated that the figure on the computer had an "OCD problem" and instructed the participants to imagine that they were that person. During the sessions, participants were asked to maneuver the computer figure that was reported to have contamination obsessions and washing rituals, performing exposure procedures such as touching dirt and then preventing the figure from hand washing. The computer world consisted of a hotel, a street, a back yard garden, and a house with a sink for washing. As the computer figure performed different actions, a thermometer displayed its comfort level from "comfortable" to "panic, very anxious." As the participant guided the computer figure to perform more exposures without allowing it to wash, he or she scored more points. As these exposures occurred, the thermometer registered an increase in anxiety. The participant's ability to continue the exercise in spite of the computer figure's anxiety represents a simulated "habituation" to the task.

This vicarious exposure generalized to real world tasks, in particular for the 7 OCD (out of 13) participants who were washers. Positive results were also achieved for the checkers but were not as significant. (These two OCD subtypes, *washers,* who perform washing rituals to prevent contamination obsessions, and *checkers,* who perform checking rituals to reduce contamination fears, are often seen as having significant overlap. As a result, many consider the terms to be misnomers.) The positive results with the washers could reflect the program exposed participants to what washers experience in the real world—exposure to germs without being able to wash. The washers also reported the program to be similar to actual daily experiences. This feedback is important and should be examined by therapists and program developers to determine the level of detail of real-life experiences that is necessary to achieve positive treatment results using computer simulations.

BAT scores improved following treatment: Only 7 of the OCD participants washed their hands after planting the real daffodil bulb as opposed to 12 who washed prior to treatment. Scores on both the Padua Inventory and the Beck Depression Inventory decreased significantly before and after, but not on the Yale–Brown Obsessive–Compulsive Scale, which is thought to reflect "symptom severity." Most traditional OCD treatment protocols require a minimum of 20 sessions (Stanley & Turner, 1995); this protocol was only three sessions and did not require a therapist to be present, yet it still resulted in significant improvement as measured by the Beck Depression Inventory and Padua Inventory and to some extent by the Yale–Brown Obsessive–Compulsive Scale. These results may indicate that VR treatment could be a cost-effective alternative to traditional treatment of OCD.

One strength of the VR program is that it records every mouse stroke and movement of the participant. The real-time data allow the researcher to determine how quickly and with how many steps the participants exposed themselves to dirt, and whether they washed immediately or waited for several minutes. The number of repetitions performed by the participant did in fact correlate with outcome in a dose-response relationship. Kirkby et al. (2000) recommended further studies to investigate "ceiling" effects that might occur and also the impact of intelligence level on therapeutic response. In their initial study, those with lower intelligence took longer than those with a normal level of intelligence to begin using therapeutic strategies (exposure without washing) but were able to increase their usage over the three sessions.

VR therapy has been applied in the treatment of "checking" compulsions as well. One case study done in 1999 at Clark Atlanta involved a student who was late to class every day because she continually checked and rechecked her book bag. The virtual environment used in this case contained a room with books, pencils, and other school materials. Sessions were conducted for 10 to 15 minutes, once a week for 8 weeks. She was asked to place virtual objects in a book bag and to repeat the process until she no longer had doubts about forgetting an object. She was then asked to navigate outside the house and was again asked if she had any doubts about forgetting an object. If she had anxiety, and she did report experiencing subjective anxiety as well as sweaty palms and an increase in heart rate, she was given the opportunity to go back into the house and repack her book bag. She was allowed to continue this process until her anxiety level came down to zero. After her final treatment she reported being able to go to classes without the previous obsessive thoughts taking control (North, North, & Coble, 1996a; vrpsych-l@usc.edu posting to list serv, 6/13/99).

The North group in Georgia is also exploring the efficacy of treating OCD with virtual reality graded exposure therapy (VRGET) for other situations where obsessions might arise (North, North, & Coble, 1996c; M. North, personal communication, March 2003). North and colleagues have suggested that VR could be used for desensitization, for example, a person could continually rearrange books on a bookshelf in the VR world until desensitization occurs. It is thought the VR world would be more appealing for treating OCD because it occurs in a nonjudgmental environment. Future VR applications for OCD treatment that have been proposed include the use of a dataglove, with tactile augmentation, which could be used by the patient to "touch" virtual doorknobs, or shaking virtual strangers' hands, allowing for "contamination" to occur. In addition, with the addition of smell to virtual environments, olfactory cues could be added to increase the sense of realism. Patients could smell and feel themselves planting a virtual daffodil, thus building on the success of the Kirkby et al. study detailed above.

Summary

OCD is widespread across populations and cultural groups. It is most commonly treated with exposure and response prevention. In some cases, medications prove effective, but the results achieved are usually lost when medication is discontinued. The application of VRGET to OCD, although still limited, has shown great promise. The unlimited potential for exposure in the absence of real-world consequences renders VRGET a powerful tool in the treatment of this disorder.

Posttraumatic Stress Disorder

10

Posttraumatic stress disorder (PTSD) is a heterogeneous disorder that may occur following a traumatic event such as serious injury or threat of injury or death to self or others. Symptoms can include increased anxiety or arousal, dissociation, and flashbacks of the event. Duration of these symptoms must be at least once a month (American Psychiatric Association, 2000). Anxiety-reducing medications, antidepressants, support from friends and family, and cognitive–behavioral therapy (CBT; with some exposure involved) can help with recovery (Barlow, 1988). In treating those with PTSD following a motor vehicle accident, it is important to carefully assess whether the person is experiencing "accident phobia," which would be a specific phobia, or PTSD. Reports of treating accident phobias can be found as far back as 1962 (Wolpe) and have traditionally included some sort of exposure therapy. In the treatment of PTSD, exposure also seems to be included in most all treatment regimens. In fact, a panel of experts recently published a consensus opinion that exposure therapy is the most appropriate therapy for PTSD; the possibility of "retraumatizing" the individual was not considered cause for concern (Ballenger et al., 2001).

Prevalence

PTSD is estimated to affect between 1% and 14% of the populations of the U. S. during their lifetimes, depending on the population sampled. When at-risk individuals, such as combat veterans and victims of natural disasters or criminal violence, are sampled, prevalence rates range from 3% to 58% (American Psychiatric Association, 2000). Although there may be a delayed onset of symptoms following a trauma, most symptoms of PTSD occur within three months; often, patients receive a diagnosis of acute stress disorder.

Risk Factors

Researchers have tried to explain what predisposes some individuals but not others to develop PTSD following a traumatic event. Researchers have looked at both the potential for being exposed to traumatic events and tendency to develop PTSD following this exposure. For example, alcohol and drugs were found to be risk factors for exposure to adverse events (such as automobile accidents), but the dependence on these substances per se was not a risk factor for the development of PTSD in exposed populations. A prior history of depression was not a risk factor for exposure to adverse events but was a risk factor for PTSD in an exposed population (Breslau, Davis, Andreski, & Peterson, 1991). In addition, predisaster anxiety disorders may constitute a risk factor for postdisaster PTSD symptoms (Asarnow et al., 1999).

Based on a study of 90 combat veterans, Macklin et al. (2002) have suggested that people with lower IQ who experience trauma are more likely than others to develop PTSD symptoms. Conversely, individuals with a higher IQ may believe in their own ability to cope with the experience and thus not develop PTSD.

Posttraumatic Stress Disorder in Vietnam Veterans

Approximately 8.5% of women and 15.2% of men who served in Vietnam still meet the *Diagnostic and Statistical Manual of Mental Disorders*

(4th ed., *DSM–IV*; American Psychiatric Association, 2000) criteria for PTSD 15 or more years after their service. Because PTSD has varied symptoms and is resistant to treatment, many treatment modalities have been investigated (Kizer, 1996). These include behavioral treatments, such as systematic desensitization; flooding (prolonged exposure to feared stimulus); both forms of exposure therapy; electromyography (EMG) biofeedback; eye movement desensitization; stress inoculation therapy; cognitive therapy; psychodynamic treatment; and hypnotherapy. However, few controlled studies have been conducted (Blanchard & Hickling, 1997). Currently, only 66% of persons with PTSD fully recover (Kessler, Sonnega, Bromet, Hughes, & Nelson, 1995). Biochemical markers associated with PTSD have been identified by Veterans Affairs researchers. Researchers have also found psychophysiological instruments to be reliable and valid at discriminating between individuals who have PTSD and those who do not. Using virtual reality graded exposure therapy (VRGET) and physiological feedback may lead to treatments that benefit not only veterans but also those whose PTSD was triggered by natural disasters, violent crimes, and terrorism (Kizer, 1996).

Most approaches to treating PTSD have used some form of exposure therapy as part of the treatment regimen. Hodges et al. (1999) have begun exploring VRGET at the Atlanta Veterans Affairs Hospital to treat PTSD. Five case studies have been reported to date. This treatment involves nine 60-minute individual sessions over a period of 5 weeks in which veterans are exposed to virtual Huey helicopters that fly them over the jungles of Vietnam (Salyer, 1997). The Virtually Better, Inc. (Decatur, Georgia) software used in these treatments offers two environments. In the "open field" environment, the participant stands on a platform that is surrounded by handrails. The patient can walk through the field by pushing a button on a joystick. This virtual field is surrounded by jungle, and the patient can hear sounds in the jungle including helicopter noise, gunfire, explosions, and soldiers yelling. Visuals include a swampy area, a hilly area, trees and jungle area, fog, helicopters, and daytime and nighttime conditions (Figure 10.1).

The second environment is a helicopter environment during which users wear a head-mounted display and sit in a Thunderseat™. The helicopter environment seats the patient behind a pilot in a Huey helicopter with the side door open. The helicopter can remain on the ground, take off, fly over different types of terrain, and land. The therapist can control the duration and sequence of each scenario. Visual stimuli in this environment include rice paddies, jungles, rivers, mountains, and a forest. Auditory effects include the Huey helicopter sounds, B52s, explosions, radio chatter, and machine guns. The therapist controls all sounds.

FIGURE 10.1.

This Virtual Vietnam was developed by Virtually Better, Inc. to treat veterans with PTSD.

While exposed to the virtual environments, the patient is asked to recount memories of the war. The therapist tries to match these memories with visual and auditory stimuli in the virtual world. Although the therapist cannot match all stimuli precisely, a close enough fit occurs to allow the patient to process the trauma. In an initial case study, patients who had been exposed to both environments experienced a 34% decrease in PTSD symptoms as rated by the clinician and a 45% decrease in their self-ratings. At 6-month follow-up, these gains were maintained (Hodges et al., 1999; Rothbaum et al., 1999).

Hyperarousal to presentation of combat-related stimuli has been shown in several physiological measurements, including heart rate (Blanchard, Kolb, & Prins, 1991) and electrodermal activity (Brende, 1982; Pitman, Orr, Forgue, de Jong, & Claiborn, 1987). Veterans with PTSD clearly show an increased physiological response as compared to veterans without PTSD. To build on this research, Attias, Bleich, Furman, and Zinger (1996) measured visual event-related potentials in both a control group and a group of PTSD patients. Event-related potentials reflect neural activity that is associated with information processing. The P3 component of the event-related potentials reflects stimulus relevance, and its amplitude and latency are thought to be determined by the subjective value of a stimulus (Donchin & Coles, 1988). The N1 component of the event-related potentials reflects early stage selection, and its amplitude is dependent on the physical attributes of a stimulus (Duncan-Johnson & Donchin, 1982). PTSD patients showed increased P3 and N1 amplitudes in response to combat-related pictures. They did not show this increase when presented with neutral pictures. The control group of combat veterans who did not have PTSD did not show these patterns. It is important to further explore these measures as VRGET begins to be used to treat this population. It has been hypothesized that event-related potentials could be used as a diagnostic tool for PTSD. The three-dimensional nature of the VR stimuli could allow for more accurate representation of stimuli and would allow for systematic presentation of the relevant stimuli (Attias et al., 1996).

Posttraumatic Stress Disorder in Motor Vehicle Accident Survivors

Motor vehicle accidents are the most common trauma that occurs in the United States; 3.5 million persons are injured in accidents each year (Butler & Moffic, 1999). According to a study by Norris (1992), 23.4% of Americans will be involved in a motor vehicle accident at some point in their lifetimes. Of the individuals in Norris's study who had been in one, 11.5% developed PTSD. In a more recent National Institute of Mental Health-funded study, 39.2% of the motor vehicle accident survivors assessed met the criteria for PTSD and 28.5% met the criteria for subsyndromal PTSD (Blanchard & Hickling, 1997, 1998). During follow-up, 11% of those with subsyndromal PTSD had developed full PTSD, as measured by the Clinician Administered Post-Traumatic Stress Disorder Scale (Blake et al., 1996). Among those who developed PTSD, 43.5% also developed major depression, compared with only 2% of those who did not develop PTSD. Comorbid panic disorder was developed by 4.8% of the PTSD survivors compared to none of those without PTSD. In the PTSD group, 21% had specific phobias. (The study does not give a breakdown of these phobias.) The study does identify two groups of phobic individuals: those who developed a driving phobia (15.3%) and those who began avoiding certain driving situations (93.2%). The long-term follow-up showed that of the 55% of the PTSD individuals who responded, 24% still met full criteria 2 years after the accident. Persons with PTSD seem to have a high level of sympathetic arousal when exposed to cues of the previous trauma.

Psychophysiological assessment of the car accident survivors included both heart rate and skin resistance measures. These measures have proven helpful in assessing both Vietnam veterans and sexual assault victims with PTSD and also appeared to be robust measures in this study. The measures correctly identified two thirds of the car accident survivors with PTSD. At 1-year follow-up, those whose PTSD had not remitted continued to show physiological arousal when exposed to the cues, whereas those whose PTSD had remitted did not show arousal. Those who still had PTSD had in fact shown a higher rate of arousal when first assessed 1 to 4 months after their accidents as compared with those who no longer had PTSD (Blanchard & Hickling, 1997, 1998).

In the above-mentioned study, a subsample of the group was treated with a manual-based CBT program that included relaxation training and in vivo and imaginal exposure. Reports indicate that the treatment was successful in helping all the participants overcome some or all of their PTSD symptoms.

As discussed in chapter 13 ("Fear of Driving"), VR seems to work well with those who have had a motor vehicle accident and are experiencing PTSD symptoms.

Virtual Reality Applications for Other Types of Posttraumatic Stress Disorder

Therapists are interested in using VR therapy to treat PTSD resulting from on-the-job injuries. Work simulation tasks have proven useful in helping those with PTSD as a result of an on-the-job injury. An occupational therapist and a psychologist working as a team can often provide a safe environment where patients can expose themselves to graded tasks that are within their physical limits. These tasks could be undertaken in a virtual world, with such things as height situations or driving scenarios serving to help recreate the "accident" scene (Phillips, Bruehl, & Harden, 1997).

Therapists are also interested in using VR therapy to treat survivors of natural disasters. One such program has been developed and has undergone initial testing in Greece (Tarnanas, 2001). The program is used to teach anxiety management skills to individuals who have experienced earthquakes. The virtual world is run on a personal computer and viewed through a VPL EyePhone (VPL Research, Inc., Redwood City, California), with a motion capture system to study emotional state. This study involved preschool children and children with Down's syndrome. The children were exposed to a virtual earthquake disaster and were trained to control their anxiety responses using an avatar to model ideal behavior. The study found that 87% of the children were able to lower their anxiety levels and that these gains were maintained at 3 months after treatment. This study suggests that phobias developed in response to natural disasters, such as earthquakes, could be treated using VRGET. Such treatments have thus far been limited to imaginal exposure, with the accompanying limitations. Here VRGET is the method of exposure where the in vivo recreation is not an option.

VR may also be useful in the treatment of rape victims. Although each victim's experience is unique, clinicians have found that many "generalizations" about scenarios may be made. The addition of smell may be important for some patients and could be added or removed from the room for others. VR treatment allows therapists to overcome one of the difficulties with treating PTSD patients, namely, getting them to stay on task. It is much more difficult to disassociate when the world is "surrounding" you with three-dimensional visual and auditory components and realistic scents.

Those experiencing PTSD find it especially important to learn coping skills before exposure for any phobia. The person with PTSD should be taught self-soothing and grounding techniques prior to re-experiencing the trauma so that he or she is not resensitized to the trauma. Patients with PTSD may require a longer period of recovery before leaving an exposure session, and this should be accommodated. In addition, those who have had a trauma may feel a greater need for control in their treatment and exposure than those who have not, and therapists should allow for this (Winston, 1996).

Summary

Initial reports have shown VR technology to be a helpful therapeutic tool in the treatment of PTSD. Using VRGET to treat Vietnam veterans with PTSD has shown initial successes, as has treatment of PTSD related to motor vehicle accidents. Preliminary work also suggests that VRGET could be an effective treatment for survivors of natural disasters or as a "stress inoculation training" tool to teach individuals how to respond during emergency events. Areas still to be explored include PTSD resulting from on-the-job injuries, rape, and child abuse. Because it is not realistic to expose someone to the trauma stimuli in vivo, in these areas VR holds great promise. Although research done in PTSD treatment using VR is very scanty, the results thus far show that VR therapy may decrease the length of treatment and may increase the likelihood of long-term reduction of symptoms.

Specific Phobias and Social Phobia | 11

Specific Phobias

The criteria that must be met for a diagnosis of Specific Phobia according to the *Diagnostic and Statistical Manaul of Mental Disorders* (4th ed., *DSM–IV*; American Psychiatric Association, 1994) are as follows:

A. A marked and persistent fear that is excessive, unreasonable, and cued by the presence or anticipation of a specific object or situation, with
B. Exposure to the phobic stimulus provoking an anxiety response
C. The person recognizes that the fear is excessive
D. And the phobic situation(s) is avoided or else endured with intense anxiety
E. The anxiety response interferes significantly with the person's normal functioning.

Those experiencing a specific phobia have anxiety that is provoked by confronting a specific stimulus or by anticipating such a confrontation. More than 200 phobias have been identified. The *DSM–IV* Subtypes for specific phobias are as follows:

- Animal Type, which generally has a childhood onset. Female individuals account for 75%–90% of those with this subtype.
- Natural Environment Type, which includes fear of heights, water, and storms and generally has a childhood onset. Female individuals account for 75%–90% of this subtype.
- Blood-Injection-Injury Type, which includes fear of invasive medical procedures other than just injections and is accompanied by a vasovagal response. Female individuals account for 55%–70% of this subtype.
- Situational Type, which includes fear of flying, bridges, elevators, driving, or enclosed places. The age at onset of this subtype is either during childhood or in the mid-20s. This is the most frequent subtype seen in adults; 75%–90% of those with this subtype are female.
- Other Types, which include fear of falling down when away from walls, fear of vomiting, fear of contracting an illness, fear of loud sounds, and fear of costumed characters (in children).

People with a specific phobia subtype are more likely to have another phobia within the same subtype. Panic disorder with agoraphobia is frequently found in individuals who have specific phobias. Situational-type phobias are the subtype most commonly seen in clinical settings; however, this does not reflect the actual prevalence in society, because only a minority of those with phobias ever seek professional treatment (Reich, 1986).

PREVALENCE

Phobias are the most common psychiatric disorder, more common than major depression, alcohol abuse, or alcohol dependence. It is estimated that 9% of the U. S. population will be diagnosed with a phobia during any given year, with lifetime prevalence estimated at between 10% and 11.3% (Boyd et al., 1990). Prevalence rates are found to be significantly higher in women, with women making up 75% to 90% of people who seek treatment for phobias. Community samples show a 3.8:1.0 ratio of women to men with phobias. In general, 83.4% of those with a specific phobia also report having had another mental health disorder at some time in their lives. Phobias are strongly comorbid with each other, with other anxiety disorders, and with affective disorders (such as mania and depression). Age of onset may be either in childhood or young adulthood (mid-20s). Specific phobias are negatively related to education but not to income, and prevalence is significantly elevated among Hispanics, among those who are not employed, and among those who live with their parents (Magee et al., 1996). Less than 15% of those with a specific phobia ever seek treatment (Agras et al., 1969; Boyd et al., 1990). Without treatment, only 20% of cases that persist into adulthood will remit (http://www.nimh.nih.gov).

RISK FACTORS

The strongest risk factor associated with phobias is the presence of another psychiatric disorder, and the most frequent co-occurrence is with panic disorder (Boyd et al., 1990). There is a strong familial pattern with phobias; first-degree relatives of phobic individuals have a greater than average likelihood of also having a phobia of the same specific subtype. In addition, fear of blood and injury have strong familial ties. The women to men ratio for specific phobias is 2:1, but this ratio varies slightly over the different sub-types (*DSM–IV–TR*; American Psychiatric Association, 2000). A particularly threatening experience may put a person at risk for developing a specific phobia. Witnessing a traumatic event in which others experience harm or extreme fear is another risk factor for specific phobia as well as receiving repeated information or warnings about potentially dangerous situations from an authority figure. Another predisposing factor is experiencing an unexpected panic attack in a certain situation (*DSM–IV–TR*; American Psychiatric Association, 2000)

TREATMENT

Exposure therapy, sometimes in combination with relaxation therapy, is generally used to treat phobias. Medication may also be used as an adjunct (Barlow, 1988). Pharmacological treatments include oral medications, such as antianxiolytics and antidepressants. The difficulty with using medication is that the anxiolytic effect is only short-term. Once the medication is discontinued, research has shown that the patient's anxiety returns to pre-treatment levels. In addition, pharmacological treatment is often contraindicated due to pre-existing health conditions. Some medications have been shown to cause memory impairment and other problematic side effects (Uinsworth, 1984). Slovin has argued that psychological interventions need to be implemented in order for the phobia to be overcome in the long term (Slovin, 1997).

There are many psychological treatments available for specific phobias. Hypnosis has been shown to successfully decrease fear related to phobias; however, it has been estimated that only 20% of individuals are capable of attaining a deep trance (Benson, 2000). Eye Movement Desensitization and Reprocessing has been shown to be a promising treatment, but only if the phobia has been related to a trauma (De Jongh, van den Oord, & ten Broeke, 2002). The most commonly researched behavioral psychological therapies are relaxation training, modeling, cognitive therapy, and exposure therapy. However, there is a wide body of research that has shown that phobias are most successfully treated by using a broad-based therapy that incorporates cognitive, behavioral, and psychophysiological components into cognitive–behavioral therapy (CBT).

Traditional exposure therapies, although effective in treating anxiety and phobias in general, do have some deficiencies. *In vivo* exposure to the many situations a phobic patient typically fears can involve considerable cost and time, safety risks, and a loss of confidentiality. In addition, it may be too overwhelming or frightening as a first step in treatment.

To address the many problems with *in vivo* exposure, researchers developed imaginal exposure methods to help people desensitize to fear-inducing situations. One problem with this approach, however, is that many people are unable to effectively visualize the situations that cause them anxiety. It is estimated that only 15% of patients can visualize effectively (Kosslyn, Brunn, Cave, & Wallach, 1984). Poor visualizers are unable to feel present in the phobic situation and since the fear response is not activated, disconfirming information cannot be introduced to change it, and habituation does not occur (Foa & Kozack, 1986). However, as stated earlier, virtual reality can offer solutions to many of these problems.

Social Phobia

Social phobia is defined as a "marked and persistent fear of one or more social or performance situations in which the person is exposed to unfamiliar people or to possible scrutiny by others" (American Psychiatric Association, 2000, p. 450). This phobia may involve specific settings or activities as eating in public, signing checks in front of others, public speaking, or taking tests. It may also be generalized to include most situations. People with social phobia are at increased risk for alcohol abuse and alcohol dependence compared to those with other anxiety disorders (Amies, Gelder, & Shaw, 1983). In addition, suicidal ideation has been shown to occur frequently in individuals with social phobia; weaker evidence suggests a higher frequency of suicidal attempts in this population (Amies et al., 1983; Schneier, Johnson, Hornig, Liebowitz, & Weissman, 1992).

PREVALENCE

Social phobia has a lifetime prevalence of 13.3% and a reported 30-day prevalence of 4.5% (Kessler et al., 1994). Fifty-nine percent of those with social phobia meet the diagnosis for a co-morbid specific phobia (Magee et al., 1996). Shyness is often a useful descriptor of social phobia. Shy and social phobic people report similar cognitions, and both report a fear of negative evaluation when engaged in social interactions (Ludwig & Lazarus, 1983). Social phobia is found more frequently among first-degree biological relatives of those with social phobia compared with the general population (American Psychiatric Association, 2000).

RISK FACTORS

Research suggests that a complex variety of components are involved in the etiology of social phobia. Temperamental characteristics like shyness, behavioral inhibition, self-consciousness, and embarrassment are commonly thought to be predispositional factors (Beidel & Morris, 1995; Beidel & Randall, 1994; Crozier, 1990; Heimberg, Hope, Dodge, & Becker, 1987; Kagan & Moss, 1962; Leary & Kowalski, 1995; Rosenbaum, Biederman, Pollock, & Hirshfeld, 1994; Stemberger, Turner, Beidel, & Calhoun, 1995), and social phobia is sometimes even considered their severe form. Heredity (Beidel & Morris, 1995; Beidel & Randall, 1994; Bruch, 1989; Greist et al., 1997; Rosenbaum et al., 1994; Stemberger et al., 1995) and a biochemical predisposition to social anxiety and selective attention are also implicated (Greist et al., 1997; Heimberg et al., 1987; Jefferson, 1996; Johnson & Lydiard, 1995; Liebowitz et al., 1988; Rosenbaum et al., 1994; Stemberger et al., 1995; van Vliet, den Boer, & Westenberg, 1994). Traumatic conditioning, on the other hand, is assumed to factor more heavily into the development of circumscribed social phobia (Beidell & Randall, 1994; Rosenbaum et al., 1994; Stemberger et al., 1995).

GENERALIZED SOCIAL PHOBIA

The specifier *Generalized* refers to a form of social phobia wherein the individual fears most social situations (American Psychiatric Association, 2000). In some cases these individuals may also qualify for a diagnosis of avoidant personality disorder, which refers to the avoidance of most social situations and fear of judgment, or they may have agoraphobia with or without panic disorder. In fact, several studies show that 50% to 89% of those with generalized social phobia also meet diagnostic criteria for avoidant personality disorder, whereas only 21%

to 23% of those with more discrete forms of social phobia, such as fear of public speaking, meet avoidant personality disorder criteria (Herbert, Hope, & Bellack, 1992; C. S. Holt, Heimberg, & Hope, 1992; Schneier, Spitzer, Gibbon, Fyer, & Liebowitz, 1991). Although anecdotal reports have shown clinical effectiveness of (VR) therapy with this disorder, effectiveness has not yet been established through controlled clinical trials. Though no therapy will be effective for every patient, this is an area for future research focus (Wiederhold, 2001).

FEAR OF PUBLIC SPEAKING (GLOSSOPHOBIA)

According to the American Psychiatric Association (www.psych.org), the most common social phobia is fear of public speaking. Fear of public speaking is the third most common psychiatric disorder and was listed by the *Book of Lists* as the number 1 fear among Americans (Greist, 1995). An article by Furmark (1997) reported that "stage fright" afflicts 13% of people at some point during their lifetimes. Treatment typically involves CBT or medication or a combination of the two. CBT often involves exposure, reframing thoughts associated with the social scene, social skills training, and relaxation training. Beta-blocker anti-anxiety drugs, such as propranolol, can be used on an as-needed basis (e.g., on the day of performance; Barlow, 1988) and have been used for years with apparent success for many individuals in decreasing the physiological effects of stage fright, such as hand tremors, rapid heart rate, and sweaty palms. Thirteen percent of speakers at an American College of Cardiology meeting admitted to having used beta-blockers prior to giving their presentation at the conference (Jefferson, 1995). Although beta-blockers do not act directly on the cognitive component of the fear, it has been speculated that reduction in physical symptoms helps boost the glossophobic individual's confidence, which in turn may lead to improved performance abilities (Heimberg et al., 1995). Anti-depressants, such as monoamine oxidase inhibitors or Paxil, are now also being explored as treatment methods; their drawback is that they must be taken on a daily basis to work and may have undesirable side effects. Although medication is a valid option for those who experience a fear of public speaking, there is no indication that the use of drugs, once discontinued, has any lasting effect on curing or preventing stage fright. Thus, for some, behavior therapy, which involves learning the skills and techniques needed to overcome this disorder, may prove a better long-term solution (Tanouye, 1997).

A good use of VR technology is to have the patient role-play in a VR environment where different scenarios can be acted out and then discussed. This provides a starting point for meaningful dialogue between therapist and patient. Because it can be difficult to arrange in vivo exposure for many social phobia situations (e.g., those that involve confronting authority figures), treatment must resort to imaginal exposure (Barlow, 1988). The more powerful and convenient approach offered by VR technology is to digitize the authority figure's face into the virtual world and allow the patient to do repeated role-plays. With intelligent software, perhaps driven by neural networks, the virtual personae of the authority figure could react differently according to how the patient handled himself or herself. Such treatment would provide systematic desensitization and help the patient develop social skills and self-assertion techniques.

North and his colleagues in Atlanta have actively used VR therapy to treat fear of public speaking. Participants in their initial study were exposed to a virtual audience and experienced many of the same symptoms as might be experienced when in front of a real audience—dry mouth, sweaty palms, and increased heart rate (North, North, & Coble, 1996c). In a second study, 16 participants were randomized into either a VR treatment group (virtual reality graded exposure therapy, VRGET) or a no-treatment control group (North, North, & Coble, 1998). Attitude Toward Public Speaking Questionnaire (North, North, & Coble, 1998), the Marks and Mathews' Fear Questionnaire (1979), self-reported anxiety (subjective units of distress) levels, and heart rate were used as measures. The no-treatment group was allowed to navigate through "trivial" VR scenes and were told to manage their fear and try to expose themselves to situations that they had been avoiding. No other instructions were given on relaxation or coping skills. The VRGET group was exposed to a variety of virtual scenarios, including speaking in front of an empty auditorium, speaking to an uninterested audience, speaking to an audience who laughed at them and told them to "speak up," and speaking to an audience that smiled and applauded. Size of audience was varied from 0 to 100. Treatment was given over a period of 5 weeks. A significant correlation was found between self-reported distress scores and heart rate, indicating both subjective and objective arousal during exposure. Results of this study indicated no decrease in anxiety for participants in the "control" group; however, the scores of VRGET group members were statistically significantly lower on the Attitude Toward Public Speaking Questionnaire and Fear Questionnaire.

An important pilot study was done to assess the level of immersion in VR environments and its affect on anxiety using both desktop and head-mounted display systems (Slater, Pertaub, & Steed, 1999). Ten people were placed in front of a virtual audience, and the results indicated a clear correlation between immersion and anxiety. The study was followed up by a larger one using both a between and within-group design. Forty participants were randomized into either a head-mounted-display group or a desktop-using group, and audience response was friendly, neutral, or hostile (Pertaub, Slater, & Barker, 2001). To test this design, all participants gave two speeches; three groups were randomized and gave speeches while in a head-mounted display, and another three groups gave the same speeches while viewing an audience on a three-dimensional desktop display. One group in each condition (head-mounted display vs. desktop) gave both speeches to a neutral audience. A second group gave their first talk to a hostile audience and their second talk to a friendly audience. A third group gave the first talk to the friendly audience and the second talk to the hostile audience (see Figure 11.1). An order effect was found, with the

FIGURE 11.1.

Therapists can choose between small or large, and attentive or inattentive audiences to help the patient progress through treatment of public speaking phobia. Software developed by Virtually Better, Inc.

second talk generating less anxiety; except where the second talk was to the hostile audience. Overall, those in the head-mounted display group reported lower scores as measured by the Personal Report of Confidence as a Speaker questionnaire (Paul, 1991). This would seem to fit with what has been found in other experiments comparing head-mounted displays and desk-top VR systems: The VR system seems more realistic and the participant experiences more arousal (anxiety), both subjectively and objectively (Wiederhold, Davis, & Wiederhold, 1998).

With the idea of developing more accessible treatment options, a number of projects have looked toward making programs available through the World Wide Web. One project proposed by Hans Sieburg at University of California at San Diego involves a virtual reality modeling language (VRML) environment for treating those with social phobias. This world could be accessed over the Internet, and behaviors, such as coughing, whispering, fidgeting, crowd noise, and other "audience" interactions, could be programmed in at appropriate times by the therapist (North, North, & Coble, 1996c).

A self-help program, aptly named "Talk to me," is in the early stages of pilot testing on a group of university students in Valencia, Spain, have a fear of public speaking (Botella, Baños, et al., 2000; Riva et al., 2001). The "Talk to me" program is offered over the Internet using nonimmersive two-dimensional computer simulations. (Three-dimensional stimuli are planned for future versions.) For now, the program offers video and audio streaming in real-time through the Internet, making this easily accessible to patients in their home. The video presentation is controlled and when threatening stimuli are presented, appropriate help and guidance are made available, or the program may be aborted if it becomes too overwhelming. When the patient first begins treatment using this system, a patient file is created and he or she is not allowed to progress unless certain criteria are met. To enable this, there is a bi-directional flow of data between the client and a server. During treatment, patients have access to a team of psychologists through e-mail, fax, or telephone. The system uses an outcome protocol that assesses treatment effectiveness throughout the process. It includes the basic elements of patient education, exposure through auditory and visual stimuli, attentional focus, and cognitive restructuring techniques. The following exposure scenarios have been included thus far: a classroom setting, a group of friends conversing, an oral presentation, an oral exam, speaking before Congress, and a congratulatory speech at a lunch gathering. In each scenario, a hierarchy is built and shown to the participant in an order determined by assessment results.

TEST ANXIETY

In a *DSM–IV* sub-workgroup, a review of papers on test anxiety indicated that persons who have test anxiety have high rates of "social evaluative anxiety," with one social phobia study reporting a 19% rate of test anxiety among study participants. When physiology was examined, those with test anxiety tested very similarly to those with social phobia. The workgroup concluded that test anxiety should be considered as a discrete social phobia if other criteria for social phobia are met, such as intense distress and impairment (Heimberg et al., 1995).

VR therapy may have a role in helping to reduce test anxiety in college students. Test anxiety is a major concern for many college students, particularly in math and science courses. Virtual worlds, with electromyography (EMG) feedback, have been proposed as a tool for helping students recognize and relieve their test anxiety. The EMG electrodes measure muscle tension; individuals can use it to recognize signs of tension and then develop techniques to reduce the tension. Students could go into the virtual test environment, see the EMG response, and learn to lower their arousal levels. These techniques also show promise in training students to improve performance (Knox, Schacht, & Turner, 1993). Virtual classrooms have been created by two groups, under the direction of Sun Kim at Hanyang University and Skip Rizzo at University of Southern California, as a possible assessment tool and treatment mechanism for those with attentional difficulties (Rizzo, Bowerly, Schultheis, Shahabi, & Buckwalter, 2002). The same software may also be used as an in vivo exposure tool for those with test anxiety.

SOCIAL SKILLS TRAINING

Those with social phobia may also have a deficit in social skills, and therapy may thus include social skills training. Current social skills training programs involve techniques such as behavior modeling and directive teaching strategies. Students using programs do gain social skills; however, these behavior gains do not transfer to natural environments, such as the playground, classroom, and community. It is therefore suggested that VR treatment may allow for more transfer of learning because the immersive, interactive quality allows the user to experience a sense of presence through more naturalistic scenarios that are created and practiced by students. The flexibility of a VR approach that includes different scenarios, multiple users, scaling, and active problem-solving capabilities could test students' skills by varying the scenarios depending on their actions and teach them the consequences associated with different behavioral choices.

Muscott and Gifford (1994) proposed that VR therapy be used to train children to enhance social skills. Work with phobic individuals shows that skills learned in the virtual world do indeed generalize to the real world, and so there is every indication that VR therapy could also be successful with social skills training. Social environments could allow virtual personae-characters to interact with the patient either autonomously or in a guided manner. A guided virtual personae-character is under the complete control of the therapist, where an autonomous one could be pre-programmed with a set of algorithms built into the VR software system (Glantz et al., 1996). Persons in the virtual world could be systematically made to respond differently depending on the actions taken by the patient. For instance, if the patient did not make eye contact or did not begin a conversation, the therapist could control the world so that the virtual character would walk away. Conversely, if the patient made eye contact and started a conversation, the virtual character could be made to smile and give a preprogrammed answer. By providing positive reinforcement in simulations duplicating real-life scenarios, patient self-efficacy and sense of mastery could be improved. Patients would likely feel more comfortable confronting social situations in the real world because their responses had been practiced many times in the virtual world. The virtual world is a nice step because the responses to the patient can be controlled— with the virtual character being pleasant in the beginning if the patient responds appropriately, and slowly becoming neutral or rude as the patient gains skill in handling this behavior. Building the patient's self-confidence, combined with the realization that the behavior of others is independent of their control, are useful lessons.

Wiederhold and Wiederhold (2000) described a 32-year-old man who referred himself to the Virtual Reality Medical Center after becoming increasingly uncomfortable with social functions. He had actually been unable to attend some recent events and had begun to feel as though he was being held back both professionally and personally by this anxiety. Treatment began with a combination of patient education, cognitive coping techniques, and breathing retraining. As treatment proceeded the patient was exposed to a variety of virtual environments—a restaurant scene, an office scene, a grocery store scene, a beach scene—in which he had to interact with people, making eye contact and initiating small talk. Between sessions he was given the assignment of practicing the skills he had learned during the therapy session. Because he had come for treatment just prior to the holiday season, he was able to find many opportunities to practice his skills in vivo. He also was encouraged to practice eye contact and small talk with new people in the office setting. He reported feeling more comfortable with trying these in vivo assignments because "he had already done it numerous times" in the virtual world. The gains made in VRGET transferred well to the real world setting, and he was able to stop avoiding social situations and begin interacting with less anxiety.

Protocols now include treatment using first the VR worlds and then progressing to Internet-based worlds, which can provide real-time audio feedback, with positive reinforcement for correct skill usage and a chance for the therapist to observe skills that may still need to be enhanced. After the patient is comfortable with the Internet-based worlds, real-time audio and visual feedback may be used through Microsoft Net Meeting, an inexpensive microphone, and an inexpensive camera placed atop the computer. In this way, the patient may practice, first with a therapist and then with fellow patients, and still feel some degree of anonymity. Homework includes practicing skills in real world settings between sessions.

BODY DYSMORPHIC DISORDER

Body dysmorphic disorder is often seen as a concomitant of social phobia. Individuals with body dysmorphic disorder (also called *dysmorphophobia*), which is classified as a Somatoform Disorder by the *DSM–IV*, have an intense preoccupation with an imagined defect in appearance. If the defect is present at all, the individual's concern about it is seen as excessive. Individuals with this disorder may avoid activities such as dating, school, and job interviews. In extreme cases, individuals may become housebound, and suicide attempts are common (American Psychiatric Association, 1994). When body dysmorphic disorder is present, along with social phobia, role-playing during therapy appears to increase the chance of successful treatment (Marks, 1995). Part of the treatment used currently in the VR eating disorders research is to digitize patients' actual body into the VR world (Figure 11.2) and help them to deal with body image distortion and dissatisfaction (Riva, 1998b). Other software allows patients to "deform" parts of their body, including breast size, hips, and waist. It has been proposed that this could be used to help the patient deal with deformities that might occur from surgery, such as mastectomy (Alcaniz et al., 2000).

SOCIAL PHOBIA AND AVOIDANT PERSONALITY DISORDER

Some studies suggest that the presentation of generalized social phobia and avoidant personality disorder share many similarities and represent more of a quantitative than a qualitative difference in symptoms. This is not surprising; an essential issue in both avoidant personality disorder and social phobia is fear of negative evaluation (C. S. Holt et al., 1992;

FIGURE 11.2.

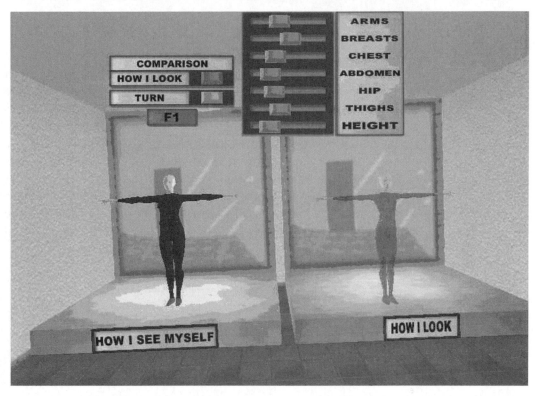

Patients use this software to become aware of body image distortion and dissatisfaction as part of eating disorder treatment. Software developed by PREVI.

S. M. Turner, Beidel, & Townsley, 1992). Other studies report that almost 50% of the U.S. population has a problem with shyness; some have speculated that the increase in shyness may be due in part to the surge in Internet usage (Schrof & Schultz, 1999). Persons with social phobia or avoidant personality disorder may find that the virtual world can offer an anonymous venue in which therapy can proceed, where they can be immersed in a scenario and allowed to interact with non-judgmental virtual humans. The head-mounted display also allows the patient to be relieved of the uncomfortable situation of talking face-to-face with the therapist. Some studies show that this may allow for more open dialogue to occur (King & Poulos, 1998). In most psycho-therapeutic situations we are accustomed to talking to the patient face-to-face; however, psychoanalytic settings use the back-to-face orientation as the traditional therapy position, which, some believe, may allow for more open disclosure (Gillieron, 1981).

Summary

Social phobia, in its various manifestations, is widespread in the population. Social phobias, such as public speaking or test anxiety, affect large numbers of people. Traditional methods of treatment include medication, carrying the risk of side effects, and CBT. VRGET offers a viable alternative allowing the patient to gain confidence through repeated exposures. Exposure situations can also be varied and the intensity increased according to the patient's needs. There is no risk to the patient as VRGET is completed in the therapist's office under controlled conditions. Other venues for treatment include a treatment program run by a clinical facility, which can be accessed through the Internet. VRGET also shows promise in treating patients with social skills deficits and those with body dysmorphic disorder.

Aviophobia

12

The *Diagnostic and Statistical Manual of Mental Disorders* (4th ed., Text Revision; *DSM–IV–TR*; American Psychiatric Association, 2000) classifies a*viophobia,* the fear of flying, under the heading of Anxiety Disorders as a Specific Phobia of the Situational subtype. Phobias of this subtype involve fear that is cued by a specific situation, such as elevators, driving, or flying. Persons presenting for treatment of fear of flying may have either a specific phobia, or the fear of flying may be part of their agoraphobia. Persons with a specific phobia are afraid of crashing, whereas those with agoraphobia are afraid of having a panic attack (McNally & Louro, 1992).

Prevalence

An estimated 10% to 20% of the general population is affected by aviophobia, although this fear may not always reach the intensity required to meet *DSM* criteria for a specific phobia (Agras et al., 1969). Of those who do fly, approximately 20% use sedatives or alcohol to deal with their anxiety (Greist & Greist, 1981). Fear of flying may result in social stigmatization for some, but for others it may result in lost job opportunities because of an inability to travel. If these figures are accurate, the opportunity cost of this disorder to the airline industry is $1.6 billion per year (Roberts, 1989).

Treatment

Systematic desensitization is the most commonly used method for treating aviophobia. Systematic desensitization consists of pairing relaxation exercises with imaginal exposure to the phobic stimuli (Wolpe, Brady, Serber, Agras, & Liberman, 1973).

The first controlled study of fear of flying with a civilian population was conducted by Solyom, Shugar, Bryntwick, and Solyom in 1973. Individuals were given one of four treatments: (a) habituation, (b) systematic desensitization, (c) aversion relief, or (d) group therapy. The first three behavior therapies were equally effective in reducing fear of flying; group therapy, however, proved ineffective. Several subsequent controlled studies have shown that exposure-based treatments are effective for fear of flying (Denholtz, Hall, & Mann, 1978; Denholtz & Mann, 1975; Howard, Murphy, & Clarke, 1983; Solyom et al., 1973). As you can see, the research using in vivo exposure is fairly old. This is due to the fact that in vivo exposure is expensive, so few controlled treatment studies were executed after the idea was proven.

Other researchers have attempted to approximate flight experiences through advanced audio-visual sensations. Denholtz and Mann (1975) used a combination of techniques (desensitization, modeling, and positive reinforcement) as part of an automated audiovisual program to treat individuals with flight phobia. Four treatment groups were included in the study: (a) individuals who performed 30 minutes of relaxation training each session, followed by audiovisual exposure to phobic stimuli, proceeding further only if no anxiety was experienced and receiving relaxation instructions if anxiety was experienced; (b) individuals who underwent relaxation training and then all scenes in the hierarchy, one after the other with no intervening relaxation exercises during presentation or control of hierarchy presentation; (c) individuals who experienced the same procedure as Group 1, but without relaxation training provided; and (d) individuals who received only relaxation training.

Results of the study revealed that 65% of those in Group 1 were able to fly alone on a free posttreatment flight, compared to only 15% of Group 2, and 27% of Group 3; none of the Group 4 members could fly alone. Significant changes in favor of the Group 1 treatment were also measured by the Taylor Manifest Anxiety Scale (Taylor, 1953). In all groups combined, only 19 of the 51 participants (37%) agreed to fly alone after treatment. However, there were significant problems with dropouts in this study, which compromises the generalization of its results. A total of 81 individuals began the six-treatment session protocol, but 30 of these dropped out prior to the sixth session. Furthermore, of the 51 who completed treatment, 24 had taken part in an earlier study designed to assess film scenes, 80 scenes of which were thought to provoke anxiety in those with fear of flying and 80 scenes that were meant to evoke pleasure.

In a follow-up study, Denholtz et al. (1978) ascertained that some (38) individuals continued to fly alone 3½ years after they completed treatment. Forty-three of the 51 individuals from the 1975 study were contacted. Of those who had taken the posttreatment flight, 88% had maintained their ability to fly as measured by a telephone interview, although 43% still continued to use alcohol or tranquilizers before flying.

Case studies using virtual reality graded exposure therapy (VRGET) to treat successfully fear of flying have appeared in the literature (Hodges, Rothbaum, Watson, Kessler, & Opdyke, 1996; North, North, & Coble, 1996b, 1997; Rothbaum, Hodges, & Kooper, 1997; Rothbaum, Hodges, Watson, Kessler, & Opdyke, 1996). Hodges and Rothbaum and their colleagues studied a 42-year-old woman who had grown increasingly fearful of flying over the last 5 years and who had not been able to fly at all for the past 2 years. She was given the Questionnaire on Attitudes toward Flying (Howard, Mattick, & Clarke, 1982), the Fear of Flying Inventory (Scott, 1987), the Self-Survey of Stress Responses (Forgione & Bauer, 1980), the State–Trait Anxiety Inventory (Spielberger et al., 1983), the Beck Depression Inventory (Beck, Ward, Mendelsohn, Mock, & Erbaugh, 1961), the Clinical Global Improvement Scale (Guy, 1976), and a Flight Self-Monitoring Sheet developed by the authors of the study. The woman was first given seven sessions of anxiety management training, followed by six sessions of VR exposure. She then completed a posttreatment flight after completion of the exposure therapy. She showed statistically significant decreases on all self-report measures after completion of anxiety management training and further reductions after VR exposure.

North, North, and Coble (1996c) studied a 42-year-old man who had also received VR exposure therapy for his fear of heights in 1995. A virtual helicopter was used in this exposure rather than a fixed-wing aircraft, and a virtual therapist was also placed in the virtual world. There was no formal desensitization before exposure therapy. The man was given five sessions of virtual treatment and was given only the subjective units of distress rating scale. He has flown successfully several times since ending treatment.

Wiederhold, Gevirtz, and Wiederhold (1998) also reported on a case study of a patient given four sessions of VRGET. They compared the physiological responses as well as the responses on self-report questionnaires of one nonphobic and one phobic patient. Heart rate, peripheral skin temperature, respiration rate, sweat gland activity, and brain wave activity were measured during a 5-minute eyes-closed baseline period, a 20-minute virtual flight, and a 5-minute eyes-closed recovery period. Self-report questionnaires used were the Questionnaire on Attitudes toward Flying, Fear of Flying Inventory, Self-Survey of Stress Responses, State–Trait Anxiety Inventory, Tellegen Absorption Scale, and Hypnotizability Induction Profile. During the first session, the phobic patient had a decrease in skin resistance of between 34% and 36% during various parts of the flight as compared to baseline skin resistance. During Session 4, the patient was able to stabilize her skin resistance levels and actually had an increase in skin resistance, which was 57% above baseline by the end of the VR flight, indicating physiological relaxation. The patient was subsequently able to take a real-life flight. This is in comparison to a nonphobic individual who was placed in the virtual world for a 20-minute exposure session, similar to that used for VRGET. Her skin resistance levels went from a baseline of 224 to a level of 281 by the end of the flight (a 25% increase).

In the first controlled study on aviophobia, Wiederhold (1999) studied 30 participants, ranging in age from 24 to 55, who met the *DSM–IV* criteria for fear of flying. The study compared VRGET to imaginal therapy. After an initial phone screening, qualified participants were scheduled for an initial intake session. A participant was excluded from the study if he or she had a history of heart disease, migraines, seizures, or concurrent diagnosis of severe mental disorders, such as psychosis or major depressive disorder as determined by the intake interview.

Participants were randomly assigned (according to a previously generated random numbers table) to one of three groups when they arrived for the initial intake session. The three groups consisted of VRGET with no physiological feedback (VRGETno), VRGET with physiological feedback (VRGETpm), and systematic desensitization with imaginal exposure therapy. The equipment used for the VR portion of the study was a Pentium II 300 Mhz personal computer, a Liquid Image head-mounted display, an office chair with a subwoofer and an attached airplane seatbelt, and computer simulation software created by Virtually Better, Inc. (Figure 12.1).

FIGURE 12.1.

Scene from a window seat over the left wing in a virtual reality simulation. Software developed by Virtually Better, Inc.

In the initial intake session all three groups received, instruction in diaphragmatic breathing, and a relaxation tape for home practice. In addition, all groups received a second 45-minute session to answer further questions about the study and to practice breathing techniques prior to beginning desensitization training. An "individualized" fear hierarchy was constructed with the therapist's help for each participant randomized into the imaginal exposure therapy group.

The changes in flying behavior from intake to follow-up for each group were as follows: 20% of those in the imaginal exposure therapy group (2 out of 10) had a positive change in flying behavior from intake to follow-up; 80% of those in the VRGETno group (8 out of 10) had a positive change in flying behavior from intake to follow-up; and 100% of those in the VRGETpm group (10 out of 10) had a positive change in flying behavior from intake to follow-up.

Although all three groups' self-report scores showed a decrease when measured after Session 8, the participants in the imaginal group did not translate this change in attitudes toward flying into a behavioral change; 90% of the group still could not fly without medication or alcohol. This may suggest that the imaginal exposure treatment was not sufficiently effective to result in a change in flying behavior. This conclusion is supported by two case studies. One participant, wanting very desperately to fly, continued with six additional sessions of imaginal exposure and biofeedback training after discontinuing the research study. By the end of treatment, he was able to fly, although still with the help of a prescription medication. A second participant from the imaginal exposure group, after reporting an inability to fly when contacted at 3-month follow-up, agreed to participate in VR exposure therapy with physiological feedback. After completing six exposure sessions, he was able to fly successfully without the use of prescription medication or alcohol and with considerably less anxiety than he had previously experienced.

In a second controlled study funded by the National Institute of Mental Health, Rothbaum, Hodges, Smith, Lee, and Price (2000) found that VRGET was as effective as standard in vivo exposure at 6-month after treatment; patients who had received either method did better than those in the wait-list control group. Participants for this study were randomly assigned to one of the two treatment groups or to the control group. The same VR equipment and software were used for this study as were used for the Wiederhold (1999) study. Forty-nine participants began the study with 45 completing the treatment. Participants were given eight treatment sessions over a period of 6 weeks, with four sessions consisting of breathing retraining, cognitive restructuring, and thought-stopping techniques. This was followed by four sessions of exposure, either in real-life or in VR. At the end of treatment, 53% of VRGET participants, 67% of real-life exposure participants, and 6.6% of the control participants were able to take a group graduation flight from Atlanta to Houston. At the end of a 6-month follow-up period, 79% of VRGET participants, and 69% of the real-life exposure participants reported having flown again since the graduation flight. In total, at the end of a 6-month follow-up period, 93% of participants in both the VRGET and real-life exposure groups had flown at least once.

Richard Klein reported on the use of VR exposure therapy in his private practice setting. Instruments used to evaluate patients included the Questionnaire on Attitudes toward Flying, Fear of Flying Inventory, State–Trait Anxiety Inventory, Self-Survey of Stress Responses, VR Airplane Scenarios, and the Minnesota Multiphase Personality Inventory (Hathaway & McKinley, 1983). Treatment began with traditional cognitive–behavioral therapy (CBT) techniques, such as relaxation training and thought-stopping techniques, with the exposure component being done in VR (Klein, 1998, 1999). Kahan, Tanzer, Darvin, and Borer (2000) also reported success in treating fear of flying with VRGET in a private practice setting. This group conducted a small clinical noncontrolled study of 31 patients and used as its measure of success whether the patients could or could not fly at the end of treatment. Their results showed that 68% of patients flew after treatment. These patients were seen for an average of six sessions of VRGET. Some of these patients also received CBT including anxiety management training and psychoeducation. Some were given medication; others were not. Klein's study shows that VR can be effective in private practice, not just in a structured research setting.

Studies are now being conducted in Valencia, Spain, with software developed by PREVI, to look at three different scenarios in the treatment of aviophobia: the anticipatory anxiety encountered and the anxiety felt during safety instructions, taxiing, takeoff, flying over land and water, flying during turbulence, and landing (Botella et al., 2002).

VR Systems

The PREVI system includes anticipatory anxiety scenes—packing a suitcase in your room, listening to the radio, watching the weather outside, sitting in the terminal listening to other flights being announced and boarding, hearing other waiting passengers discussing the flight, and seeing other planes take off outside the airport terminal windows, viewing the weather (good or bad) during daytime or nighttime. The flight then includes a radio, which can be turned on or off and tuned to different stations, a drop down screen that shows a flight attendant giving safety instructions, a magazine that can be taken from the seatback and "flipped through," a window whose covering can be opened or closed, and a seatbelt that can be fastened and unfastened. The passenger cabin is filled with people, and the participant has the choice of choosing a male or female body. This is thought to anchor the participant in the virtual environment and allow for more complete immersion or presence. The flight goes through engines on, taxi, takeoff, turbulence, flying in good weather, flying over the ocean, and landing. By moving their head, users can look around the virtual world, and joystick navigation is also provided.

The Hodges Virtually Better, Inc. software includes a passenger cabin where one is seated in the left window seat over the wing. The person can look around the cabin by turning his or her head. The cabin is empty in this software. The flight includes the following conditions: engines off, engines on, taxi, takeoff, turbulence, flying in good weather, and landing.

Other software available for flying includes a system from Austria entitled "CYBERmed" by Insight Instruments. This system combines

VR and biofeedback into one product, and the virtual experience is augmented with a motion simulator.

Summary

All fear of flying studies found in the literature include imaginal, in vivo, or virtual exposure as part of treatment. Because of the initial success with studies involving VR graded exposure in the treatment of specific phobias, and because VR potentially offers advantages over both imaginal and in vivo exposures, VRGET may be an efficient and cost effective alternative to traditional exposure therapies. That VR exposure allows for audio, visual, vestibular, and vibratory stimuli to be presented simultaneously to the participant may account for its success in alleviating fears.

Fear of Driving

13

Virtual driving systems have three main clinical applications in psychotherapy: (a) the treatment of posttraumatic stress disorder (PTSD) associated with individuals recovering from motor vehicle accidents who require, as part of treatment, exposure to driving scenarios; (b) the treatment of specific driving phobias; and (c) as part of a general treatment for agoraphobia, one manifestation of which is the inability to drive long distances from home. In the privacy of the therapist's office, driving exposure is achieved systematically and safely for both the patient and therapist. Tasks of increasing difficulty can be assigned to the patient, and the patient's reactions can be measured and observed. Another clinical application in the health psychology field is to provide treatment for individuals who have had a traumatic brain injury, stroke, or other physical trauma who need to relearn driving skills. Nonclinical applications are various and include training new drivers and assessing and retraining older drivers; this approach could also be used as a disciplinary treatment for drivers charged with road rage infractions.

The research on clinical applications of virtual reality (VR) for the treatment of accident-related PTSD, specific driving phobias, and agoraphobia is not as well developed as research on many other specific phobias, but some studies indicate that virtual reality graded exposure therapy

(VRGET) can be a successful therapeutic option. The importance of these studies derives from the observation that the physiological responses at work in driving anxiety are similar to those in other phobias that respond positively to VRGET. The breadth of these studies provides a sense of the potential for this application of VR treatment.

Fear of Driving Studies

Research on VR applications for driving phobias has begun, and the preliminary results are promising. Can VR adequately engage phobic drivers? Schare, Scardapane, Berger, and Rose (1999) examined levels of immersion and emotional reactions to the VR driving environments in 8 phobic and 9 nonphobic drivers. They used three questionnaires: the Fear Survey Schedule II (Geer, 1965); driving screening form to assess typical driving behaviors; and a VR driving assessment to assess emotion, comfort, and immersion in the virtual world. Subjective distress level ratings were taken during the experience, and pulse and blood pressure were measured. A Virtual I/O head-mounted display was used with Imago Systems driving software, a Thrustmaster T2 Driving control with a Ford Mustang steering wheel attached, and an actual seat from a Saab automobile. The program allowed a change in view with head tracking, steering wheel movements, and change in speed. Visuals included the interior of the car, speedometer, steering wheel, road signs, traffic lights, other vehicles, buildings, and grass. The system also included auditory stimuli (the engine sound and the braking sounds), which changed in response to accelerating or decelerating. Participants were first allowed to maneuver through a "practice course" twice and were then placed in a "test course." The test course included more traffic and road hazards as well as a more complex environment. In some scenarios, the participant had to deal with such things as merging traffic and a sloping road.

The study showed that phobic individuals reported higher levels of immersion and higher emotional reactions to the environment than the controls. The subjective ratings of distress levels for the two groups differed significantly; however, both groups did show similar patterns of changes with an increase in distress from pretest to the first practice, a decrease from the first to the second practice, and an increase from second practice to "test." The increases were much more pronounced for phobic individuals. This pilot study indicates that the VR environment is capable of eliciting both subjective anxiety and physiological arousal, which differs between phobic and nonphobic individuals. The authors suggested that future research should compare the cost-benefit ratio of therapist-generated imaginal exposure and VR exposure.

A study by Turner et al. (1997) addressed the issue of the quality of immersion and the physiological responses of virtual drivers. This study placed 18 nonphobic individuals in a VR car-driving scenario ("Need for Speed" by Electronic Arts/Pioneer Productions, Burnaby, British Columbia) for 10 minutes on two separate occasions. Participants wore a Kaiser Electro-Optics head-mounted display and used a hand-held pad to control steering, acceleration, and braking. Each participant was placed in the "virtual cockpit of a car" and was driving behind another automobile. The participants drove along a coastal highway with mountains on one side and the ocean on the other; they encountered blind hills, curves, corners, and two-way traffic. The scenario included both visual and auditory stimuli. Blood pressure, cardiac output, and total peripheral resistance were obtained during a 5-minute baseline period and during the 10-minute VR task. The monitors recorded an increase in both systolic and diastolic pressure, cardiac output, and peripheral resistance during the task. Participants also self-reported moderate levels of immersion and realism.

In a study examining the effects of pictorial realism, the delay of visual feedback, and observer interactivity on the subjective sense of presence (Welch et al., 1996), 20 participants were placed in a driving simulators and were asked to drive as quickly as possible along a winding road. Each participant acted either as a passenger or as driver of the car, and each drove in either a low realism, black and white simulated world, or a more realistic world with colors and with other cars on the road. Within-subject analyses of variance of 2 (interactivity: passenger or driver) × 2 (realism: high or low) × 2 (order) were run with both interactivity and realism being statistically significant for more feelings of presence. Interactivity was rated as more important to feelings of presence than was pictorial realism of the scene. Sixty-five percent of participants stated that they became unaware of the laboratory environment during the simulation, indicating a high degree of presence and immersion. A second experiment used 20 participants as their own controls in a 2 (delay of visual feedback: no delay, delay) × 2 (pictorial realism: high or low) × 2 (order) analysis of variance design. The most presence was indicated with a no delay, high-realism world, with order showing no effect. Again, participants rated realism as less important than delay effects. These studies did not use a head-mounted display or head tracking to interact with the virtual world. Future experiments should include these elements to determine whether they have an effect on presence and task performance.

Janelle (1998) examined the influence of distraction and anxiety on driving abilities during a simulated driving task. Forty-eight women were randomly assigned to one of six groups, each with varying levels of peripheral distraction and anxiety instruction sets. Cognitive anxiety, visual search patterns, performance, and arousal were measured for all groups. Overall, those who were highly anxious did poorest, with a decrease in concentration, implying a reduced ability to process peripheral information. They also made more driving errors and showed poorer driving proficiency than those who were less anxious.

In a related study, Matthews et al. (1998) assessed a person's vulnerability to driving stress through questionnaires and performance in a driving simulator. They found that those who dislike driving (possibly because of their anxiety) have reduced driving control skills, experience a greater mood disturbance while driving, and drive with greater caution. Individuals who measured high on aggressive driving were more prone to errors related to confrontive passing strategies.

Posttraumatic Stress Disorder

Automotive accidents often cause trauma in survivors. Of the approximately 3 million people involved in car accidents each year, some 45% develop PTSD symptoms (Blanchard & Hickling, 1997). These individuals may have recurrent flashbacks to the accident, nightmares, avoidance behaviors, and a generalized increase in anxiety. Cognitive–behavioral therapy has been shown to be successful in the treatment of driving-related PTSD (Blanchard & Hickling, 1997). Effective treatments include relaxation training and in vivo and imaginal exposure therapy. Because a virtual environment can mimic the circumstances of an accident where the use of in vivo exposure would be impractical and that of imaginal exposure nonimmersive, the use of VRGET with car accident victims may decrease the length of treatment and increase treatment efficacy.

Specific Phobia

Drivers who have been in bad car accidents may develop specific driving phobias. One study found that 15% of car accident victims developed such a phobia (Blanchard & Hickling, 1997). Driving phobias may be so severe that individuals are unable to drive at all, or their driving may be limited to very short distances. Using VRGET to treat driving phobias is very similar to its use with other specific phobias, focusing on gradual exposure and cognitive and behavioral modifications.

CASE STUDY

Wiederhold, Wiederhold, Jang, and Kim (2000) found that VRGET was helpful in treating PTSD caused by a motor vehicle accident. In one case study, a patient who was self-referred had been involved in a very bad accident and had been unable to drive for 5 years. An inability to successfully elicit anxiety during imaginal visualization and a refusal to participate in real-life exposure because of a feeling of lack of control and safety had prevented successful processing of the trauma. After teaching the patient anxiety management techniques, including breathing retraining, the VRGET began. The patient began stabilizing physiologically in the virtual world and subsequently began initial exposure in the real world, sitting in her car and actually starting the engine. During the fifth session, however, a left turn was suggested. This simple act caused the patient to re-experience the trauma of her previous accident where the taxi she was riding in had veered head-on into oncoming traffic. She was removed from the virtual world and the remainder of the treatment session was devoted to processing the emotions and memories that had resurfaced. She was able to fully process this trauma as a result of re-exposure in the virtual world, and her nightmares about the accident ended. After three more VRGET sessions, she was able to once again attempt in vivo driving. At 1-year follow-up, she was able to drive anywhere with little or no anxiety. The system has since been used clinically to treat other patients with PTSD resulting from car accidents. The VR tool offers these patients a safe environment in which they can make a slow transition back to driving.

AGORAPHOBIA

As we discussed in chapter 8, a system has been developed and was tested at Hanyang University in Seoul, Korea (Figure 13.1). That system is now being used at the Virtual Reality Medical Center in San Diego, California to treat patients with driving difficulties related to panic and agoraphobia. One case study using this system has been reported. The patient, a 42-year-old woman, had developed agoraphobia over the preceding 8 years, and when therapy commenced, she was unable to drive further than 1 mile from her home. At intake, she also reported being unable to fly or ride "old" elevators. After learning anxiety management techniques, she was introduced to a VR world containing a

FIGURE 13.1.

This driving simulation is used for treating driving phobia as well as driving rehabilitation. Driving Software developed by Dr. Sun Kim at Hanyang University, Seoul, Korea.

beach scene and an open plaza. These scenes caused no subjective anxiety and only a small amount of physiological arousal. The driving scenario was then attempted. After 4 minutes in the environment, she became nauseous and the VR session was discontinued. She reported feelings similar to motion sickness but no feelings of panic. During the next session, VR driving was again attempted and she once again became nauseous, this time within 2 minutes of exposure. She was removed from VR and a joint decision was made by the therapist and patient to discontinue VR treatment. During subsequent sessions, driving was continued in vivo.

Since this incident, we have treated many patients who have been able to use the VR system to successfully overcome their driving anxiety related to agoraphobia. We also had several other patients who were unable to complete VR therapy because of "cybersickness." These patients were referred to an otolaryngologist and were found to be with a vestibular disorder. Thus, the VR system may prove useful as a diagnostic tool. Studies have shown that 5% to 42% of patients with panic disorder may have abnormalities in their balance system, compared to up to 5% of healthy controls. There also appears to be a link between subclinical balance abnormalities and the development of agoraphobia (Jacob, Furman, Durrant, & Turner, 1996; Perna et al., 2001).

DRIVING RETRAINING FOLLOWING BRAIN INJURY

In an application for health psychologists, VR driving simulations can be useful for evaluating the visual–motor skills of individuals recovering from brain injury and for retraining them. Wald, Liu, and Reil (2000) used an Imago System DriVR to assess a variety of driving skills in 28 adults with brain injury. The DriVR allows playback of the participant's performance, compiles quantitative statistics of the session, and simulates various driving routes in a variety of weather conditions, road conditions, and times of day. The system includes head tracking with a head-mounted display and tracker, a steering wheel, brake, gas pedal, and graphics of open road scenarios as well as driving among tall buildings. The system can easily be adapted for other driving tasks, such as systematic desensitization of those with phobias or PTSD and for educating young drivers. This study's findings revealed generalization of skills mastered from DriVR to real world driving skills.

TECHNICAL CONSIDERATIONS

Understanding the level of detail required in the virtual environment for driving simulations is important particularly because of the level of interest and to guide the many programs being developed. The greater the detail, the more the simulation costs and, therefore, the less likely that it will receive widespread use among therapists and rehabilitation specialists. Kappe, van Erp, and Korteling (1999) looked at three types of images: those with a head-slaved display (HSD), a display that allows the virtual environment to be scanned serially by changing the orientation of the head, surrounded with detailed peripheral images; those without a HSD surrounded with less detailed peripheral images; and those with HSD surrounded with less detailed peripheral images. Results indicate that a discrete moving HSD system with less detailed peripheral images in a low-cost simulator is more efficient and effective in lane-keeping performance and spatial orientation. Moreover, an HSD allowed for better steering performance.

PRESENCE AND DRIVING

In a study of presence, Liu and Pentland (1996) used a driving simulator to determine correlation of eye fixation and detection of unexpected motion. They found that adding texture to the virtual world increases this correlation. Although not used as a therapeutic tool here, this work tells us something about how people look for things, such as other vehicles or pedestrians, which might move into their path while driving. Often patients who have a fear of driving, whatever the cause, may have grown to avoid driving by the time they present for treatment. In therapy, the goal is dual: to overcome their fear and to make sure they have adequate driving skills. This skill set could more objectively be judged with simulators that are able to systematically add obstacles in the path of the patient's car during the driving task. The therapist's office provides a safe starting place for both patient and therapist to assess the skills of the patient, increase the skill set if necessary, and improve self-efficacy.

DRIVING AND ELDERLY POPULATIONS

As people age, they often develop difficulties with the demands of driving. This can lead to some anxiety about driving and insecurity about one's abilities. Interactive simulators, which can simulate various road conditions, traffic density, and weather conditions, may be used to determine whether these individuals are capable of safe driving, as well as to reassure them that their abilities are still intact. By interacting in an environment that allows for safe assessment and "instant replays," the patient is able to see objectively what their true abilities are. The virtual environment appears to provide a good representation of real world driving skills, and anecdotal reports suggest that patients readily accept weaknesses that are pointed out by simulation tasks (Schold-Davis & Wachtel, 2000).

Moreover, decrements in cognitive processing speed may make people less able to handle difficult driving situations as they grow older. By using a driving simulator and offering training to improve such people's processing speed over 10 training sessions, improvements are transferred to real-world driving skills, according to a study funded by the National Institute of Aging and the National Institute on Nursing Research (Clay, 2000). Visual processing decrements, including visual processing speed and impaired visual attention skills, have been blamed for the decline in driving skills in older individuals (Owsley et al., 1998). A driving simulator can more objectively test these skills in a safe, systematic manner.

MOTION SICKNESS ISSUES

Motion sickness is pertinent for users of VR driving environments. One study examined the effects on postural stability of immersion in a virtual environment. The relationship of postural instability to simulator sickness and its effect on safety of postimmersion activities have not been adequately sorted out or studied. One study, for example, measured postural instability after a 20-minute interactive virtual environment task (Cobb, 1999). Mild, transitory effects on posture were found among some individuals; with no relationship found between simulator sickness and instability. However, it is also interesting to note that the combination of a "real" steering wheel and the virtual steering wheel seen in many VR simulators was very well accepted by users. In addition, the use of other peripherals such as brake, gas, and turn signals did not cause any decrement in performance.

Summary

There is great interest among researchers and clinicians in using VR technology to address a range of driving-related issues. Clinical applications include PTSD as a result of motor vehicle accidents, specific driving phobias, and driving phobias that are related to agoraphobia. Other areas include retraining patients who have had brain injury and assessing driving ability in elderly populations. Although more work is required to standardize VR driving test applications, preliminary results show promise.

Acrophobia

14

A crophobia, or the fear of heights, is categorized as a specific phobia by the *Diagnostic and Statistical Manual of Mental Disorders* (4th ed., *DSM–IV*; American Psychiatric Association, 1994). This disorder is characterized by an irrational fear of heights, resulting in the avoidance of elevations or marked distress when unable to avoid heights.

Prevalence

In an epidemiological study conducted by Agras et al. (1969), 12.4% of those surveyed had a fear of heights—ranging from an intense fear at elevations to a phobia (disruption of everyday functioning because of fear and avoidance). Some can handle heights, although they are clearly distressed, whereas others experience such intense fear that height situations must be avoided altogether. Imagine a person not being able to go to a physician if his office is on the 5th floor, not taking a job because the office is on the 10th floor, or not visiting friends who move into an apartment three stories up.

Virtual Reality and Heights Studies

Virtual environments were first created to treat fear of heights. Lamson (1994) exposed 30 participants to simulated height situations. After 1 week of exposure, 90% (27 participants) were able to expose themselves to real world height situations. Thirty months posttreatment, 90% were still able to ride in a glass elevator while looking out. This seems to indicate that treatment gains may be long lasting (Lamson, 1997; "Scared of Heights," 1994; "Virtual Therapy," 1994).

Rothbaum et al. (1995a) used virtual reality graded exposure therapy (VRGET) to treat acrophobia in 17 college students. This study compared computer-generated graded exposure ($n = 10$) to a waiting-list control group ($n = 7$). Participants were screened using the Acrophobia Questionnaire (Cohen, 1977), a screening questionnaire, the Attitude Towards Heights Questionnaire (Abelson & Curtis, 1989a), the Rating of Fear Questionnaire (Marks & Matthews, 1979), and a Subjective Units of Discomfort Scale. Participants with concomitant panic disorder, agoraphobia, or claustrophobia were not accepted in the study.

Participants were exposed to several computer-simulated height situations: a series of balconies with varying heights (ground level, 2nd floor, 10th floor, and 20th floor); a series of bridges suspended over water with varying heights (7, 50, and 80 meters) and degrees of stability; and a glass elevator modeled after an actual elevator in the Atlanta Marriott Marquis convention hotel.

These measures were completed prior to treatment and again after seven sessions of exposure therapy (one per week). In the first session, participants were familiarized with VR equipment by putting on the VR helmet and moving around in a virtual room. In subsequent sessions (35–45 minutes long), participants were allowed to proceed at their own pace through VR height scenarios. Participants verbally disclosed physical anxiety symptoms during treatment sessions. Decreases in anxiety and avoidance to heights were found to be significant for the treatment group following the sessions but not for the control group. Seven of the 10 students who completed the VR graded exposure treatment exposed themselves to actual heights during treatment although they were not specifically asked to do so. No behavioral change was reported for those in the wait-list control group. This seems to imply that real-world behavior was modified by treatment experienced in the virtual world (Rothbaum et al., 1995a).

Rothbaum et al. (1995b) reported successful treatment of an acrophobic undergraduate student with VR therapy. The 19-year-old student was given a screening questionnaire, Acrophobia Questionnaire (Cohen, 1977), Attitude Towards Heights Questionnaire (Abelson & Curtis, 1989), Marks and Mathews's Fear Questionnaire (1979a), and a Behavioral Avoidance Test in a glass elevator. He reported that he remained engaged as if he were receiving in vivo therapy rather than imaginal therapy; he also reported physical sensations similar to those experienced in vivo. On all measures his levels of avoidance, anxiety, and distress decreased significantly.

These studies showed that VRGET can successfully desensitize a patient with acrophobia; however, these studies did not compare VR exposure to imaginal or in vivo exposure therapies. To address the question of whether VRGET is equally efficacious, or more efficacious, than the more traditional exposure treatments of systematic desensitization or in vivo exposure, Huang, Himle, Beier, and Alessi (1998b) conducted a study that compared real life (in vivo) exposure to VR exposure in the treatment of acrophobia. The virtual height situations are modeled after an actual staircase located at the University of Michigan, Ann Arbor. For the study, nine participants were randomized into two groups; one group received VRGET and the other group received in vivo exposure (Huang, Himle, Beier, & Alessi, 1998a).

The virtual height situation in this study is presented in a CAVE™ Virtual Environment that projects a three-dimensional image on three 10 × 10 foot walls and a 10 × 10 foot floor. To view the images, the participant wears a set of liquid crystal display glasses.

Measures used include the Vividness of Visual Imagery Questionnaire (second ed.; Marks, 1973), the Tellegen Multidimensional Personality Questionnaire (Tellegen, 1982), the Beck Depression Inventory (Beck, Steer, & Brown, 1996), and the Phenomenology of Consciousness Inventory (Pekala, 1985). The Multidimensional Personality Questionnaire includes one scale that deals with absorption. Initial findings include a positive correlation between vividness of visualization and fear as measured by the Phenomenology of Consciousness Inventory. Only one 90-minute session was administered for this study (Huang et al., 2000; http://www.umich.edu/~ewsinfo/MT/99/Spr99/mt18s99.html).

In another study, Bullinger, Roessler, and Mueller-Spahn (1998b) compared in vivo exposure with VR exposure using an elevator cabin, with objects such as other buildings and cars serving as depth cues for the participants. The objects were added to a Silicon Graphics Demonstration Environment called "Performer Town." The participants were able to travel up a semi-transparent elevator mounted to the outside of a 40-floor building.

Hans Seiburg's City Project (Fenly, 1996a, 1996b) proposed to treat acrophobic individuals with technology developed with VRML programming language, designed to be used over the Internet. The virtual world would enable users to hear wind noise and muffled voices appearing to come from the street below. It involved a transparent elevator leading to a rooftop.

In a series of studies performed jointly between University of Amsterdam and Delft University of Technology, developers asked 6 individuals with acrophobia to evaluate the virtual worlds (Schuemie, 2000; Schuemie et al., 2000). They were first immersed in the virtual world and were asked not to make any comments. A second immersion was done with each individual, but this time they were asked to make comments, and their comments were used to revise the VR worlds. The use of patients' comments to help guide the therapists and developers allows an even richer environment to be shaped, one that elicits an appropriate amount of anxiety while allowing for desensitization to occur gradually.

With the revised virtual environments, a second study was begun with 10 participants. The aim of the study was to evaluate the effectiveness of low-budget VR exposure versus exposure in vivo in a within-subjects design using 10 participants with acrophobia. Participants were given two sessions of VRGET and then two sessions of in vivo exposure. Researchers measured their sense of realism, interaction, presence, and immersion with the Acrophobia Questionnaire (Cohen, 1977), the Attitude Towards Heights Questionnaire (Abelson & Curtis, 1989), and the Fear and Presence Questionnaire by Slater, Usah, and Steed (1994). The questionnaires were completed prior to treatment, after VRGET, and after in vivo sessions. VRGET was found to be as effective as in vivo on both anxiety and avoidance; the two sessions of in vivo did not enhance effects already achieved with VRGET (Emmelkamp, Bruynzeel, Drost, & van der Mast, 2001).

The virtual worlds were generated on a 200 MHz personal computer with a Matrox graphics card and Windows® 95. Superscape software was used to do the VR modeling. The head-mounted display was by Virtual I-O and included a 3-degrees of freedom tracker for rotation. A piece of black cloth was placed over the visor to prevent the user from seeing any part of the actual room and to make the experience more immersive. The user was required to stand on a metal grid suspended several inches above the ground and surrounded by a metal railing to give more of a feeling of height.

The virtual worlds used were a roller coaster, swimming pool with a diving tower, and a glass elevator. In the roller coaster scenario, the participant sat in a car on the track and was able to look around the world while the roller coaster moved along the track. Sounds of a real roller coaster were included along with three-dimensional images. The swimming pool world included a bridge and two diving towers. In this world the therapist controlled movement up the towers with a joystick. In the glass elevator, the therapist also controlled movement with a joystick. The sound of the wind and people talking were used to add more realism, with the sounds of the wind becoming more pronounced as height increased and the voices becoming less pronounced (Figure 14.1).

During this study, the swimming pool virtual environment proved most effective, with patients rating it highest on fear, realism, and presence. This study did show a high correlation between presence and fear in the virtual world, which was consistent with earlier work (Regenbrecht, Schubert, & Friedman, 1998). However, there was no significant correlation between presence and effectiveness of the therapy. The authors suggested that this could be due to the small sample size and the mild levels of acrophobia before treatment. Other researchers have discussed the necessity of a high level of presence for effective treatment (Carlin et al., 1997; Hodges et al., 1994). This question requires more research to be answered conclusively. What is clear is that patients begin to "fill in the pieces" of the virtual environment themselves. This is promising in that less expensive environments may be sufficient for successful therapy; those with fewer details may evoke enough anxiety to then allow patients to desensitize and habituate. It seems clear that the details provided must be consistent with those in the real world but may not need to be exhaustive.

Emmelkamp, Bruynzeel, Drost, and van der Mast (2001) used a between-groups design to evaluate the effectiveness of VRGET versus in vivo exposure in 33 participants with acrophobia. The virtual environments were modeled exactly after real environments used in the in vivo exposure. Participants were randomly assigned to either in vivo or VRGET. Patients were given the Acrophobia Questionnaire (Cohen, 1997), the Attitude Toward Heights Questionnaire (Abelson & Curtis, 1989), the Fear and Presence Questionnaire (Slater et al., 1994), and the Symptom Checklist (Derogatis, 1977) before and after treatment and at a 6-month follow-up interval. Participants were asked to complete the Behavioral Avoidance Test before and after treatment. Participants received three exposure sessions. Data are currently under analysis. Results at posttreatment and 6 months follow-up suggest that VRGET may be as efficacious as in vivo. The use of the Behavioral Avoidance Test helps determine observable behavior improvement (M. Krijn, personal communication, August 14, 2000).

Krijn (2001) compared treatment in either a virtual environment using a head-mounted display or with a CAVE-type system. The same

FIGURE 14.1.

A. Photograph of an actual staircase. B. Digital reproduction of the same staircase. As you can see, virtual reality has come very close to reproducing real environments. Software developed by M. J. Sheumie, Delft University of Technology, The Netherlands.

questionnaires used in the previous studies will again be completed by participants in this study (Krijn, 2001).

A virtual scaffolding elevator (Figure 14.2) designed by a team at Hanyang University (Ku et al., 2001) in Seoul, Korea, has proved effective in the treatment of a man with a 40-year history of acrophobia who could not go beyond the third floor of buildings if he could see outside the window or elevator. Initially he was scheduled to receive eight VR therapy sessions (three times a week for 3 weeks). The realism of the virtual world was enhanced by the sound of wind, the movement of the elevator, and the "clanking of steel" when the elevator came to rest at various height levels. In addition, in the real world, he stood in an enclosed steel balcony that mimicked that shown in the virtual world. To enhance the feeling of immersion, he was placed alone in a darkened room and the therapist monitored the progress through a

FIGURE 14.2.

This Virtual Scaffolding Elevator, developed by Dr. Sun Kim at Hanyang University in Seoul, Korea, is used to treat fear of heights.

video camera, speakers, and microphone. The head-mounted display for this environment was by Kaiser Electro-Optics, with a Polhemus tracker. A Biopac system was used to gather physiological data. Prior to beginning VRGET, he received four sessions of relaxation training; later he received six sessions of VRGET, followed by an in vivo session. The proposed eight sessions were not completed because he felt ready to try in vivo exposure. He was accompanied to the top of an observation tower and stayed there looking out for 45 minutes. His subjective units of distress level never exceeded 30. The patient later reported that the following week he performed the same task unaccompanied (Choi, Jang, Ku, Shin, & Kim, 2001). This same system is now being used for treatment at the VRMC in San Diego, California.

Summary

VRGET appears to be an effective method for treating acrophobia, showing equal efficacy with in vivo treatment in the controlled studies completed to date. These studies have included a relatively small number of participants. Considering that environments on both inexpensive personal computers and silicon graphics workstations have shown successful desensitization, a larger scale, multicenter study is the next logical step.

Claustrophobia

15

Whereas agoraphobia is usually associated with the fear of being trapped alone in an open space, *claustrophobia* is the fear of being trapped in an enclosed place. There is often a strong association between the two phobias; many of those who are fearful of large, open spaces also seem frightened of small, enclosed spaces. One hypothesis posits that both phobias are vestiges of primitive fears—the danger of being attacked was great while in either a large, unsheltered place or in a small, enclosed space. About 10% of the population have a mild to marked form of claustrophobia, and about 2% have severe claustrophobia. In about 33% of individuals with claustrophobia, the fear begins in childhood; more women appear to experience this disorder than men (Rachman, 1978). Claustrophobia can be a concomitant of agoraphobia, aviophobia, or post-traumatic stress disorder (PTSD).

One of the most common manifestations of claustrophobia is a refusal to ride in an enclosed elevator. Other common precipitators of claustrophobia include closets, tunnels, airplanes, and certain medical testing machinery and procedures, such as magnetic resonance imaging, hyperbaric oxygen treatment, and computed tomography (CT) scan (Beck, Emery, & Greenberg, 1985; Botella, Quero, et al., 1998).

Virtual Reality
Claustrophobia Studies

Botella, Baños, et al. (1998) reported on a 43-year-old woman with claustrophobia who had been referred to them because she had been unable to undergo a CT scan that was necessary to detect a possible growth on her spinal column. She reported that since childhood, she had been afraid of all closed spaces, including elevators, closed windows during sleep, and airplanes. She was treated successfully with eight individual virtual reality graded exposure therapy (VRGET) sessions over a 3-week period. All self-report measures showed a decrease in anxiety following VR treatment, and treatment gains were maintained at 1-month follow-up. This study is significant in that VR therapy alone was used.

She was given several self-report questionnaires and measures before and after treatment and at 1-month follow-up: a Spanish adaptation of the Marks and Mathews's Fear Scale (1979a), the Fear of Closed Spaces Measure, the Problem-Related Impairment Questionnaire (Borda & Echeburúa, 1991), the Self-Efficacy Towards the Target Behavior Measure, and the Attitude Towards CTS [CT scan] Measure. Subjective units of distress ratings (0 to 10) were assessed every 5 minutes during the VRGET. The virtual environment was run on a Silicon Graphics workstation with a Virtual Research head-mounted display and Polhemus tracker. (This environment, though originally created to run on a Silicon Graphics workstation, was recreated to run on an inexpensive PC to allow for wider commercial use. A Virtual Research head-mounted display was also used for peripherals with the PC-based system.) Four virtual environments were provided during therapy: (a) a balcony that was 2 × 5 meters; (b) a 4 × 5 meter room with doors and windows that could be opened and closed; (c) a 3 × 3 meter room that could be made smaller by moving a wall closer and closer to the patient until it was only 1 meter in width, which also had a door that the patient could lock; and (d) an elevator that could be made smaller, that could be used to ride up and down to different floors, and that the patient could be blocked from exiting for specified periods of time.

In another study, Botella, Villa, Baños, Perpina, and Garcia-Palacios (1999a) reported on the treatment of a 37-year-old woman who has claustrophobia, fear of storms, and panic disorder with agoraphobia. Her fear of enclosed places had begun 12 years earlier as a result of a crowded mall. The crowd had come in to avoid a storm, and so her phobia included a fear of storms. She had begun to avoid unknown places and shopping alone. She was treated using the same virtual environments as described above. She answered the same question-naires that were given to the patient who had been unable to take a CT scan; she took them before and after treatment and at a 3-month follow-up. The patient was given eight treatment sessions using VRGET alone. Not only did her fear of enclosed places diminish, but so too did her fear of storms and avoidance of shopping alone. The generalizability of treatment for claustrophobia to her other fears was thought to be due to changes in her self-efficacy. The VR made the patient feel more capable about her abilities to face situations in general and not just those with a claustrophobic element.

Botella, Villa, Baños, Perpina, and Garcia-Palacios (1999b) com-pleted a controlled multiple-baseline study of four claustrophobic patients who were treated successfully with the use of virtual environ-ments. Duration of symptoms ranged from 3 months to 14 years; with three participants also meeting *Diagnostic and Statistical Manual of Mental Disorders* (4th ed., *DSM–IV*; American Psychiatric Association, 1994) criteria for panic disorder with agoraphobia. Hardware consisted of a Silicon Graphics High Impact computer workstation, Virtual Research head-mounted display, and Fastrak head tracking system from Polhe-mus. Software was modeled using Autocad software by Autodesk, Inc. Participants in the study were given eight VRGET sessions lasting 35–45 minutes each. No other cognitive or behavioral techniques were in-cluded in the treatment regimen. Virtual scenarios included (a) a house with windows and doors that could be closed as treatment progressed and which could be made smaller by virtue of a moving a wall and (b) an elevator, which could be made larger or smaller, viewed from a hallway, and entered and exited during the session.

Patients completed a Behavioral Avoidance Test before and after treatment and at a 3-month follow-up. In addition, self-report ques-tionnaire data was collected at the three time periods. These question-naires included the following: Beck Depression Inventory, State–Trait Anxiety Inventory (Spielberger et al., 1983), and the Fear Question-naire (Marks & Mathews, 1979a). During the exposure sessions, subjec-tive units of distress scores (Wolpe & Lang, 1964) were collected. Results indicated treatment success for all four participants; gains were maintained at the 3-month follow-up. In addition there was a decline in agoraphobic avoidance in the three participants who had met the panic disorder with agoraphobia diagnosis and an increase in self-efficacy for all four participants (Botella, Baños, et al., 2000).

Bullinger, Roessler, and Mueller-Spahn (1998a) exposed 13 non-phobic participants and 2 claustrophobic participants to claustrophobic virtual environments in one 45-minute exposure session. Physiological parameters measured included pulse and oxygen saturation of the blood using an infrared sensor and blood pressure using a blood pressure cuff. A Critikon Dinamap/OXYTRAK version CB was used to measure the physiological signals and every 3 minutes the readings were printed out. The researcher took a self-rating of simulator sickness every 3 minutes. After a 6-minute baseline during which the participant sat quietly with the head-mounted display on, the simulation was started. The participants were seated at the rear wall of the VR world and were able to look around the room by turning their heads. They were allowed to stay in this scenario for 45 minutes, after which the head-mounted display remained on without the simulation for a 6-minute period, after which it was removed and the exposure was ended.

For the 13 nonphobic participants, both physiological and subjective measures of anxiety or impairment were within normal ranges. The 2 claustrophobic participants experienced a rise in pulse rate during stimulus presentation. However, values for blood pressure, pulse, and oxygen saturation were within the normal range. The claustrophobic environment for this study was created and run on a Silicon graphics (SGI) workstation with a Virtual Research head-mounted display and Ascension tracker. The environment used was a virtual room with a movable front wall, which allowed the room to be shrunk as desensitization occurred (Riva, Wiederhold, & Molinari, 1998). The room was modeled with Truespace three-dimensional modeling software, and radiosity Lightscape software was used to add more realistic lighting to the virtual scenes.

A second study using the SGI Onyx2 Infinite Reality Deskside and a head-mounted display and tracker compared virtual reality (VR) exposure therapy and in vivo exposure in phobic and nonphobic participants (Bullinger, Bergner, Roessler, Estoppey, & Mueller-Spahn, 1999). Five exposure sessions were performed for the groups, lasting at least 45 minutes each. Physiological measures were taken to determine whether, in fact, virtual exposure to phobic stimuli causes similar physiological reactions as real world exposure. Heart rate, oxygen saturation, and blood pressure were monitored during the exposure sessions. Temporal EMG (electromyography) provided a measure of stimulus avoidance by determining when participants' eyes were closed during the exposure session. Catecholamines were also measured before, after, and during the presentation. Self-report questionnaires used for the study included the Montgomery and Asberg Depression Rating Scale (Montgomery & Asberg, 1975), the Hamilton Anxiety Scale (Guy, 1976), and the Questionnaire Concerning Body-Related Anxieties, Cognitions, and Avoidance. No statistically significant differences were found between participants receiving the in vivo exposure and participants receiving the VR exposure. The results at 6-months posttreatment follow-up showed that the treatment gains had been maintained.

Wiederhold and Wiederhold (2000) also reported successful treatment of claustrophobia using software developed by Giuseppe Riva, consisting of a virtual elevator environment (Figure 15.1). A 75-year-old Caucasian woman presented for treatment of severe claustrophobia. She had been referred to the clinic by her physician because she needed to have an MRI (magnetic resonance imaging) for a medical condition. Because of comorbid conditions, she and her physician had agreed that she would try to undergo the MRI without the use of intravenous Valium. She had a 40-year history of fear of elevators and other small, enclosed places, and had chosen to always climb stairs—up to 15 flights at times—rather than take

FIGURE 15.1.

This virtual environment is used to help patients who experience claustrophobia. Software created by Dr. Giuseppe Riva, Milan, Italy.

elevators. She had undergone hip replacement surgery three years earlier and had subsequently confined her activities to locations no more than three stories high. She was, however, able to ride in glass elevators with little or no apparent anxiety. An initial history revealed no comorbid psychological disorders and a high level of motivation to overcome this fear.

The patient was first taught diaphragmatic breathing to use as a coping mechanism during VRGET. Physiological measurements taken during the sessions included peripheral skin temperature, heart rate, respiration rate, and sweat gland activity. She learned relaxation techniques by seeing the changes in physiology on the screen real-time when she was sitting relaxed and when she was performing a stressful task; this allowed her to differentiate between relaxation and physiological arousal. She was then taught thought-stopping and distraction techniques.

Although she had severe claustrophobia, the head-mounted display caused no problem during sessions. The patient, who had never used a computer, became accustomed quite easily to the joystick and display used for navigation. Initial virtual exposure consisted of familiarization with a virtual beach, which would not cause anxiety but which would allow for practice in navigational abilities. During her first exposure to the virtual elevator scene, she walked forward and opened the door of the elevator but did not initially want to go inside. She commented that it "looked very small." She reported that her subjective units of distress rating was "80 out of 100." After several minutes of facing the virtual elevator door and doing diaphragmatic breathing, physiological stabilization occurred, and she was able to venture inside. She stood in the elevator briefly and then exited. The rest of the 20-minute VRGET session was spent walking around the lobby, facing the elevator, entering the elevator, and closing the doors. Subsequent sessions included VRGET, and, finally, in vivo exposure using the elevator in the clinic. At the end of seven treatment sessions, she was able to successfully stand in the elevator for 15 minutes with little or no anxiety. She was subsequently able to successfully undergo the MRI without the use of medication.

Another virtual environment with claustrophobic stimuli is made by Fifth Dimensions Technologies (www.5dt.com). The module includes a set of passageways that have decreasing dimensions. Either the patient (using a joystick) or therapist (using keyboard commands) can maintain control of how quickly the passageways decrease in size. No published studies on the use of this software with clinical populations are currently available.

Summary

Claustrophobia, the fear of being trapped in enclosed spaces, commonly manifests itself in reluctance to ride in elevators. It is also related to aviophobia, PTSD caused by motor vehicle accidents, and fear of medical testing equipment, such as MRI. Treatment for claustrophobia has traditionally used in vivo exposure, which has the drawback of eliciting patient resistance and fear. VRGET offers an effective alternative that can be implemented in the safety and convenience of the therapist's office. Results from the application of VRGET to claustrophobia have indicated that the treatment reduces anxiety about claustrophobic situations and helps patients confront their fears in real life.

Arachnophobia

16

Arachnophobia, or fear of spiders, is under the *Diagnostic and Statistical Manual of Mental Disorders* (4th ed., *DSM–IV*) classification of a specific phobia (American Psychiatric Association, 1994). About 40% of specific phobias can be classified as belonging to the category of "bugs, snakes, bats, or mice" (Chapman, 1997, p. 415). Those with a fear of spiders show anxiety on exposure to spiders or avoid spiders and situations in which they might encounter a spider. These phobias normally begin in childhood and affect twice as many women as men (Ost, 1987).

Because the stimulus for this phobia is so specific, it is well suited to virtual replication. A study at the University of Nottingham plans to use VR treatment for arachnophobia. Current treatment begins with exposing the anxious patient to pictures of spiders and finally getting that patient to handle a real tarantula. This study is being done in conjunction with the Maudsley Institute of Psychiatry (London); it explores replacing the real tarantula with a virtual one (http://www.crg.cs.nott.ac.uk/research/projects/Spiders/).

Virtual Reality and
Arachnophobia Studies

In a study at the Norwegian University of Science and Technology, eight patients underwent virtual reality (VR) exposure therapy (Goetestam, Hollup, & Graawe, 1996; Lindboel, 1996). They wore stereoscopic glasses to view a computer-generated spider on a computer screen, which gave the spider a three-dimensional look. Participants wore a VR glove that allowed them to move a virtual arm toward the virtual spider. Both before and after the VR session, participants were exposed to live spiders; after treatment all eight reported a significant reduction in anxiety or no anxiety at all.

Kirkby and associates (Kirkby, 1996) have used nonimmersive VR techniques to treat several individuals with arachnophobia. In this approach, the patient acts as a therapist and guides an "on-screen phobic patient" around a house, exposing the virtual patient to spiders. The computer registers an anxiety response and keeps a running score of exposures performed. In this way, the patient learns therapeutic skills through an interactive symbolic modeling process, which may then be applied to his or her phobia in vivo.

A case study completed by Carlin et al. (1997) combined VR and augmented reality to add to the realism of exposure for an individual who had had arachnophobia for 20 years. Treatment involved exposing the participant to a tarantula and a black widow in the virtual world and then having her touch a furry toy spider while she was viewing a spider in the virtual world. After 12 one-hour sessions, the patient was able to go camping in the woods and successfully encounter a spider in her home. One-year follow-up indicated that treatment gains were still intact (Hoffman, 1998).

Having a patient touch something in the real world while viewing the same thing in the virtual world is referred to as *tactile augmentation*. This apparently adds to the realism of the experience (Carlin et al., 1997; Hoffman, 1998).

In another study, 45 participants who had spider phobia were given three 40-minute computer exposure sessions, with one session being administered every 2 weeks (Smith, Kirkby, Montgomery, & Daniels, 1997). The participants were randomized into one of three treatment groups: relevant exposure with feedback (REF group), irrelevant exposure with feedback (IEF group), or relevant exposure with no feedback (RENoF group). The relevant exposure environment was interactive animation of spiders, whereas the irrelevant exposure was interactive animation involving elevators. The REF group was exposed to spider scenarios with an "anxiety thermometer" showing increased anxiety as exposure situations were undertaken. The RENoF group participants were exposed to spider scenarios but were given points only when they left the exposure situation or walked into rooms of the simulated house that contained no spiders. Each participant was instructed to guide the computer character around a home that had spiders of varying degrees of reality, both dead and alive. The IEF group participants were instructed to expose the computer character to elevator scenarios. The program began with a very brief explanation of exposure therapy in the treatment of phobias and then the participants were instructed to expose the computer character to the phobic situations shown on-screen to help the character overcome its fear.

To assess the levels of phobic severity, participants completed the following questionnaires before and after treatment and at 6-month and 12-month follow-up: The Spider Questionnaire (Klorman, Weerts, Hastings, Melamed, & Lang, 1974), The Spider Questionnaire (Watts & Sharrock, 1984), Phobic Targets, Work and Adjustment Rating Scales (Watson & Marks, 1971), and a Homework Questionnaire (created by the authors) about in vivo spider exposure. All three groups showed significant improvement on these outcome measures. The RENoF group reported the fewest new in vivo activities, but this difference did not reach statistical significance. This seems to suggest that feedback is more important in exposure than is the stimuli presented during exposure. A sense of mastery that is properly reinforced may transfer to other situations. However, this was a small sample and the study should be repeated with a larger sample to determine whether these results generalize to the whole population (Smith et al., 1997).

Garcia-Palacios, Hoffman, Carlin, Furness, and Botella (2002) conducted an initial controlled study on the efficacy of VR exposure therapy for treating fear of spiders. Undergraduate students who scored very high in fear of spiders scale (but many of whom were not clinically phobic) were randomly assigned to one of three VR exposure therapy treatment conditions: virtual spiders with tactile augmentation, virtual spiders with no tactile cues, and a no-treatment control group who went into KitchenWorld (a virtual kitchen environment) but encountered no spiders (Figure 16.1).

A Behavioral Avoidance Test, which provides an objective measure of fear of spiders, was conducted before VR treatments and after participants completed their VR exposure therapy. The test measured how close (in feet and inches) participants would walk toward a live tarantula that was enclosed in a terrarium. Participants were told this was

FIGURE 16.1.

SpiderWorld is a virtual environment in which patients interact with realistic spiders in a kitchen setting. Software developed by Dr. Hunter Hoffman at HIT Lab, University of Washington.

not part of their treatment, and they should only get as close to the tarantula as they felt comfortable They received identical instructions for the posttreatment test.

This preliminary study showed that, on average, the 12 participants in the group who received VR therapy with tactile augmentation (three 1-hour VR sessions) stopped 5.5 feet away from the live tarantula prior to VR exposure therapy and were able to approach to within 6 inches of the tarantula after VR treatment (where they had the illusion of physically touching the virtual spider).

The 12 participants assigned to the "ordinary SpiderWorld" (whose real hand felt nothing when they touched the virtual spider with their cyber hand during three 1-hour VR treatments) approached to within about 5 feet of the live tarantula prior to VR treatment and were able to approach to within 2.5 feet of the tarantula after treatment. Although this was a significant improvement, it was approximately half as effective as the tactile augmentation VR exposure treatment.

The 12 participants in the control condition (who received no VR exposure therapy) showed no reduction in the distance at which they would approach the spider. Because only 6 of the 36 participants in the first study (just described) were clinically phobic, this research team has a second, more carefully controlled clinical study underway at the Human Interface Technology Lab at the University of Washington to determine whether the results could be replicated and whether they extend to clinically phobic patients (H. Hoffman, personal communication, August 8, 2000; Garcia-Palacios et al., 2002).

Two studies performed by Garcia-Palacios, Hoffman, See, Tsai, and Botella (2001) indicate participants' preference for virtual exposure over in vivo exposure. In the first study, 423 undergraduate students were given a shortened version of the Attitude Towards Spiders Questionnaire (Szymanski & O'Donahue, 1995). Six questions were scored on a rating scale that ranged from 1 (*does not apply to me*) to 7 (*very much applies to me*). The participants were then given a written explanation of what exposure therapy is and were asked if they would consider free treatment with either in vivo or VR exposure. The answers to these two questions again were ranked (1 = *would not consider*, 7 = *definitely would do this*). Finally, they were asked a forced-choice question on which therapy, in vivo or VR, they would choose. The order of presentation of questions was switched for one-half of the participants to avoid order effects. The results indicated that 21% of the students (87 students) scored more than 1 standard deviation above the mean on the ATSQ, which put them in the category "high in fear of spiders." Students' scores were then analyzed. On the question of whether they would consider free treatment conducted in vivo, 17.4% of the students said they would definitely not (compared to only 4.6% who said they would definitely not try VR). Of those who said they definitely would do treatment, 31% said they would definitely do VR compared to only 7% who said they would definitely do in vivo. On the forced-choice question, 81% chose VR compared with only 19% who chose in vivo.

The second study by this group (Garcia-Palacios et al., 2001) involved 354 undergraduate students who were given the ATSQ. They were given a brief description of a one-session, 3-hour in vivo exposure treatment and a description of a VR treatment consisting of three sessions of 1 hour each. They were then asked the same questions as in the first study. Of the 75 participants who scored as having a fear of spiders in this study, 34.7% said they would definitely not do in vivo, compared to 8% who said they would not do VR therapy. This is compared with 27% who said they definitely would do VR therapy and only 10.7% who said they would do in vivo. When forced to choose a treatment, 89.2% chose VR therapy with only 10.8% choosing in vivo.

Gilroy, Kirkby, Daniels, Menzies, and Montgomery (2000) evaluated 45 participants randomly assigned to "computer" exposure, in vivo exposure, or a relaxation placebo group. This nonimmersive VR allowed the participant to view a virtual world through the window of the computer screen. Prior to treatment, a Behavioral Assessment Test was administered; the test was progressively more challenging, with the last step being to approach and hold a spider. Each group was given three sessions of treatment. Symptom severity was measured both before and after treatment as well as at a 3-month follow-up assessment using the Spider Questionnaire (Watts & Sharrock, 1984), Behavioral Assessment Test with a Subjective Units of Distress rating scale (from 0 to 100), a Phobic Targets and Work Adjustment Ratings Scale (Gelder & Marks, 1966; Watson & Marks, 1971), and a Fear Questionnaire (Marks & Matthews, 1979a). The results indicated that both VR exposure and in vivo exposure were equally effective in reducing phobic symptoms, and both treatments proved to be more effective than the relaxation placebo.

In contrast with the success shown with VR therapy, Muris, Merckelbach, Holdrinet, and Sijsenaar (1998) found computerized exposure to be ineffective in treating children with spider phobia. Their conclusion was based on a 2½-hour exposure session during which children viewed four types of spiders: a cartoonish spider, a spider on a string, a house spider, and a tarantula. The exposure was neither interactive nor immersive, and it was short-lasting; the other studies included in this chapter all used interactive computer simulations and proved successful in treating arachnophobia.

One of the authors (Brenda Wiederhold) used in vivo exposure with several patients who had a fear of tarantulas. The pet tarantula that was kept at the clinic had to be fed "live" food (crickets) three times a week, had to be cared for even over holiday clinic closings, and had to have its cage cleaned once a week. One research assistant at the clinic developed a severe allergy to the tarantula, and the room had to be thoroughly cleaned and the tarantula relocated off-site. Another assistant, who had a fear of tarantulas, refused to participate in treating patients who had the same fear.

Summary

The studies support the argument that patients should be exposed to their fear in a nonthreatening manner, such as in VR therapy, before they confront that fear in real life. Phobic patients may find VR therapy appealing, which improves the likelihood that they would actually seek help. Computer simulations for arachnophobia have many advantages, including decreased length of treatment, reduced cost of treatment, and the absence of complications that arise with the use of live specimens.

Fear of Medical Procedures   17

Virtual reality (VR) therapy has a number of uses in medical applications. One use is to help reduce anxiety related to certain medical procedures, such as dental work, injections, and MRI (magnetic resonance imaging) testing. The fear of medical procedures may cause individuals to avoid medical treatment, thereby putting their health at risk. Another use of VR therapy in medical-related phobias is to distract patients from the discomfort associated with various medical treatments, such as chemotherapy and wound care.

Dentophobia

In an epidemiological study done in 1969, Agras et al. found that 2% of those surveyed had an intense fear of dental procedures. This fear may become so intense, and the anticipatory anxiety so great, that persons avoid going to the dentist altogether or faint as soon as the dental procedures begins.

A 1997 article ("Dentists try to ease panic") reported that 40 million Americans avoid or postpone dental visits because of fear. This can lead to loss of teeth from gum disease, and, as new studies are showing, poor dental health can lead to other health problems. Dentists have begun looking at new ways to help these phobic patients, including using quieter air drills to treat cavities, teaching patients relaxation and guided imagery techniques, using needle-free anesthesia, and, finally, using VR distraction techniques.

One of these dentists, Michael Krochak of New York, uses VR therapy as a routine procedure. Because VR provides both auditory and visual stimuli, it is a powerful distraction that helps patients relax and complete the treatment with little or no anxiety or distress. In his opinion, "it is the best distraction tool I have seen in 18 years of practice" (M. Krochuk, personal communication, August 25, 2000). Moreover, he is able to interrupt the virtual stimuli when necessary to communicate with the patients. When patients first come in, he spends time establishing a trusting relationship with them before suggesting that they try VR. Only after patient confidence and trust have been established does he have them begin the VR session. This method of treatment is now widely available (J. Westin, personal communication, March 2002).

Corah (1988) discussed a series of investigations that were conducted to determine which methods were successful in reducing patient anxiety. The only two successful strategies were relaxation and distraction techniques. The distraction techniques used were video games. Patient anxiety, as measured by the Dental Anxiety Scale (Corah, 1969), was reduced only through use of the video games. All other techniques proved unsuccessful. In another study, Seyrek, Corah, and Pace (1984) compared three distraction techniques—a video game, a video-comedy program, and an audio-comedy program—during amalgam restorations. The video games and video-comedy programs were equally effective at distracting the patients and reducing anxiety; both were superior to the audio program. This study also found that physiological arousal increased as distraction level increased, in contrast to earlier study findings.

Needle Phobia

Needle phobia is the extreme fear and avoidance of needles associated with medical injections. The *Diagnostic and Statistical Manual of Mental Disorders* (4th ed., Text Revision; *DSM–IV–TR*; American Psychiatric Association, 2000) categorizes needle phobia as a Specific Phobia under the subtype Blood-Injection-Injury and notes: "This subtype is highly familial and is often characterized by a strong vasovagal response" (pp. 445–446), leading to fainting in 75% of these individuals. The phobic response includes avoidance of all situations associated with medical treatments, including obtaining routine health care. The consequences of such avoidance can be exacerbation of existing medical conditions or delayed diagnosis of serious medical conditions.

Common treatment for needle phobia uses imaginal or in vivo exposure, where desensitization and training in relaxation techniques are applied. VR therapy can provide an enhanced exposure technique that bypasses the difficulties of imaginal or in vivo therapy. One study examined the fear response of individuals with needle phobia in a virtual environment (Hamza, Jones, Lesaoana, & Blake, 2000). In it, needle-phobic participants entered a virtual environment consisting of a doctor's office, with reception and examination rooms. Participants were greeted in the reception room and then taken to the examination room by a virtual doctor who was controlled by the researchers. The participants communicated with the "doctor" by microphone. In the examination room, the injection needle was located at the far end of the doctor's desk. The participants were then asked to move the needle closer to their own position at their own pace. Ultimately, the participants were asked to raise their arms (seen on screen in the form of an avatar arm) and were given a pre-injection swab and the injection itself; then they observed the removal of the needle from their arms. Results showed that anxiety was induced during the period when the participants drew the needle closer to themselves and during the injection itself. These initial results suggest a potential application of VR therapy in this field. Areas of future research and improvement in the virtual experience include adding tactile and olfactory stimuli, such as the feel and smell of the pre-injection swab.

Magnetic Resonance Imaging Procedures

Last year more than one million MRI procedures were performed in the United States. The incidence of claustrophobic reaction during MRI procedures is estimated at 20% (Klonoff, Janata, & Kaufman, 1986). Some individuals become too anxious to complete MRI scans. Klonoff et al. (1986) used imaginal desensitization to generate a hierarchy for MRI procedures. The patient in their study was instructed in relaxation techniques and then gradually inserted her head into a box to simulate entering the MRI tube. She was able to successfully complete the MRI following this intervention without sedation. On the basis of this result, the authors recommended that even patients with little or no anxiety undergo a 10-minute imaginal assessment as a means for uncovering underlying claustrophobia and anxiety.

Rosenberg et al. (1997) evaluated the effect of using a scanner simulator to avoid sedation during MRI imaging of children. Sedation can have side effects and "may also interfere with cognitive function and alter brain physiology" (pp. 853–854). Sixteen children between the ages of 6 and 17 years were exposed to an MRI simulator in a non-threatening, relaxed environment before actual MRI scanning was attempted. During the simulation, the researchers played typical sounds from the MR imaging device. All participants were able to complete the MRI scanning procedure subsequent to treatment. Most participants experienced decreased levels of anxiety and distress, and none of the participants required sedation. The only disadvantage of this program is that construction of the simulation scanner costs approximately $10,000, and it occupies a 9- × 12-foot room. It is interesting to speculate whether the construction of a VR scanner could be as effective as the simulated scanner, considering that the cost and space requirements would be significantly reduced.

Chemotherapy

Cancer is one of the leading causes of death in children. The expected survival rate among children with cancer is 75%, with survival chances greatly increased when patients follow appropriate treatment regimens (Jemal et al., 1975–2000). Some children, however, have great anxiety and distress in the form of nausea, vomiting, and other side effects of chemotherapy. These children may prematurely discontinue treatment, delay treatment, or be given smaller dosages of chemotherapy. If children experience side effects during chemotherapy, they are likely to begin developing anticipatory anxiety associated with each subsequent treatment. Schneider and Workman (1999) at Case Western Reserve University used VR exposure to reduce anxiety in 11 children during their chemotherapy procedure. Previous studies have shown video-games, relaxation, and guided imagery to be helpful in reducing distress and serving as a distraction technique (Dahlquist, Gil, Armstrong, Ginsberg, & Jones, 1985; Redd et al., 1987). However, these techniques do not work for everyone. It is thought that the immersive, interactive nature of VR may enable more individuals to remain engaged and distracted.

Schneider and Workman (1999) found that Symptom Distress Scale (McKorkle & Young, 1978) scores and State–Trait Anxiety Inventory for Children (Spielberger, 1973) scores were lower while participants were using the VR exposure. Eighty-two percent of the participants indicated that the chemotherapy done in conjunction with VR treatment was not as bad as it had been without the treatment. No participants indicated that the treatments with VR were worse than previous treatments without VR. Of note is that three of the participants did indicate transitory headaches that were alleviated by removing the head-mounted display. This could have been associated with the participants' alopecia and should be taken into consideration if this study is replicated (Schneider, 1999).

In a follow-up, Schneider (2001) studied 46 women receiving chemotherapy for treatment of breast cancer. The women were randomly assigned to a group that received VR exposure during one treatment, followed by a treatment with no exposure, or to a group that received a treatment with no exposure, followed by a treatment with exposure. The State Anxiety Inventory, Symptom Distress Scale, and Revised Piper Fatigue Scale were used to measure anxiety and symptom distress.

Oyama, Kaneda, Katsumata, Akechi, and Ohsuga (2000) have developed the Bedside Wellness System, which is a system composed of three wide-angle liquid crystal displays, a three-dimensional sound system, and headphone and speakers that deliver a virtual experience to bed-ridden patients (Figure 17.1). The system also is capable of delivering a gentle breeze and the aroma of flowers or of the forest triggered by foot devices as the patient "walks" through a simulated forest scene. The system contains vital sign monitoring capability that can measure electrocardiogram, blood pressure, and respiration. Thirty patients who underwent chemotherapy drug infusions were treated during exposure to the Bedside Wellness System. Responses to questionnaires and analysis of vital sign data indicated that patients had reduced levels of nausea, fatigue, anxiety, and depression after using the system. The authors believe that intervention using the system as part of therapy will result in more effective treatment and greater benefits to patients.

Wound Care

VR treatment is being used as a distraction technique to reduce pain associated with wound care in burn victims. Because pain requires conscious attention, researchers felt that the immersive, interactive

FIGURE 17.1.

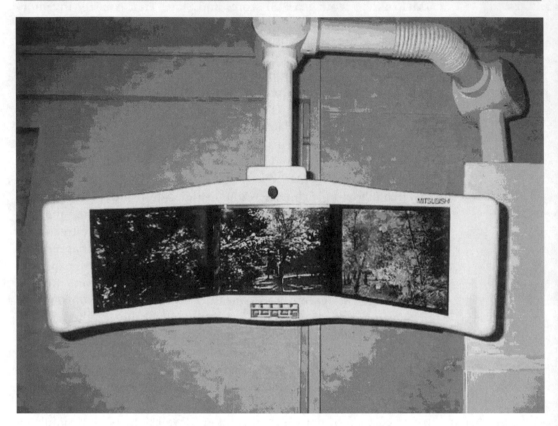

On the Bedside Wellness System, patients view a wraparound scene of a relaxing walk in the forest. They hear birds chirping, feel a warm breeze on their face, and smell forest flowers in bloom. Image courtesy of National Cancer Hospital, Tokyo, Japan.

nature of VR would reduce the patient's attentional resources that would otherwise be focused on the pain. During an initial study by Hoffman, Doctor, Patterson, Carrougher, and Furness (2000), two patients explored a "SpiderWorld" originally created to treat those with arachnophobia, which included a kitchen with virtual objects (pans, plates, etc.) and cabinet doors that could be opened and closed. Each patient also physically picked up real objects that were represented virtually, adding to the realism of the experience. The patients had staples removed from their wounds both while playing Nintendo and while in the VR world. Both patients reported dramatic decreases in pain only during the VR condition (http://www.hitl.washington.edu/research/burn/).

In a second study, Hoffman, Patterson, and Carrougher (2000) used VR distraction for 12 patients with burns during physical therapy procedures. The patients ranged in age from 19 to 47 and performed physical therapy exercises for 3 minutes during a VR condition and for 3 minutes during a no-VR condition. During the VR condition, patients showed dramatic decreases in pain and "time spent thinking about pain." In addition to decreasing pain, anxiety during physical therapy was also decreased. Researchers believe that VR will serve as a motivating factor to help patients try harder to do their exercises. For instance, patients using a fighter-jet simulation can get a "virtual reward" ("more gas for their jet" so they can run the simulation longer) if they complete a certain number of the requested physical therapy exercises, such as "gripping and ungripping their healing hand 10 times" (Hoffman, Patterson, & Carrougher, 2000, p. 245).

To determine whether VR therapy was subject to demand characteristics (such as social desirability), Hoffman, Garcia-Palacios, Kapa, Beecher, and Sharar (2003) subjected student participants to laboratory-induced ischemic pain. Participants were placed in either a "low technology VR condition," a "high technology VR condition," or a control condition with no VR. None of the participants was aware that there were two VR conditions. As the researchers had predicted, those in the "high tech" condition reported less pain and reported feeling more "present" in the virtual world. This lends support to the hypothesis that VR reduces pain by means of an attentional mechanism and not as a result of demand characteristics.

Neurorehabilitation

Cunningham and Krishack (1999) used VR therapy to improve cognitive and perceptual dysfunctions in a group of patients with cerebrovascular accidents. The nonimmersive VR platform consisted of a large screen television, a video camera, and video gesture control technology. This technology is used to digitize the patient's movements, which are then projected onto the large screen television. Patients stand in front of the television and their actions are mirrored directly on the screen. In this particular study, a head-mounted display is not used, allowing for greater freedom of movement in elderly and debilitated patients. Patients are encouraged to practice a variety of neurocognitive skills, including eye–hand coordination, right–left discrimination, visual attention concentration, visual tracking scanning, divided attention, and visual neglect. The patient is asked to complete specific maneuvers, for example, to touch a red balloon or the blue balloon or to follow the red balloon, and so on. When the patient correctly follows a command, auditory feedback can be generated, which was shown to improve patient acceptance and enjoyment. The authors reported that many of the elderly patients enjoyed performing these sessions while listening to Frank Sinatra and Bing Crosby. The potential benefit of this technique is very exciting because many patients with acute injury are often fearful of reinjuring themselves, and some become increasingly resistant to therapeutic intervention over time. This type of interactive system improves coordination, training, and skills assessment but also has a very significant social skills and stress reduction components.

Ohsuga, Miwa, and Hashima (2001) at the Advanced Technology R & D Center, Mitsubishi Electric Corporation, who originally developed the Bedside Wellness System, is now extending and expanding the concept to include physical and occupational therapy. The researchers are devising a prototype system capable of presenting three-dimensional visual, auditory, and vibrational feedback to the patient. The image is viewed on a 60-inch Mitsubishi LVP-X300 liquid crystal projector. Patients with neurocognitive deficits will be shown three-dimensional objects of various sizes and colors, and they will be instructed to touch, follow, or in some cases to break or pop an object such as a balloon (to build muscle strength). In this system, they will attempt to devise an auditory and force feedback component that can be used to measure progression of muscle strength and coordination.

Summary

VR therapy can be a great service to patients undergoing various medical procedures. VR exposure therapy is an alternative to medication or in vivo exposure therapy for patients who are unable or unwilling to use them to reduce their anxiety surrounding medical procedures, such as dental work, injections, or MRI testing. Applied as a distraction technique, VR therapy can also help reduce patient anxiety and discomfort during painful medical procedures such as chemotherapy and burn care. There is strong interest in all of these applications, and new technologies are under continuous development.

IV
Conclusion

Final Comments and Future Directions

18

nitial studies have shown that virtual reality (VR) treatment is effective for many anxiety disorders. Virtual reality graded exposure therapy (VRGET) can reduce the length of treatment, on average, from 12 or more sessions (for CBT) to only 8 to 12 sessions. Moreover, traditional cognitive–behavioral therapy (CBT) has an average relapse rate of 11% (Stuart, Treat, & Wade, 2000), whereas VR therapy has a 90% rate of improvement of symptoms (Lamson, 1997). In a small study of 30 participants treated with VR therapy, none had relapsed at 36 months posttreatment (Wiederhold & Wiederhold, 2003). Furthermore, VR therapy can offer options to patients who cannot use imaginal therapy or who are resistant to in vivo treatment. There are, nevertheless, a number of issues related to VRGET that clinicians must take into consideration. These issues include cost, technological capability of the therapist, side effects in some patients, the inability of the programs as yet to be tailored to individual patient needs, the question of the realism of the virtual environment, and the problem of obtaining objective measurements of desensitization.

Until recently, the cost of VR software and equipment was approximately $150,000. Now, some systems are available for under $5,000 and can be deployed on a personal computer, and prices are decreasing rapidly with the development of newer and less complicated systems. Augmenting the VR program with devices such as data gloves is still expensive, and using such devices adds a significant level of complexity to an office-based system. Other additions such as the technology to recreate smell, heat, wind, or breeze (as in driving) would not require significant investment.

The operation of PC-based VR programs does require basic computer skills, and the therapist must be willing to invest time to learn these basic operations. There are several key technical issues that must be addressed as research in VR treatments continues. Some software programs contain bugs, and systems do occasionally crash or freeze up. Assembling systems requires knowledge of computer peripheral devices and how to appropriately interface them to computers. Safety issues remain a problem because of the bewildering array of wires from the system to the head-mounted display worn by the patient. Controlling the environment through either the keyboard or mouse can at times be awkward for patients and may affect the level of immersion in the environment. Perhaps the most inconvenient aspect of current VR systems is the need to have a separate hardware platform for each environment. Because no uniform standard for the development of VR software exists, VR developers use a variety of different software programs, graphics cards, sound cards, and so on, which require that a separate computer system be assembled for each environment.

The higher end systems, such as the Cave Automatic Virtual Environment (CAVE) and Immersadesk, run simulations that require significant technical support and are not yet practical for the therapist's office. Efforts to increase realism or presence, such as by using airline or automobile seats or by adding tactile augmentation, are custom design efforts and are largely left up to the ingenuity and tenacity of individual clinicians and researchers. (To create an environment in which to treat patients who feared to fly, we had to rent a van, drive to the high desert above Los Angeles, and retrieve used airline seats from a 40-acre airplane salvage yard belonging to Mark Thompson of El Mirage, California).

To mitigate these inconveniences, some VR researchers are investigating the possibility of delivering virtual environments over the Internet. This would make access easier and broaden the array of virtual worlds available to the therapists. In addition, therapists would have access to the latest (improved) versions of the software. Eventually it will be possible to offer VR services to patients (under therapist supervision) at their homes. This may be a great asset for some populations, such as children with attention deficit disorder or patients with agoraphobia or social phobia. Other patients could benefit from occasional Internet-based "booster" sessions after successful completion of therapy for a specific phobia.

A small percentage of the population experiences side effects associated with VRGET, such as motion sickness, oculomotor problems, and VR-triggered migraines. Patients with seizure disorder and vestibular abnormalities should not use VR. The effects of VR on populations with schizophrenia and other disorders are not confirmed, but this is an active area of investigation (Ku et al., 2003).

To date, virtual environments cannot be altered to fit each client's individual fear and phobia hierarchies, and the opportunities for therapist-patient interaction remain limited. Undoubtedly, these issues will be addressed as more user-friendly software becomes available. Interactive virtual environments will allow a wider variety of disorders to be treated with VR therapy. The recent advances in "shared worlds" protocols on the Internet open the possibility of two or more individuals entering an environment together. The therapist could accompany the patient into the shared space, and family members could interact together in these virtual worlds. Certainly family therapy or group therapy would take on new dimensions in a shared virtual space.

For some people, the VR environments may not seem real enough. Some graphics are still cartoonish and may not effectively invoke the fear response; thus, improved and variable scenarios are needed to increase real-life applicability and generalizability. This concern is somewhat attenuated by the research on presence, which indicates that a highly realistic environment may not be necessary, and, in some cases, may not even be optimal for effective therapy.

Although objective measures of presence are not yet widely available, clinicians have shown that heart rate variability, skin conductance, and electroencephalogram (EEG) are useful analogs of absorption and presence. It is clear that self-report measures do not produce the desirable level of accuracy and can be colored by a variety of patient and event specific confounds. A high level of presence and immersion seems to be correlated with quicker movement through therapy, a higher level of therapeutic success, and from preliminary data less recidivism. At present two systems are necessary to present visual stimuli and to measure physiology. Future systems may combine both tasks into an easy-to-use product that makes this form of therapy easy to deliver.

Many therapists who perform imaginal exposure or systematic desensitization currently use physiological monitoring. Patients are progressed through the fear hierarchy only as physiological stabilization occurs. Studies have reported that when the phobic individual's fear structure is activated, autonomic arousal (such as increased heart rate or sweat gland activity) occurs. Physiological monitoring helps to determine whether the patient's fear structure is activated and, therefore, open to change. It also indicates whether the patient is getting "too" aroused, a possible indication of flooding, which is not desirable. Physiological monitoring gauges whether the patient has become desensitized to a certain aspect of the phobic scenario and whether the patient should be encouraged to move on to the next level of the fear hierarchy.

Advanced data analysis may allow underlying trends in patients' physiology to be monitored as they move through the virtual world. An integrated system incorporating a virtual world and physiological monitoring may allow real-time data analysis to occur. The ultimate goal might be to have VR systems that are driven by the patient's own physiology. This may even include intelligent software that could automatically control the level of difficulty the patient experiences in achieving desired parameters in training. Newer and less invasive methods to measure patient physiology should be developed, because current methods are intrusive to some patients and may affect their levels of immersion in the virtual environment.

It must be acknowledged here that the use of VR therapy in the area of mental health is still in its infancy. To further proceed and become a recognized part of therapy, more controlled studies are needed to determine whether VR therapy is indeed quicker, cheaper, and more efficient than conventional treatments. Clinicians should use available VR treatments with a view toward producing the evidence that would confirm or disconfirm the validity of VR as a successful method of treatment.

Future Directions

VR therapy has made significant progress in four major areas: anxiety disorders and phobias, eating and body dysmorphic disorders, neuropsychological assessment and rehabilitation, and as a distraction technique for painful or unpleasant medical procedures. Many investigators are actively pursuing other areas in mental health, including using virtual environments for addiction disorders, stress management, depression, schizophrenia, sex aggression, social skills training, attention deficit disorder, and many others. One exciting development is the use of virtual environments for special education purposes. Brown, Standen, and Cobb (1998) at the Virtual Reality Applications Research Team are developing the Learning in Virtual Environments program

(LIVE), a new experiential and communication tool at a special school in Nottingham, England. They are measuring how skills learned in a virtual world transfer to the real world.

As VR video games continue to become more realistic and flexible, they may offer potential new tools for clinical use in psychotherapy. The current version of "Midtown Madness" by Angel Studios/Microsoft® is an inexpensive off-the-shelf video game VR with an excellent driving simulation that can be used for a wide variety of social, medical, and psychological performance assays. Another video game, "Half-life," by Valve, offers a fully-mouse-driven 360° realistic world, parts of which might be useful for treating war-related posttraumatic stress disorder. Modules that are easily adaptable are also available through the Internet, and such things as "spiders" can be programmed into the world for other phobias such as arachnophobia.

Other exciting developments in VR therapy include studies into how people interact in virtual worlds. The Collaborative Virtual Environments project, funded by the European Commission, focuses on the development of shared or collaborative virtual environments, bringing together expertise from human factors, networked VR, computer graphics, human computer interaction, and telecommunications infrastructure. This project looks at network requirements for the support of such shared virtual worlds (Benford, Brown, Reynard, & Greenhalgh, 1996). Bobick and others (1999) from the Massachusetts Institute of Technology are collaborating to produce The KidsRoom, "a perceptually-based, interactive, narrative playspace for children" (p. 369). In this world, sound effects, music, narration, light, and images are used to transform a child's bedroom into a fantasy land where children are guided through a reactive adventure story. Pandzic, Capin, Thalmann, and Thalmann (1997) from the MIRALab-CUI are creating the Virtual Life Network, a group that studies how humans react and interact with virtual worlds and attempts to devise more naturalistic methods for this interaction. In this setting, autonomous virtual actors can be introduced into the environment for any variety of tasks or purposes. Slater et al. (1994) devised a series of experiments where three individuals who had never met were required to collaborate to carry out tasks in the virtual environment. Group dynamics and interpersonal interaction were observed, with many human emotions (e.g., embarrassment) being generated from the required interaction.

When using new VR tools, it is important to remember that existing therapeutic concepts should form the basis for the construction of virtual worlds. VR technology must be understood in light of existing science and established paradigms. The application of VR and its cost relative to existing therapeutic approaches must be taken into consideration in assessing the clinical use of VR. Multidisciplinary teams of experts can be very helpful in the development and delivery of VR systems.

A number of Web-based resources are available or are under development and will offer information on VR therapy, resources for therapists, clinical protocols, and advice on where to purchase equipment. A Web page set up by active VR therapists will collect data on adverse effects of virtual worlds and will explore ethical issues that emerge from treating patients. Slater and his colleagues (1994) are developing the Simple Virtual Environment library. This library provides tools that assist in the development of new virtual environments. Training for therapists new to VR therapy could be easily conducted over the Internet using commercially available education platforms or other privately developed services.

VR therapy has made initial progress in treating patients with anxiety disorders and phobias. There is yet more work to be done in a number of areas including the development of easy to use and more affordable hardware and software, the development of objective measurement tools, the issue of side effects, and more controlled studies to evaluate the strength of VR therapy in comparison with traditional therapies. Wider dissemination of the technology will encourage the industry to develop tools in response to user needs.

The future of VR therapy includes applications to a wide variety of disorders in addition to the applications already in use. Future areas include treatment of addictions, depression, attention deficit disorder, stress management, and social skills training. An ongoing area of study is how people interact in virtual worlds. The information gained from such research can then be applied in clinical contexts, such as family or group therapy. Web-based resources for VR practitioners are currently available and are in continuous development. Input on such topics as clinical protocols, equipment updates and purchases, ethical issues, and the newest research findings are easily accessed using the Internet. Training for VR therapists may also become available through the Internet, making it possible for interested individuals throughout the world to participate.

Wide dissemination of VR techniques to therapists interacting with patients rather than research participants is clearly needed to provide lessons learned in clinical practice. Although few clinicians currently use VR therapy in their practice, this is likely to change as the equipment becomes ever more sophisticated, accessible, and reasonably priced. We hope this volume encourages research in this important field.

References

Abelson, J. L., & Curtis, G. C. (1989). Cardiac and neuroendocrine responses to exposure therapy in height phobics: Desynchrony with the physiological response system. *Behavior Research and Therapy, 27,* 556–561.

Agras, S., Sylvester, D., & Oliveau, D. (1969). The epidemiology of common fears and phobias. *Comprehensive Psychiatry, 10,* 151–156.

Akhtar, S., Wig, N., Verma, V. K., Pershad, D., & Verma, S. A. (1975). Phenomenological analysis of symptoms in obsessive compulsive disorder. *British Journal of Psychiatry, 127,* 342–348.

Alcaniz, M., Botella, C., Perpina, C., Baños, R., Lozano, J. A., Montesa, J., et al. (2000). A new realistic 3D body representation in virtual environments for the treatment of disturbed body image in eating disorders. *CyberPsychology & Behavior: The Impact of the Internet, Multimedia and Virtual Reality on Behavior and Society, 3,* 433–439.

American Psychiatric Association. (1994). *Diagnostic and statistical manual of mental disorders* (4th ed.). Washington, DC: Author.

American Psychiatric Association. (1998). Practice guideline for the treatment of patients with panic disorder. *American Journal of Psychiatry, 155*(Suppl. 5), 1–34.

American Psychiatric Association. (2000). *Diagnostic and statistical manual of mental disorders* (4th ed., Text Revision). Washington, DC: Author.

American Psychological Association. (1997, November 5). *APA statement on services by telephone, teleconferencing, and Internet.* Washington, DC: Author. Retrieved May 6, 2001, from http://www.apa.org/ethics/stmnt01.html

American Psychological Association. (2002). Ethical principals of psychologists and code of conduct. *American Psychologist, 57,* 1060–1073.

Amies, P. L., Gelder, M. G., & Shaw, P. M. (1983). Social phobia: A comparative clinical study. *British Journal of Psychiatry, 142,* 174–179.

Antony, M. M., McCabe, R. E., Leeuw, I., Sano, N., & Swinson, R. P. (2001). Effect of exposure and coping style on in vivo exposure for specific phobia of spiders. *Behaviour Research and Therapy, 39,* 1137–1150.

Antony, M. M., & Swinson, R. P. (2000). *Phobic disorders and panic in adults: A guide to assessment and treatment.* Washington, DC: American Psychological Association.

Asarnow, J., Glynn, S., Pynoos, R. S., Nahum, J., Guthrie, D., Cantwell, D. P., & Franklin, B. (1999). When the earth stops shaking: Earthquake sequelae among children diagnosed for pre-earthquake psychopathology. *Journal of the American Academy of Child and Adolescent Psychiatry, 38,* 1016–1023.

Attias, J., Bleich, A., Furman, V., & Zinger, Y. (1996). Event-related potentials in posttraumatic stress disorder of combat origin. *Society of Biological Psychiatry, 40,* 373–381.

Baer, L. (1996). A telephone interface for simulated behavior therapy of an anxiety disorder. In S. J. Weghorst, H. B. Sieburg, & K. S. Morgan (Eds.), *Medicine meets virtual reality: Health care in the information age,* (pp. 718–719). Washington, DC: IOS Press.

Ballenger, J. C., Davidson, J. R., Lecrubier, Y., Nutt, D. J., Foa, E. B., Kessler, R. C., et al. (2001). Consensus statement on posttraumatic stress disorder from the International Consensus Group on Depression and Anxiety. *Journal of Clinical Psychiatry, 61*(Suppl. 5), 60–66.

Baños, R. M., Botella, C., Garcia-Palacios, A., Villa, H., Perpina, C., & Alacaniz, M. (2000). Presence and reality judgment in virtual environments: A unitary concept? *CyberPsychology & Behavior: The Impact of the Internet, Multimedia and Virtual Reality on Behavior and Society, 3,* 327–336.

Baños, R., Botella, C., Garcia-Palacios, A., Villa, H., Perpina, C., & Gallardo, M. (1999). Psychological variables and reality judgment in virtual environments: The roles of absorption and dissociation. *CyberPsychology & Behavior: The Impact of the Internet, Multimedia and Virtual Reality on Behavior and Society, 2,* 143–148.

Bard, S. R. (1991, Autumn). Virtual reality: An extension of perception. *Noetic Sciences Review, 7*–16.

Barlow, D. H. (1988). *Anxiety and its disorders: The nature and treatment of anxiety and panic.* New York: Guilford Press.

Barlow, D. H. (2002). *Anxiety and its disorders: The nature and treatment of anxiety and panic* (2nd ed.). New York: Guilford Press.

Barlow, D. H., Craske, M. G., Cerny, J. A., & Klosko, J. S. (1989). Behavioral treatment of panic disorder. *Behavior Therapy, 20,* 261–282.

Barlow, D. H., DiNardo, P. A., Vermilyea, B. B., Vermilyea, J. A., & Blanchard, E. B. (1986). Co-morbidity and depression among the anxiety disorders: Issues in diagnosis and classification. *Journal of Nervous and Mental Disease, 174,* 63–72.

Barlow, D. H., & Mavissakalian, M. (1981). Directions in the assessment and treatment of phobia: The next decade. In M. Mavissakalian & D. H. Barlow (Eds.), *Phobia: Psychological and pharmacological treatment.* New York: Guilford Press.

Beck, A. T., Emery, G., & Greenberg, R. (1985). *Anxiety disorders and phobias: A cognitive perspective.* New York: Basic Books.

Beck, A. T., Steer, R. A., & Brown, G. K. (1996). *Manual for the Beck Depression Inventory* (2nd ed.). San Antonio, TX: The Psychological Corporation.

Beck, A. T., Ward, C. H., Mendelsohn, M., Mock, J., & Erbaugh, J. (1961). An inventory for measuring depression. *Archives of General Psychiatry, 4,* 561–571.

Beckham, J. C., Vrana, S. R., May, J. G., Gustafson, D. J., & Smith, G. R. (1990). Emotional processing and fear measurement synchrony as indicators of treatment outcome in fear of flying. *Journal of Behavior Therapy & Experimental Psychiatry, 21*(3), 153–162.

Beidel, D. C., & Randall, J. (1994). Social phobia. In T. H. Ollendick, N. J. King, & W. Yule (Eds.), *International handbook of phobia and anxiety disorders in children and adolescents* (pp. 111–130). New York: Plenum Press.

Beidel, D. C., & Morris, T. L. (1995). Social Phobia. In J. March (Ed.), *Anxiety disorders in children and adolescents* (pp. 181–211). New York: Guilford.

Being and believing: Ethics of virtual reality. (1991). [Editorial]. *The Lancet, 338,* 283–284.

Benford, S. D., Brown, C. C., Reynard, G. T., & Greenhalgh, C. M. (1996). Shared spaces: Transportation, artificiality, and spatiality. *Proceedings of the ACM Conference on Computer Supported Cooperative Work* (pp. 77–86). Boston: ACM Press.

Benson, P. E. (2000). Suggestion can help. *Annals of the Royal Australasian College of Dental Surgeons, 15,* 284–285.

Blake, D. D., Weathers, F. W., Nargy, L. M., Kaloupek, D. G., Charney, D. S., & Keane, T. M. (1996). *The Clinician-Administered PTSD scale (CAPS).* Boston: National Centre for PTSD, Boston VA Medical Centre.

Blanchard, E., Kolb, L., & Prins, A. (1991). Psychophysiological responses in the diagnosis of posttraumatic stress disorder in Vietnam veterans. *Journal of Nervous and Mental Disease, 79,* 97–101.

Blanchard, E. B., & Hickling, E. J. (1997). *After the crash: Assessment and treatment of motor vehicle accident survivors.* Washington, DC: American Psychological Association.

Blanchard, E. B., & Hickling, E. J. (1998). Motor vehicle accident survivors and PTSD. *PTSD Research Quarterly, 9*(3), 1–8.

Bobick, A. F., Intille, S. S., Davis, J. W., Baird, F., Pinhanez, C. S., Campbell, L. W., et al. (1999). The KidsRoom: A perceptually-based interactive and immersive story environment. *Presence, 8,* 369–393.

Borda, M., & Echeburúa, E. (1991). La autoexposición como tratamiento psicológico en un caso de agorafobia. *Análisis y Modificacón de Conducta, 17,* 993–1012.

Borkovec, T. D., & Nau, S. D. (1972). Credibility of analogue therapy rationales. *Journal of Behavior Therapy and Experimental Psychiatry, 3,* 257–260.

Borkovec, T. D., & Sides, J. K. (1979). The contribution of relaxation and expectancy to fear reduction via graded imaginal exposure to feared stimuli. *Behavior Research & Therapy, 17,* 529–540.

Botella, C., Baños, R., Guillen, V., Perpiña, C., Alcaniz, M., & Pons, A. (2000). Telepsychology: Public speaking fear treatment in internet. *CyberPsychology & Behavior: The Impact of the Internet, Multimedia and Virtual Reality on Behavior and Society, 3,* 959–968.

Botella, C., Baños, R. M., Perpiña, C., Villa, H., Alcaniz, M., & Rey, A. (1998). Virtual reality treatment of claustrophobia: A case report. *Behavior Research & Therapy, 36*(2), 239–246.

Botella, C., Perpiña, C., Alcaniz, M., Lozano, J. A., Osma, J., & Gallardo, M. (2002). Virtual reality treatment of flying phobia. *IEEE Transactions on Information Technology in Biomedicine, 6*(3), 206–212.

Botella, C., Quero, S., Perpiña, C., Baños, R. M., Alcaniz, M., Lozano, J. A., & Rey, A. (1998). Virtual environments for the treatment of claustrophobia. *The International Journal of Virtual Reality, 3*(3), 8–13.

Botella, C., Villa, H., Baños, R., Perpiña, C., & García-Palacios, A. (1999a). The treatment of claustrophobia with virtual reality: Changes in other phobic behaviors not specifically treated. *CyberPsychology & Behavior: The Impact of the Internet, Multimedia and Virtual Reality on Behavior and Society, 2*(2), 135–141.

Botella, C., Villa, H., Baños, R., Perpiña, C., & García-Palacios, A. (1999b, January). *Virtual reality in the treatment of claustrophobia: A controlled multiple baseline design.* Paper presented at the Virtual Reality and Mental Health Symposium, MMVR 7, Medicine Meets Virtual Reality Conference, San Francisco, CA.

Botella, C., Villa, H., Baños, R., Perpiña, C., & García-Palacios, A. (2000). Virtual reality in the treatment of claustrophobic fear: A controlled multiple baseline design. *Behavior Therapy, 31,* 583–595.

Boyd, J. H. (1986). Use of mental health services for the treatment of panic disorder. *American Journal of Psychiatry, 143,* 1569–1574.

Boyd, J. H., Rae, D. S., Thompson, J. W., Burns, B. J., Bourdon, K., Locke, B. Z., & Regier, D. A. (1990). Phobia: Prevalence and risk factors. *Social Psychiatry and Psychiatric Epidemiology, 25,* 314–323.

Breiter, H. C., Rauch, S. L., Kwong, K. K., Baker, J. R., Weisskoff, R. M., Kennedy, D.N., et al. (1996). Functional magnetic resonance imaging of symptom provocation in obsessive–compulsive disorder. *Archives of General Psychiatry, 53,* 595–606.

Brende, J. (1982). Electrodermal responses in post-traumatic syndromes. A pilot study of cerebral hemisphere functioning in Vietnam veterans. *Journal of Nervous and Mental Disease, 170*, 352–361.

Brown, D. J., Standen, P. J., & Cobb, S. V. (1998). Virtual environments: Special needs and evaluative methods. In G. Riva, B. K. Wiederhold, & E. Molinari (Eds.), *Virtual environments in clinical psychology and neuroscience* (Vol. 58, pp. 91–102). Amsterdam: IOS Press.

Bruch, M. A. (1989). Familial and developmental antecedents of social phobia: Issues and findings. *Clinical Psychology Review, 9*, 37–47.

Buffett-Jerrott, S., & Stewart, S. H. (2002). Cognitive and sedative effects of benzodiazepine use. *Current Pharmaceutical Design, 8*, 45–58.

Bullinger, A. H., Bergner, J., Roessler, A., Estoppey, K. H., & Mueller-Spahn, F. (1999, January). *Virtual reality in claustrophobia and acrophobia.* Proceedings of the Virtual Reality and Mental Health Symposium, MMVR 7, Medicine Meets Virtual Reality Conference, San Francisco, CA.

Bullinger, A. H., Roessler, A., & Mueller-Spahn, F. (1998a). 3D VR as a tool in cognitive–behavioral therapy of claustrophobic patients. *CyberPsychology & Behavior: The Impact of the Internet, Multimedia and Virtual Reality on Behavior and Society, 1*(2), 139–146.

Bullinger, A. H., Roessler, A., & Mueller-Spahn, F. (1998b). From toy to tool: The development of immersive virtual reality environments or psychotherapy of specific phobias. In G. Riva, B. K. Wiederhold, & E. Molinari (Eds.), *Virtual environments in clinical psychology and neuroscience* (Vol. 58, pp. 103–111). Amsterdam: IOS Press.

Burns, G. L., Keortge, S., Formea, G., & Sternberger, L. (1996). Revision of the Padua Inventory of obsessive-compulsive disorder symptoms: Distinctions between worry, obsessions, and compulsions. *Behavior Research and Therapy, 34*, 163–173.

Butler, D. J., & Moffic, H. S. (1999). Post-traumatic stress reactions following motor vehicle accidents. *American Family Physician, 60*, 524–531.

Camara, E. (1993). Virtual reality: Applications in medicine and psychiatry. *Hawaii Medical Journal, 52*(12), 332–333.

Carlin, A. S., Hoffman, H. G., & Weghorst, S. (1997). Virtual reality and tactile augmentation in the treatment of spider phobia: A case report. *Behavior Research & Therapy, 35*(2), 153–158.

Carlson, E. B., & Putnam, F. W. (1992). *The Dissociative Experiences scale.* Towson, MD: Sidran Press.

Carlson, N. R. (1999). *Foundations of physiological psychology* (4th ed.). Needham Heights, MA: Allyn and Bacon.

Cartwright, G. F. (1994, March–April). Virtual or real? The mind in cyberspace. *The Futurist,* 22–26.

Chambless, D. L., Caputo, G. S., Bright, P., & Gallagher, R. (1984). Assessment of fear of fear on agoraphobics. The Bodily Sensation Questionnaire and the Agoraphobic Cognitions Questionnaire. *Journal of Consulting and Clinical Psychology, 52*, 1090–1097.

Chambless, D. L., & Goldstein, A. J. (1983). *Agoraphobia: Multiple perspectives on theory and treatment.* New York. Wiley.

Chapman, D. L. (1997). The epidemiology of fears and phobias. In G. C. L. Davey (Ed.), *Phobias. A handbook of theory, research and treatment* (pp. 415–434). London: Wiley.

Childress, C. (1998). Potential risks and benefits of online psychotherapeutic interventions. *International Society for Mental Health Online.* Retrieved February 27, 2000, from http://www.ismho.org/issues/9801.htm

Choi, Y. H., Jang, D. P., Ku, J. H., Shin, M. B., & Kim, S. I. (2001). Short-term treatment of acrophobia with virtual reality therapy (VRT): A case report. *CyberPsychology & Behavior Journal, 4*, 349–354.

Clark, A., Kirkby, K. C., Daniels, B. A., & Marks, I. M. (1998). A pilot study of computer-aided vicarious exposure for obsessive-compulsive disorder. *Australian and New Zealand Journal of Psychiatry, 32*, 268–275.

Clark, D. M. (1989). Anxiety states. Panic and generalized anxiety. In K. Hawton,

P. M. Salkovskis, J. Kirk, & D. M. Clark (Eds.), *Cognitive behaviour therapy for psychiatric problems. A practical guide* (pp. 52–96). Oxford, England: Oxford Medical Publications.

Clark, D., Salkovskis, P., & Chalkley, A. (1985). Respiratory control as a treatment for panic attacks. *Journal of Behavior Therapy and Experimental Psychiatry, 16,* 23–30.

Clark, D. M., Salkovskis, P., Gelder, M., Koehler, C., Martin, M., Anastasiades, P., et al. (1988). Tests of a cognitive theory of panic. In I. Hand & H. Wittchen (Eds.), *Panic and phobias II* (pp. 78–95). Berlin, Germany: Springer-Verlag.

Clark, D. M., Salkovskis, P., Hackmann, A., Middleton, H., Anastasiades, P., & Gelder, M. (1994). A comparison of cognitive therapy, applied relaxation, and imipramine in the treatment of panic disorder. *British Journal of Clinical Psychology, 164,* 759–769.

Clay, R. A. (2000, January). Staying in control. *APA Monitor, 32–34.*

Cobb, S. V. (1999). Measurement of postural stability before and after immersion in a virtual environment. *Applied Ergonomics, 30*(1), 47–57.

Cohen, D. C. (1997). Comparison of self-report and behavioral procedures for assessing acrophobia. *Behavior Therapy, 8,* 17–23.

Communications Research Group. (n.d.). *The use of virtual reality in the treatment of phobias.* University of Nottingham project in conjunction with Maudsley Institute of Psychiatry, London. Retrieved December 2001, from http://www.crg.cs.nott.ac.uk/research/projects/Spiders/

Cook, E. W., III, Melamed, B. G., Cuthbert, B. N., McNeil, D. W., & Lang, P. J. (1988). Emotional imagery and the differential diagnosis of anxiety. *Journal of Consulting and Clinical Psychology, 56,* 734–740.

Corah, N. L. (1969). Development of a dental anxiety scale. *Journal of Dental Research, 48,* 596.

Corah, N. L. (1988). Dental anxiety: Assessment, reduction and increasing patient satisfaction. *Dental Clinics of North America, 32,* 779–790.

Costa, P. T., Jr., & McCrae, R. R. (1992). *Revised NEO Personality Inventory (NEO–PI–R) and NEO Five-Factor Inventory (FFI) manual.* Odessa, FL: Psychological Assessment Resources.

Costello, P. J. (1997). *Health and safety issues associated with virtual reality—A review of current literature* (Tech. Rep. No. 37). Loughborough, UK: Advanced VR Research Centre.

Craske, M. G., Miller, P. P., Rotunda, R., & Barlow, D. H. (1990). A descriptive report of features of initial unexpected panic attacks in minimal and extensive avoiders. *Behaviour Research and Therapy, 28,* 395–400.

Craske, M. G., Rapee, R. M., & Barlow, D. H. (1988). The significance of panic-expectancy for individual patterns of avoidance. *Behavior Therapy, 19,* 577–592.

Craske, M. G., Street, L. L., & Barlow, D. H. (1989). Instructions to focus upon or distract from internal cues during exposure treatment of agoraphobic avoidance. *Behaviour Research and Therapy, 27,* 663–672.

Crowe, R. R., Noyes, R., Wilson, A. F., Elston, R. C., & Ward, L. J. (1987). A linkage study of panic disorder. *Archives of General Psychiatry, 44,* 933–937.

Crozier, W. R. (Ed.). (1990). Shyness and embarrassment: Perspectives from social psychology. Cambridge, England: Cambridge University Press.

Cunningham, D., & Krishack, M. (1999). Virtual reality promotes visual and cognitive function in rehabilitation. *CyberPsychology & Behavior Journal, 2*(1), 19–24.

Dahlquist, L. M., Gil, K. M., Armstrong, D., Ginsberg, A., & Jones, B. (1985). Behavioral management of children's distress during chemotherapy. *Journal of Behavior Therapy & Experimental Psychiatry, 16*(4), 325–329.

Davey, G. C. L. (1997). *Phobias: A handbook of theory, research and treatment.* New York: Wiley.

Davide, F., Holmberg, M., & Lundstrom, I. (1999). Virtual olfactory interfaces: Electronic noses and olfactory displays. In G.

Riva & F. Davide (Eds.), *Emerging communications: Studies in new technologies and practices in communication* (Vol. 1, pp. 193–220). Amsterdam: IOS Press.

De Jongh, A., van den Oord, H. J., & ten Broeke, E. (2002). Efficacy of eye movement desensitization and reprocessing in the treatment of specific phobias: Four single-case studies of dental phobia. *Journal of Clinical Psychology, 58*(12), 1453–1463.

Denholtz, M. S., Hall, L. A., & Mann, E. (1978). Automated treatment for flight phobia: A 3½-year follow-up. *American Journal of Psychiatry, 135,* 1340–1343.

Denholtz, M. S., & Mann, E. T. (1975). An automated audiovisual treatment of phobias administered by non-professionals. *Journal of Behavior Therapy & Experimental Psychiatry, 6,* 111–115.

Denot-Ledunois, S., Vardon, G., Perruchet, P., & Gallego, J. (1998). The effect of attentional load on the breathing pattern in children. *International Journal of Psychophysiology, 29*(1), 13–21.

Dentists try to ease panic along with pain. (1997, October 19). *San Diego Union-Tribune,* p. A-17.

Derogatis, L. R. (1977). *Scl-90-R: Administration. Scoring and procedures manual-I for the revised version of other instruments of the Psychopathology Rating Scale Series.* Baltimore, MD: John Hopkins University of Medicine, Clinical Psychometrics Research Unit.

Diaz, M. I., Vallejo, M. A., & Comeche, M. I. (2003). Development of a multi-channel exploratory battery for psychophysiological assessment: The Stress Profile. *Clinical Neurophysiology, 114*(12), 2487–2496.

DiBartolo, P. M., Hofmann, S. G., & Barlow, D. H. (1995). Psychosocial approaches to panic disorder and agoraphobia: Assessment and treatment issues for the primary care physician. *Mind/Body Medicine, 1*(3), 133–146.

Dinh, H. W., Walker, N., Song, C., Kobayashi, A., & Hodges, L. F. (1999, March). *Evaluating the importance of multi-sensory input on memory and the sense of presence in virtual environments.* Proceedings of IEEE Virtual Reality 1999 Conference, Houston, TX.

Dolocek, Q. E. (1994). Computer-generated stereoscopic displays. *John Hopkins APL Technical Digest, 15,* 137–142.

Donchin, E., & Coles, M. (1988). Is the P300 component a manifestation of context updating? *Behavioral Brain Science, 11,* 357–374.

Duncan-Johnson, C. C., & Donchin, E. (1982). The P300 component of the event-related brain potential as an index of informational processing. *Biological Psychiatry, 14,* 1–52.

DuPont, R. L., Rice, D. P., Miller, L. S., Shiraki S. S., Rowland, C. R., & Harwood, H. J. (1996). Economic costs of anxiety disorders. *Anxiety, 2,* 167–172.

Dyer, F. J. (1992, Summer). Virtual reality: Philosophical implications of a new technology. *The Quest,* 38–46.

Eaton, W. W., Dryman, A., & Weissman, M. M. (1991). Panic and phobia. In L. N. Robins & D. A. Reiger (Eds.), *Psychiatric disorders in America: The Epidemiological Catchment Area study* (pp. 155–179). New York: Free Press.

Emes, C. E. (1997). Is Mr. Pac Man eating our children? A review of the effect of video games on children. *Canadian Journal of Psychiatry, 42,* 409–414.

Emmelkamp, P. M. G., Bruynzeel, M., Drost, L., & van der Mast, C. A. P. G. (2001). Virtual reality treatment in acrophobia: A comparison with exposure in vivo. *CyberPsychology & Behavior Journal, 4,* 335–340.

Emmelkamp, P. M. G., Krijn, M., Hulsbosch, L., de Vries, S., Schuemie, M. J., & van der Mast, C. A. P. G. (2002). Virtual reality treatment versus exposure in vivo: A comparative evaluation in acrophobia. *Behavior Research and Therapy, 40*(5), 25–32.

Faravelli, C., Pallanti, S., Biondi, F., Paterniti, S., & Scarpato, M. A. (1992). Onset of panic disorder. *American Journal of Psychiatry, 149,* 827–828.

Fenly, L. (1996a, August 14). Computer technology can virtually wipe out phobias. *The San Diego Union-Tribune*, p. E-1.

Fenly, L. (1996b, August 14). Details provide believability for virtual reality therapy. *The San Diego Union-Tribune*, p. E-3.

Fiske, A. P., & Haslam, N. (1997). Is obsessive-compulsive disorder a pathology of the human disposition to perform socially meaningful rituals? Evidence of similar content. *Journal of Nervous and Mental Disease, 185,* 211–222.

Foa, E. B., & Kozak, M. J. (1986). Emotional processing of fear: Exposure to corrective information. *Psychological Bulletin, 99,* 20–35.

Foa, E. B., Steketee, G. S., & Ozarow, B. J. (1985). Behavior therapy with obsessive-compulsives: From theory to treatment. In M. Mavissakalian, S. M. Turner, & L. Michelson (Eds.), *Obsessive-compulsive disorders: Psychological and pharmacological treatment* (pp. 49–120). New York: Plenum Press.

Foa, E. B., Steketee, G., & Rothbaum, B. O. (1989). Behavioral/cognitive conceptualizations of post-traumatic stress disorder. *Behavior Therapy, 20,* 155–176.

Forgione, A. G., & Bauer, F. M. (1980). *Fearless flying: The complete program for relaxed air travel.* Boston: Houghton Mifflin.

Furmark, T. (2002). Social phobia: Overview of community surveys. *Acta Psychiatrica Scandinavica, 105*(2), 84–93.

Fylan, F., Harding, G. F., Edson, A. S., & Webb, R. M. (1999). Mechanisms of video-game epilepsy. *Epilepsia, 40*(Suppl. 4), 28–30.

Garcia-Palacios, A., Hoffman, H., See, S. K., Tsai, A., & Botella, C. (2001). Redefining therapeutic success with virtual reality exposure therapy. *CyberPsychology & Behavior Journal, 4*(3), 341–348.

Geer, J. H. (1965). Fear survey schedule II [FSS II]. In K. Corcoran & J. Fischer. *Measures for clinical practice: A sourcebook* (3rd ed., pp. 294–295). New York: Free Press.

Gelder, M. G., & Marks, I. M. (1966). Severe agoraphobia: A controlled prospective trial of behavior therapy. *British Journal of Psychiatry, 112,* 309–319.

Gillieron, E. (1981). Influence of the setting on a psychotherapeutic relationship in analytically oriented brief psychotherapy. *Psychotherapy & Psychosomatics, 35*(1), 44–54.

Gilroy, L. J., Kirkby, K. C., Daniels, B. A., Menzies, R. G., & Montgomery, I. M. (2000). Controlled comparison of computer-aided vicarious exposure versus live exposure in the treatment of spider phobia. *Behavior Therapy, 31,* 733–744.

Glantz, K., Durlach, N. I., Barnett, R. C., & Aviles, W. A. (1996). Virtual reality (VR) for psychotherapy: From the physical to the social environment. *Psychotherapy, 33,* 464–473.

Goetestam, K. G., Hollup, S., & Graawe, R. W. (August, 1996). *Virtual reality in the treatment of spider phobia: An experimental controlled study.* Paper presented at the World Psychiatry Congress, Barcelona, Spain.

Goisman, R. M., Rogers, M. P., Steketee, G. S., Warshaw, M. G., Cuneo, P., & Keller, M. B. (1993). Utilization of behavioral methods in a multicenter anxiety disorders study. *Journal of Clinical Psychiatry, 54*(6), 213–218.

Goodman, W. K., Price, L. H., Rasmussen, S. A., Mazure, C., Delgado, P., Heninger, G. R., et al. (1989). The Yale–Brown Obsessive–Compulsive Scale II: Validity. *Archives of General Psychiatry, 46,* 1006–1016.

Gorman, J. M., & Coplan, J. D. (1996). *Journal of Clinical Psychiatry, 57*(Suppl. 10), 34–41.

Greenberg, J. L., Lewis, S. E., & Dodd, D. K. (1999). Overlapping addictions and self-esteem among college men and women. *Addiction Behavior, 24,* 565–571.

Greist, J. H. (1995). The diagnosis of social phobia. *Journal of Clinical Psychiatry, 56*(Suppl. 5), 5–12.

Greist, J. H., & Greist, G. L. (1981). *Fearless flying: A passenger guide to modern airline travel.* Chicago: Nelson Hall.

Greist, J. H., Jefferson, J. W., & Katzelnick, D. J. (2000). *Social anxiety disorder: A guide*

[Booklet]. Madison, WI: Information Centers.

Griffiths, M. D., & Hunt, N. (1998). Dependence on computer games by adolescents. *Psychological Report, 82,* 475–480.

Gudaitis, T. D. (1998). The missing link in information security: Three dimensional profiling. *CyberPsychology & Behavior: The Impact of the Internet, Multimedia and Virtual Reality on Behavior and Society, 1,* 321–340.

Gupta, S. C., Klein, S. A., Barker, J. H., Franken, R. J. P. M., & Banis, J. C. (1995). Introduction of new technology to clinical practice: A guide for assessment of new VR applications. *The Journal of Medicine and Virtual Reality, 1,* 16–20.

Guy, W. (Ed.). (1976). *ECDEU Assessment Manual for Psychopharmacology, Revised* (pp. 218–222). Rockville, MD: U.S. Department of Health and Human Service, Alcohol, Drug Abuse, and Mental Health Administration, NIMH Psychopharmacology Research Branch.

Gwinup, G., Haw, T., & Elias, A. (1983). Cardiovascular changes in video-game players. Cause for concern? *Postgraduate Medicine, 74*(6), 245–248.

Hahn, J. K., Fouad, H., Gritz, L., & Lee, J. W. (1998). Integrating sounds and motions in virtual environments. *Presence, 7*(1), 67–77.

Hales, R. E., Hilty, D. A., & Wise, M. G. (1997). A treatment algorithm for the management of anxiety in primary care practice. *Journal of Clinical Psychiatry, 53*(Suppl. 3), 76–80.

Hamilton, J. O. (1992, October 5). Virtual reality: How a computer-generated world could change the real world. *Business Week,* p. 97.

Hamilton, J. O. (1993, February 22). Trials of a cyber-celebrity. *Business Week,* p. 95.

Hamza, S., Jones, N., Lesaoana, M., & Blake, E. (2000, October 6). *Virtual reality exposure therapy for needle phobia. Does it invoke an anxiety response?* Retrieved October 6, 2000, from http:/cs.uct.ac.za/Research/CVC/projects/vrnp/NewWebpage/Documents/techpaper/techpaper.htm

Harcourt, L., Kirkby, K., Daniels, B., & Montgomery, I. (1998). The differential effect of personality on computer-based treatment of agoraphobia. *Comprehensive Psychiatry, 39,* 303–307.

Harding, G. F. A. (1998). TV can be bad for your health. *Nature Medicine, 4,* 265–267.

Harding, G. F., & Harding, P. F. (1999). Televised material and photosensitive epilepsy. *Epilepsia, 40*(Suppl. 4), 65–69.

Hathaway, S. R., & McKinley, J. C. (1983). *Manual for the Minnesota Multiphasic Personality Inventory.* New York: Psychological Corporation.

Haug, T., Brenne, L., Johnsen, B. H., Berntzen, D., Gotestam, K., & Hugdahl, K. (1987). A three-systems analysis of fear of flying: A comparison of a consonant vs. a non-consonant treatment method. *Behavior Research and Therapy, 25*(3), 187–194.

Heilig, M. (1962). Sensorama simulator, U.S. Patent #3,050,870 (Filed 28 August 1962).

Heimberg, R. G., Hope, D. A., Dodge, C. S., & Becker, R. E. (1987, November). *An examination of DSM–III–R subtypes of social phobia.* Poster presented at the annual meeting of the Association for Advancement of Behavior Therapy, Boston, MA.

Heimberg, R. G., Liebowitz, M. R., Hope, D. A., & Schneier, F. R. (Eds.). (1995). *Social phobia: Diagnosis, assessment, and teatment.* New York: Guilford Press.

Herbert, J. D., Hope, D. A., & Bellack, A. S. (1992). Validity of the distinction between generalized social phobia and avoidant personality disorders. *Journal of Abnormal Psychology, 101,* 332–339.

Hinjo, S., Hirano, C., Murase, S., Kaneko, T., Sugiyama, T., Ohtaka, K., et al. (1989). Obsessive compulsive symptoms in childhood and adolescence. *Acta Psychiatrica Scandanivica, 80,* 83–91.

Hodges, L. F., Rothbaum, B. O., Alarcon, R., Ready, D., Shahar, F., Graap, K., et al. (1999). A virtual environment for the treatment of chronic combat-related post-traumatic stress disorder. *CyberPsychology & Behavior: The Impact of the In-*

ternet, *Multimedia and Virtual Reality on Behavior and Society, 2*(1), 7–14.

Hodges, L. F., Rothbaum, B. O., Watson, B. A., Kessler, G. D., & Opdyke, D. (1996). Virtually conquering fear of flying. *IEEE Computer Graphics & Applications, 16*(6), 42–49.

Hodgson, R., & Rachman, S. (1974). Desynchrony in measures of fear. *Behavior Research and Therapy, 12*, 319–326.

Hoffman, H. (1998). VR: A new tool for interdisciplinary psychology research. *CyberPsychology & Behavior: The Impact of the Internet, Multimedia and Virtual Reality on Behavior and Society, 1*(2), 195–200.

Hoffman, H. G., Garcia-Palacios, A., Kapa, V., Beecher, J., & Sharar, S. R. (2003). Immersive virtual reality for reducing experimental ischemic pain. *International Journal of Human-Computer Interaction, 15*, 469–486.

Hoffman, H. G., Patterson, D. R., & Carrougher, G. J. (2000). Use of virtual reality for adjunctive treatment of adult burn pain during physical therapy: A controlled study. *Clinical Journal of Pain, 16*(3), 244–250.

Hoffman, H. G., Patterson, D. R., Carrougher, G. J., & Sharar, S. (2001). The effectiveness of virtual reality based pain control with multiple treatments. *Clinical Journal of Pain, 17*, 229–235.

Holt, C. S., Heimberg, R. G., & Hope, D. A. (1992). Avoidant personality disorder and the generalized subtype of social phobia. *Journal of Abnormal Psychology, 101*, 318–325.

Holt, P., & Andrews, G. (1989). Hyperventilation and anxiety in panic disorder, agoraphobia, and generalized anxiety disorder. *Behaviour Research and Therapy, 27*, 453.

Howard, W. A., Mattick, R. P., & Clarke, J. C. (1982). *The nature of fear of flying.* Unpublished manuscript, University of New South Wales.

Howard, W. A., Murphy, S. M., & Clarke, J. C. (1983). The nature and treatment of fear of flying: A controlled investigation. *Behavior Therapy, 14*, 557–567.

Huang, M. P. (1999). Introduction: Beyond presence. *CyberPsychology & Behavior: The Impact of the Internet, Multimedia and Virtual Reality on Behavior and Society, 2*, 321–324.

Huang, M. P., & Alessi, N. E. (1999a). Mental health implications for presence. *CyberPsychology & Behavior: The Impact of the Internet, Multimedia and Virtual Reality on Behavior and Society, 2*, 15–18.

Huang, M. P., & Alessi, N. E. (1999b). Presence as an emotional experience. In J. D. Westwood, H. M. Hoffman, R. A. Robb, & D. Stredney (Eds.), *Medicine meets virtual reality: The convergence of physical and informational technologies options for a new era in healthcare* (pp. 148–153). Amsterdam: IOS Press.

Huang, M. P., Himle, J., & Alessi, N. E. (2000). Vivid visualization in the experience of phobia in virtual environments: Preliminary results. *CyberPsychology & Behavior: The Impact of the Internet, Multimedia and Virtual Reality on Behavior and Society, 3*, 321–326.

Huang, M. P., Himle, J., Beier, K., & Alessi, N. E. (1998a). Challenges of recreating reality in virtual environments. *CyberPsychology & Behavior: The Impact of the Internet, Multimedia and Virtual Reality on Behavior and Society, 1*(2), 163–168.

Huang, M. P., Himle, J., Beier, K., & Alessi, N. E. (1998b). Comparing virtual and real worlds for acrophobia treatment. In J. D. Westwood, H. M. Hoffman, D. Stredney, & S. J. Weghorst (Eds.), *Medicine meets virtual reality: Art, science, technology: Healthcare ®evolution*™ (pp. 175–179). Amsterdam: IOS Press and Ohmstra.

Huang, M. P., Rajarethinam, R. P., Abelson, J. L., & Alessi, N. E. (1998). Case studies of the Internet: Experiences at an anxiety disorders program. *MD Computing, 15*, 238–241.

Hutchinson, R. C. (1992). *Development in the treatment of agoraphobia: Potential use of computers.* Unpublished masters thesis, University of Tasmania, Australia.

Inoue, Y., Fukao, K., Araki, T., Yamamoto, S., Kubota, H., & Watanabe, Y. (1999).

Photosensitive and nonphotosensitive electronic screen game-induced seizures. *Epilepsia, 40*(Suppl. 4), 8–16.

Ischimura, A., Nakajima, I., & Jusoji, H. (2001). Investigation and analysis of a reported incident resulting in an actual airline hijacking due to a fanatical and engrossed VR state. *CyberPsychology & Behavior: The Impact of the Internet, Multimedia and Virtual Reality on Behavior and Society, 4,* 355–364.

Jacob, R. G., Furman, J. M., Durrant, J. D., & Turner, S. M. (1996). Panic, agoraphobia, and vestibular dysfunction. *American Journal of Psychiatry, 153,* 503–512.

James, L. K., Lin, C. Y., Steed, A., Swapp, D., & Slater, M. (2003). Social anxiety in virtual environments: Results of a pilot study. *CyberPsychology & Behavior, 6*(3), 237–243.

Janelle, C. M. (1998). Change in visual search patterns as an indication of attentional narrowing and distraction during a simulated high-speed driving task under increasing levels of anxiety. *Dissertation Abstracts International: Section B: The Sciences and Engineering 58*(7B), 3959.

Jang, D. P., Ku, J. H., Shin, M. B., Choi, Y. H., & Kim, S. I. (2000). Objective validation of the effectiveness of virtual reality psychotherapy. *CyberPsychology & Behavior: The Impact of the Internet, Multimedia and Virtual Reality on Behavior and Society, 3*(3), 321–326.

Jefferson, J. W. (1995). Social phobia: A pharmacologic treatment overview. *Journal of Clinical Psychiatry, 56*(Suppl. 5), 18–24.

Jefferson, J. W. (1996). Social phobia: everyone's disorder? *Journal of Clinical Psychiatry, 57,* 28–32.

Johnson, M. R., & Lydiard, R. B. (1995). Personality disorders in social phobia. *Psychiatric Annals, 25,* 554–563.

Joinson, A. (1999). Social desirability, anonymity, and Internet-based questionnaires. *Behavioral Research Methods, Instruments and Computers, 31,* 433–439.

Joinson, A. N. (2001). Self-disclosure in computer-mediated communication: The role of self-awareness and visual an-

onymity. *European Journal of Social Psychology, 31*(2), 177–192.

Jonas, B. S., Franks, P., & Ingram, D. D. (1997). Are symptoms of anxiety and depression risk factors for hypertension? Longitudinal evidence from the National Health and Nutritional Examination Survey I Epidemiologic Follow-up Study. *Archives of Family Medicine, 6,* 43–49.

Kagan, J., & Moss, H. A. (1962). *Birth to maturity.* New York: John Wiley & Sons.

Kahan, M. (2000). Integration of psychodynamic and cognitive–behavioral therapy in a virtual environment. *CyberPsychology & Behavior: The Impact of the Internet, Multimedia and Virtual Reality on Behavior and Society, 3,* 179–184.

Kahan, M., Tanzer, J., Darvin, D., & Borer, F. (2000). Virtual reality-assisted cognitive–behavioral treatment for fear of flying: Acute treatment and follow-up. *CyberPsychology & Behavior: The Impact of the Internet, Multimedia and Virtual Reality on Behavior and Society, 3,* 387–392.

Kappe, B., van Erp, J., Korteling, J. E. (1999). Effects of head-slaved and peripheral displays on lane-keeping performance and spatial orientation. *Human Factors, 41,* 453–466.

Kasteleijn-Nolst Trenite, D. G., da Silva, A. M., Ricci, S., Binnie, C. D., Rubboli, G., Tassinari, C. A., et al. (1999). Videogame epilepsy: A European study. *Epilepsia, 40*(Suppl. 4), 70–74.

Kelley, R. E., Chang, J. Y., Scheinman, N. J., Levin, B. E., Duncan, R. C., & Lee, S. C. (1992). Transcranial Doppler assessment of cerebral flow velocity during cognitive tasks. *Stroke, 23*(1), 9–14.

Kennedy, R. S., Kennedy, K. E., & Bartlett, K. M. (2000). *Chapter 31: Virtual environments and products liability.* Retrieved January 31, 2000, from http://vehand.engr.ucf.edu/handbook/Chapters/Chapter%2031.htm

Kennedy, R., Lane, N., Berbaum, K., & Lilienthal, M. (1993). A Simulator Sickness Questionnaire (SSQ): A new method for quantifying simulator sickness. *International Journal of Aviation Psychology, 3*(3), 203–220.

Kennedy, R. S., Lanham, D. S., Drexler, J. M., & Massey, C. J. (1997). A comparison of cybersickness incidences, symptom profiles, measurement techniques, and suggestions for further research. *Presence, 6*, 638–644.

Kennedy, R. S., Lilenthal, M. G., Berbaum, K. S., Baltzley, D. R., & McCauley, M. E. (1989). Simulator sickness in U.S. Navy flight simulators. *Aviation, Space, and Environmental Medicine, 60*, 10–16.

Kent, C. (1996, December 2). NIMH spearheads new anxiety education campaign. *American Medical News*, 5–6.

Kessler, R. C., McGonagle, K. A., Zhao, S., Nelson, C. B., Hughes, M., Eshelman, S., et al. (1994). Lifetime and 12-month prevalence of *DSM–III–R* psychiatric disorders in the United States. *Archives of General Psychiatry, 51*, 8–19.

Kessler, R. C., Sonnega, A., Bromet, E., Hughes, M., & Nelson, C. B. (1995). Posttraumatic stress disorder in the National Comorbidity Survey. *Archives of General Psychiatry, 52*, 1048–1060.

Khanna, S., & Channabasavanna, S. (1987). Toward a classification of compulsions in obsessive compulsive neurosis. *Psychopathology, 20*, 23–28.

King, S. A., & Poulos, S. T. (1998). Using the Internet to treat generalized social phobia and avoidant personality disorder. *CyberPsychology & Behavior: The Impact of the Internet, Multimedia and Virtual Reality on Behavior and Society, 1*(1), 29–36.

Kirkby, K. C. (1996). Computer-assisted treatment of phobias. *Psychiatric Services, 47*(2), 139–140, 142.

Kirkby, K. C., Berrios, G. E., Daniels, B. A., Menzies, R. G., Clark, A., & Romano, A. (2000). Process-outcome analysis in computer-aided treatment of obsessive–compulsive disorder. *Comprehensive Psychiatry, 41*(4), 259–265.

Kirkby, K. C., Daniels, B. A., Harcourt, L., & Romano, A. J. (1999). Behavioral analysis of computer-administered vicarious exposure in agoraphobic subjects: The effect of personality on in-session treatment process. *Comprehensive Psychiatry, 40*(5), 386–390.

Kizer, K. W. (1996). Progress on posttraumatic stress disorder. *Journal of the American Medical Association, 275*, 1149.

Klein, R. A. (1998). Virtual reality exposure therapy (fear of flying): From a private practice perspective. *CyberPsychology & Behavior: The Impact of the Internet, Multimedia and Virtual Reality on Behavior and Society, 1*(3), 311–316.

Klein, R. A. (1999). Virtual reality exposure therapy in the treatment of fear of flying. *Journal of Contemporary Psychotherapy, 30*(2), 195–208.

Klonoff, E. A., Janata, W. J., & Kaufman, B. (1986). The use of systematic desensitization to overcome resistance to magnetic resonance imaging (MRI) scanning. *Journal of Behavior Therapy & Experimental Psychiatry 17*(3), 189–192.

Klorman, R., Weerts, T. C., Hastings, J. C., Melamed, B. G., & Lang, P. (1974). Psychometric description of some specific-fear questionnaires. *Behaviour Therapy, 5*, 401–409.

Knox, D., Schacht, C., & Turner, J. (1993). Virtual reality: A proposal for treating test anxiety in college students. *College Student Journal, 27*, 294–296.

Kooper, R. (1994a). *Virtually present: Treatment of acrophobia by using virtual reality graded exposure.* Retrieved May 15, 2000, from http://www.cc.gatech.edu/gvu/people/Masters/Rob.Kooper/Thesis/

Kooper, R. (1994b). *Virtual reality exposure therapy.* Retrieved May 13, 2000, from http://www.cc.gatech.edu/gvu/virtual/Phobia/phobia.html

Kosslyn, S. M., Brunn, J., Cave, K. R., & Wallach, R. W. (1984). Individual differences in mental imagery ability: A computational analysis. *Cognition, 18*(1–3), 195–243.

Kowachi, I., Sparrow, D., Vokonas, P. S., & Weiss, S. T. (1994). Symptoms of anxiety and risk of coronary heart disease: The Normative Aging Study. *Circulation, 90*, 2225–2229.

Krijn, M. (2001, January). *Review of three Dutch studies on virtual reality treatment of acrophobia.* Proceedings of the Virtual Reality and Mental Health Symposium of the Medicine Meets Virtual Reality Conference, Newport Beach, CA.

Krueger, M. (1983). *Artificial reality.* Reading, MA: Addison-Wesley.

Krueger, M. W. (1991). *Artificial reality II.* New York: Addison-Wesley.

Ku, J., Cho, W., Kim, J. J., Peled, A., Wiederhold, B. K., Wiederhold, M. D., Kim, I. Y., et al. (2003). A virtual environment for investigating schizophrenic patients' characteristics: Assessment of cognitive and navigation ability. *CyberPsychology & Behavior, 6*(4), 397–404.

Ku, J., Jang, D. P., Jo, H. J., Shin, M. B., Choi, Y. H., & Kim, S. I. (2001, January). *Development of virtual reality therapy system for the treatment of acrophobia.* Proceedings of the Virtual Reality and Mental Health Symposium of the Medicine Meets Virtual Reality Conference, Newport Beach, CA.

Kubzansky, L. D., Kawachi, I., & Spiro III, A. (1997). Is worrying bad for your heart? A prospective study of worry and coronary heart disease in the Normative Aging Study. *Circulation, 95,* 818–824.

Lamson, R. (1994). Virtual therapy of anxiety disorders. *CyberEdge Journal, 4*(2), 1, 6–8.

Lamson, R. J. (1997). *Virtual therapy.* Montreal, Canada: Polytechnic International Press.

Lamson, R. J., & Meisner, M. D. (1996, January). Clinical application of virtual therapy to psychiatric disorders: Theory, research, practice. *Proceedings of Medicine Meets Virtual Reality,* San Diego, CA.

Lang, P. J., Melamed, B. G., & Hart, J. (1970). A psychophysiological analysis of fear modification using an automated desensitization procedure. *Journal of Abnormal Psychology, 76,* 220–234.

Larijani, L. C. (1993). *The virtual reality primer.* New York: McGraw-Hill.

Lawson, B. D., & Mead, A. M. (1997, June). *The sopite syndrome revisited: Drowsiness and mood changes during real or apparent motion.* Invited papers from the 12th Annual Man in Space Symposium on the Future of Humans in Space, Washington, DC.

Leahy, R. L., & Holland, S. J. (2000). *Treatment plans and interventions for depression and anxiety disorders.* New York: Guilford Press.

Leary, M. R., & Kowalski, R. M. (1995). *Social anxiety.* New York: Guilford Press.

Ley, R. (1991). The efficacy of breathing retraining and the centrality of hyperventilation in panic disorder: A reinterpretation of experimental findings. *Behavior Research and Therapy, 29,* 301–304.

Liebowitz, M. R., Gorman, J. M., Fyer, A. J., Campeas, R., Levin, A. P., Sandberg, D., et al. (1988). Pharmacotherapy of social phobia: An interim report of a placebo-controlled comparison of phenelzine and atenolol. *Journal of Clinical Psychiatry, 49*(7), 252–257.

Lindboel, S. (1996). Virtual reality vs. arachnophobia. *Gemini-Research News From the SINTEF Group and NTNU, 4.* Retrieved June 17, 2000, from http://www.ntnu.no/gemini/1996-04/

Liu, A., & Pentland, A. P. (1996). Detection of unexpected motion while driving: From psychophysics to real world via virtual environments. *Presence, 5*(2), 163–172.

Ludwig, R. P., & Lazarus, P. J. (1983). Relationship between shyness in children and constricted cognitive control as measured by the Stroop color–word test. *Journal of Clinical and Consulting Psychology, 51,* 386–389.

Macklin, M. L., Metzger, L. J., Lasko, N. B., Orr, S. P., Pitman, R. K., Litz, B. T., & McNally, R. J. (2002). Lower precombat intelligence is a risk factor for posttraumatic stress disorder. *Journal of Consulting and Clinical Psychology, 66,* No. 2, 323–326.

McCauley, M. E., & Cook, A. M. (1986). Simulator sickness research program at NASA-Ames Research Center. *Proceedings of the Human Factor Society 31st Annual Meeting* (pp. 502–504). Santa Monica, CA: Human Factors Society.

McCauley, M. E., & Sharkey, T. J. (1992). Cybersickness: Perception of self-motion in virtual environments. *Presence: Teleop-*

erators and Virtual Environments, 1, 311–318.

McCorkle, R., & Young, K. (1978). Development of a symptom distress scale. *Cancer Nursing, 1*(5), 373–378.

McGlynn, F. D., Rose, M. P., & Lazarte, A. (1994). Control and attention during exposure influence arousal and fear amont insect phobics. *Behavior Modification, 18*, 347–364.

McNally, R. J. (1987). *Panic disorder: A critical analysis.* New York: Guilford Press.

McNally, R. J., & Louro, C. E. (1992). Fear of flying in agoraphobia and simple phobia: Distinguishing features. *Journal of Anxiety Disorders, 6*, 319–324.

Magee, W. J., Eaton, W., Wittchen, H. U., McGonagle, K. A., & Kessler, R. C. (1996). Agoraphobia, simple phobia, and social phobia in the national comorbidity survey. *Archives of General Psychiatry, 53*, 159–168.

Mager, R. (2001, January). *Real time monitoring of brain activity in patients with specific phobia during exposure therapy, employing a stereoscopic virtual environment.* Proceedings of the Virtual Reality and Mental Health Symposium, Medicine Meets Virtual Reality Conference, Newport Beach, CA.

Mager, R., Bullinger, A. H., Roessler, A., Mueller-Spahn, F., & Stoermer, R. (2000). Monitoring brain activity during use of stereoscopic virtual environments. *CyberPsychology & Behavior Journal, 3*, 407–415.

Maloney, J. (1997). Fly me to the moon: A survey of American historical and contemporary simulation entertainments. *Presence, 6*, 565–580.

Mantovani, G. (1995). Virtual reality as a communication environment: Consensual hallucination, fiction, and possible selves. *Human Relations, 48*, 669–683.

Mantovani, G., & Riva, G. (1999). "Real" presence: How different ontologies generate different criteria for presence, telepresence, and virtual presence. *Presence, 8*, 540–550.

Marks, D. F. (1973). Visual imagery differences in the recall of pictures. *British Journal of Psychology, 64*, 17–24.

Marks, I. M. (1987). *Fears, phobias, and rituals.* New York: Oxford University Press.

Marks, I. M. (1995). Advances in behavioral–cognitive therapy of social phobia. *Journal of Clinical Psychiatry, 56*(Suppl. 5), 25–31.

Marks, I. M., & Mathews, A. M. (1979a). Fear questionnaire [FQ]. In M. M. Antony, S. M. Orsillo, & L. Rocmcr (2001). *Practitioner's guide to empirically based measures of anxiety* (pp. 55–56, 310, 329–330). New York: Plenum Press.

Marks, I. M., & Mathews, A. M. (1979b). Brief standard self-rating for phobic patients. *Behavior Research and Therapy, 17*, 263–267.

Marks, I. M., & O'Sullivan, G. (1988). Drugs and psychological treatments for agoraphobia/panic and obsessive–compulsive disorder. A review. *British Journal of Psychiatry, 153*, 650–658.

Masters, J. C., Burish, T. G., Hollon, S. D., & Rimm, D. C. (1987). *Behavior therapy: Techniques and empirical findings* (3rd ed.). New York: Harcourt Brace Jovanovich.

Mathews, A. M., Gelder, M. G., & Johnston, D. W. (1981). *Agoraphobia. Nature and treatment.* New York: Guilford Press.

Matthews, G., Dorn, L., Hoyes, T. W., Davies, D. R., Glendon, A. I., & Taylor, R. G. (1998). Driver stress and performance on a driving simulator. *Human Factors, 40*(1), 136–149.

Mavissakalian, M., Turner, S. M., & Michelson, L. (Eds.). (1985). *Obsessive–compulsive disorders: Psychological and pharmacological treatment.* New York: Plenum Press.

Meehan, M., Pugnetti, L., Riva, F., Barbieri, E., Mendozzi, L., & Carmagnani, E. (2000). Peripheral responses to a mental-stress inducing virtual environment experience. In P. M. Sharkey, A. Cesarani, L. Pugnetti, & S. Rizzo (Eds.), *Proceedings of the 3rd International Conference on Disability, Virtual Reality and Associated Tech-*

nologies (pp. 305–310). Reading, UK: University of Reading.

Michelson, L., Mavissakalian, M., & Marchione, K. (1985). Cognitive and behavioral treatments of agoraphobia: Clinical, behavioral and psychophysiological outcomes. *Journal of Consulting and Clinical Psychology, 53*, 913–925.

Millet, C. J., Fish, D. R., Thompson, P. J., & Johnson, A. (1999). Seizures during video-game play and other common leisure pursuits in known epilepsy patients without visual sensitivity. *Epilepsia, 40*(Suppl. 4), 59–64.

Moe, B. (2001). *Coping with mental illness.* New York: Rosen

Moline, J. (October, 1995) *Virtual environments for health care.* A White Paper for the Advanced Technology Program (ATP). National Institute of Standards and Technology.

Montgomery, S. A., & Asberg, M. A. (1975). A new depression scale designed to be sensitive to change. *The British Journal of Psychiatry, 134*, 382–389.

Moody, E. J. (2001). Internet use and its relationship to loneliness. *CyberPsychology & Behavior, 4*, 393–401.

Mukaetova-Ladinska, E. B., & Lawton, C. (1999). The bridge player—A brief acute psychotic episode in an elderly man due to playing computer games [Letter]. *International Journal of Geriatric Psychiatry, 14*, 1075–1076.

Muris, P., Merckelbach, H., Holdrinet, I., & Sijsenaar, M. (1998). Treating phobic children: Effects of EMDR versus exposure. *Journal of Consulting and Clinical Psychology, 66*(1), 193–198.

Muscott, H. S., & Gifford, T. (1994). Virtual reality and social skills training for students with behavioral disorders: Applications, challenges, and promising practices. *Education and Treatment of Children, 17*, 417–434.

Myers, J. K., Weissman, M. M., Tischler, C. E., Holzer, III, C. E., Orvaschel, H., Anthony, J. C., et al. (1983). Six-month prevalence of psychiatric disorders in three communities. *Archives of General Psychiatry, 41(10)*, 959–967.

Norris, F. H. (1992). Epidemiology of trauma: Frequency and impact of different potentially traumatic events on different demographic groups. *Journal of Consulting and Clinical Psychology, 60*, 409–418.

North, M. M., North, S. M., & Coble, J. R. (1995a). An effective treatment for psychological disorders: Treating agoraphobia with virtual environment desensitization. *CyberEdge Journal, 5*(3), 12–13.

North, M. M., North, S. M., & Coble, J. R. (1995b). Effectiveness of virtual environment desensitization in the treatment of agoraphobia. *International Journal of Virtual Reality, 1*(2), 25–34.

North, M. M., North, S. M., & Coble, J. R. (1996a). Effectiveness of virtual environment desensitization in the treatment of agoraphobia. *Presence, 5*(3), 346–352.

North, M. M., North, S. M., & Coble, J. R. (1996b). Virtual environments psychotherapy: A case study of fear of flying disorder. *Presence, 5*(4), 1–5.

North, M. M., North, S. M, & Coble, J. R. (1996c). *Virtual reality therapy: An innovative paradigm.* Ann Arbor, MI: IPI Press.

North, M., North, S., & Coble, J. R. (1997). Virtual reality therapy for fear of flying [Letter to the editor]. *American Journal of Psychiatry, 154*(1), 130.

North, M. M., North, S. M., & Coble, J. R. (1998). VR therapy: An effective treatment for the fear of public speaking. *International Journal of Virtual Reality, 3*(3), 2–7.

Ohsuga, M., Miwa, S., & Hashima, K. (2001, January). *VR system for mental and physical activation.* Proceedings of the Mental Health Symposium: 9th Annual Medicine Meets Virtual Reality Conference, Newport Beach, CA.

Ost, L. G. (1987). Age at onset in different phobias. *Journal of Abnormal Psychology, 96*, 223–229.

Oyama, H., Kaneda, M., Katsumata, N., Akechi, T., & Ohsuga, M. (2000, January). *Effectiveness of decreasing fatigue and emesis of cancer patients by bedside wellness system during chemotherapy.* Proceedings of the Mental Health Symposium: 8th Annual Medicine Meets Virtual Reality Conference, Newport Beach, CA.

Pandzic, I. S., Capin, T. K., Thalmann, N. M., & Thalmann, D. (1997). Virtual life network: A body-centered networked virtual environment. *Presence, 6,* 676–686.

Parent, A. (2001). Unpublished questionnaires. Retrieved from http://www.trytel.com/~aparent

Paul, G. L. (1991). Personal report of confidence as a speaker. In J. P. Robinson, P. R. Shaver, & L. S. Wrightsman (Eds.), *Measures of personality and social psychological attitudes* (pp. 188–190). San Diego, CA: Academic Press.

Paulhus, D. L. (2002). Socially desirable responding: The evolution of a construct. In H. I. Braun & D. N. Jackson (Eds.), *The role of constructs in psychological and educational measurement* (pp. 37–48). Mahwah, NJ: Erlbaum.

Pekala, R. J. (1985). A phenomenological approach to mapping and diagramming states of consciousness. *The Journal of Religion and Psychical Research, 8*(4), 199–214.

Pellouchoud, E., Smith, M. E., McEvoy, L., & Gevins, A. (1999). Mental effort-related EEG modulation during videogame play: Comparison between juvenile subjects with epilepsy and normal control subjects. *Epilepsia, 40*(Suppl. 4), 38–43.

Perna, G., Dario, A., Caldirola, D., Stefania, B., Cesarani, A., & Bellodi, L. (2001). Panic disorder: The role of the balance system. *Journal of Psychiatric Research, 35*(5), 279–286.

Perpiña, C., Botella, C., Baños, R., Marco, H., Alcaniz, M., & Quero, S. (1999). Body image and virtual reality in eating disorders: Is exposure to virtual reality more effective than the classical body image treatment? *CyberPsychology & Behavior, 2*(2), 149–155

Pertaub, D.-P., Slater, M., & Barker, C. (2001). An experiment on fear of public speaking in virtual reality. In J. D. Westwood, H. M. Hoffman, G. T. Mogel, D. Stredney, & R. A. Robb (Eds.), *Medicine meets virtual reality* (Vol. 81, pp. 372–378). Amsterdam: IOS Press.

Peterson, R. A., & Reiss, S. (1992). *Anxiety sensitivity index manual* (2nd ed.). Worthington, OH: International Diagnostic Systems.

Phillips, M. E., Bruehl, S., & Harden, R. N. (1997). Work-related post-traumatic stress disorder: Use of exposure therapy in work-simulation activities. *American Journal of Occupational Therapy, 51,* 696–700.

Pitman, R., Orr, S., Forgue, D., de Jong, J., & Claiborn, J. (1987). Psychophysiologic assessment of posttraumatic stress disorder imaginary in Vietnam combat veterans. *Archives of General Psychiatry, 44,* 970–975.

Plusquellec, M. (2000). Are virtual worlds a threat to the mental health of children and adolescents? *Archives of Pediatrics, 7*(2), 209–210.

Pugnetti, L., Meehan, M., & Mendozzi, L. (2001). Psychophysiological correlates of virtual reality: A review. *Presence, 10,* 384–400.

Rachman, S. J. (1978). *Fear and courage.* New York: W.H. Freeman.

Redd, W. H., Jacobsen, P. B., Die-Trill, M., Dermatis, H., McEvoy, M., & Holland, J. C. (1987). Cognitive/attentional distraction in the control of conditioned nausea in pediatric cancer patients receiving chemotherapy. *Journal of Consulting and Clinical Psychology, 55,* 391–395.

Regan, E. C., & Ramsey, A. D. (1996). The efficacy of hyoscine hydrobromide in reducing side-effects induced during immersion in virtual reality. *Aviation, Space, and Environmental Medicine, 67*(3), 222–226.

Regenbrecht, H. T., Schubert, T. W., & Friedmann, F. (1998). Measuring the sense of presence and its relations to fear of heights in virtual environments. *International Journal of Human–Computer Interaction, 10*(3), 233–249.

Regier, D. A., Narrow, W. E., & Rae, D. S. (1990). The epidemiology of anxiety disorders: The epidemiological catchment area (ECA) experience. *Journal of Psychiatric Research, 24*(2), 3–14.

Reich, J. (1986). The epidemiology of anxiety. *Journal of Nervous and Mental Disease, 174*(3), 129–136.

Renaud, P., & Bouchard, S. (2001, January). *Visual tracking of virtual objects as a dynamic measurement of behavioral avoidance in arachnophobia.* Paper presented at the 9th Annual Medicine Meets Virtual Reality Conference, Newport Beach, CA.

Rheingold, H. (1991). *Virtual reality: The revolutionary technology of computer-generated artificial worlds—And how it promises and threatens to transform business and society.* New York: Summit Books.

Ricci, S., & Vigevano, F. (1999). The effect of video-game software in video-game epilepsy. *Epilepsia, 40*(Suppl. 4), 31–37.

Rice, D. P., & Miller, L. S. (1998). Health economics and cost implications of anxiety and other mental disorders in the United States. *British Journal of Psychiatry, 173*(34), 4–9.

Rich, P. (May 7, 1996). There are reasons to panic over panic disorders. (Based on the work of Dr. Jerrold Rosenbaum, Harvard Medical School) *The Medical Post,* Retrieved from http://www.mentalhealth.com/mag1/p5m-pan2.html

Richman, W. L., Kiesler, S., Weisband, S., & Drasgow, F. (1999). A meta-analytic study of social desirability distortion in computer-administered questionnaires, traditional questionnaires, and interviews. *Journal of Applied Psychology, 84,* 754–775.

Rinalducci, E. J. (1980). Effects of aircraft motion on passengers' comfort ratings and response times. *Perceptual Motor Skills, 50*(1), 91–97.

Riva, G. (Ed.). (1997). *Virtual reality in neuropsycho-physiology: Cognitive, clinical, and methodological issues in assessment and rehabilitation.* Amsterdam: IOS Press.

Riva, G. (1998a). Virtual reality in psychological assessment: The body image virtual reality scale. *CyberPsychology & Behavior, 1*(1), 37–44.

Riva, G. (1998b). Virtual reality vs. virtual body: The use of virtual environments in the treatment of body experience disturbances. *CyberPsychology & Behavior, 1*(2), 129–138.

Riva, G. (2001). Virtual reality as communication tool: A socio–cognitive analysis. In G. Riva & F. Davide (Eds.), *Communications through virtual technology: Identity, community, and technology in the Internet age* (Vol. 1, pp. 47–56). Amsterdam: IOS Press.

Riva, G., Alcañiz, A., Anolli, L., Bacchetta, M., Baños, R., Beltrame, F., et al. (2001). The VEPSY updated project: Virtual reality in clinical psychology. *CyberPsychology & Behavior, 4*(4), 449–455.

Riva, G., Bacchetta, M., Baruffi, M., Cirillo, G., & Molinari, E. (2000). Virtual reality environment for body image modification: A multidimensional therapy for the treatment of body image in obesity and related pathologies. *CyberPsychology & Behavior, 3,* 421–431.

Riva, G., Wiederhold, B. K., & Molinari, E. (Eds.). (1998). *Virtual environments in clinical psychology and neuroscience: Methods and techniques in advanced patient–therapist interaction.* Amsterdam: IOS Press.

Rizzo, A. A., Bowerly, T., Schultheis, M. T., Shahabi, C., & Buckwalter, J. G. (2002, September). *Virtual environments for the assessment of attention and memory processes: Results from the virtual classroom and office.* The 4th International Conference on Disability, Virtual Reality and Associated Technology, Veszprem, Hungary.

Rizzo, A. A., Buckwalter, J. G., Neuman, U., Chua, C., Rooyen, M. A., Larson, P., et al. (1999). Virtual environments for targeting cognitive processes: An overview of projects at the University of Southern California. *CyberPsychology & Behavior, 2*(2), 89–100.

Roberts, R. J. (1989). Passenger fear of flying: Behavioral treatment with extensive in-vivo exposure and group support. *Aviation, Space, and Environmental Medicine, 60,* 342–348.

Rose, M. P., McGlynn, F. D., & Lazarte, A. (1995). Control and attention influence snake phobics' arousal and fear during laboratory confrontations with a caged snake. *Journal of Anxiety Disorders, 9,* 293–302.

Rosenbaum, J. F., Biederman, J., Pollock, R. A., Hirshfeld, D. R. (1994). The etiology of social phobia. *Journal of Clinical Psychiatry, 55*(Suppl. 6), 10–16.

Rosenberg, D. R., Sweeney, J. A., Gillen, J. S., Kim, J., Varanelli, M. J., O'Hearn, K. M., et al. (1997). Magnetic resonance imaging of children without sedation: Preparation with simulation. *Journal of the American Academy of Child and Adolescent Psychiatry, 36,* 853–885.

Rothbaum, B. O., Hodges, L. F., Alarcon, R., Ready, D., Shahar, F., Graap, K., et al. (1999). Virtual reality exposure therapy for PTSD Vietnam veterans: A case study. *Journal of Traumatic Stress, 12*(2), 263–271.

Rothbaum, B. O., Hodges, L., Anderson, P. L., Price, L., & Smith, S. (2002). Twelve-month follow-up of virtual reality and standard exposure therapies for the fear of flying. *Journal of Consulting and Clinical Psychology, 70*(2), 428–432.

Rothbaum, B. O., Hodges, L., & Kooper, R. (1997). Virtual reality exposure therapy. *Journal of Psychotherapy Practice and Research, 6*(3), 291–296.

Rothbaum, B. O., Hodges, L. F., Kooper, R., Opdyke, D., Williford, J. S., & North, M. (1995a). Effectiveness of computer-generated (virtual reality) graded exposure in the treatment of acrophobia. *American Journal of Psychiatry, 152,* 626–628.

Rothbaum, B. O., Hodges, L. F., Kooper, R., Opdyke, D., Williford, J. S., & North, M. (1995b). Virtual reality graded exposure in the treatment of acrophobia: A case report. *Behavior Therapy, 26,* 547–554.

Rothbaum, B. O., Hodges, L., Smith, S., Lee, J. H., & Price, L. (2000). A controlled study of virtual reality exposure therapy for the fear of flying. *Journal of Consulting and Clinical Psychology, 68,* 1020–1026.

Rothbaum, B. O., Hodges, L., Watson, B. A., Kessler, G. D., & Opdyke, D. (1996). Virtual reality exposure therapy in the treatment of fear of flying: A case report. *Behaviour Research and Therapy, 34*(5/6), 477–481.

Rubin, R. T., Ananth, J., Villanueva-Meyer, J., Trajmar, P. G., & Mena, I. (1995). Regional Xenon cerebral blood flow and cerebral Tc-HM-PAO uptake in patients with obsessive–compulsive disorder before and during treatment. *Biological Psychiatry, 38,* 429–437.

Saeed, S. A., & Bruce, T. J. (1998). Panic disorder: Effective treatment options. *American Family Physician, 57,* 2405–2412.

Salkovskis, P., Clark, D., & Hackmann, A. (1991). Treatment of panic attacks using cognitive therapy without exposure or breaching retraining. *Behaviour Research and Therapy, 29,* 161–166.

Salyer, S. (1997, July 18–20). The dawn of "virtual therapy." *USA Weekend,* p. 10.

Sanchez, J., & Lumbreras, M. (1999). Virtual environment interaction through 3D audio by blind children. *CyberPsychology & Behavior, 2,* 101–111.

Scared of heights? Virtual therapy may be on the way. (1994, November/December). *Virtual Reality World, 7.*

Schare, M. L., Scardapane, J. R., Berger, A. L., & Rose, N. (1999, November 11–14). *A virtual reality based anxiety induction procedure with driving phobic participants.* Symposium on the Virtual Reality Applications for Cognitive/Behavioral Assessment and Intervention, Proceedings of the Association for the Advancement of Behavior Therapy Conference, Toronto, Canada.

Schneider, S. M. (1999). I look funny and I feel bad: Measurement of symptom distress. *Journal of Child and Family Nursing, 2,* 380–384.

Schneider, S. M. (2001, January). *Effect of virtual reality on symptom distress in breast cancer patients.* Proceedings of the Virtual Reality and Mental Health Symposium, Medicine Meets Virtual Reality Conference, Newport Beach, CA.

Schneider, S. M., & Workman, M. L. (1999). Effects of virtual reality on symptom distress in children receiving chemotherapy.

CyberPsychology & Behavior: The Impact of the Internet, Multimedia and Virtual Reality on Behavior and Society, 2(2), 125–134.

Schneier, F. R., Johnson, J., Hornig, C. D., Liebowitz, M. R., & Weissman, M. M. (1992). Social phobia: Comorbidity and morbidity in an epidemiologic sample. *Archives of General Psychiatry, 49,* 282–288.

Schneier, F. R., Spitzer, R. L., Gibbon, M., Fyer, A. J., & Liebowitz, M. R. (1991). The relationship of social phobia subtypes and avoidant personality disorder. *Comprehensive Psychiatry, 32,* 496–502.

Schold-Davis, E., & Watchel, J. (2000, January 27–30). *Interactive driving simulation as a tool for insight development and immersion in a rehabilitation setting.* Proceedings of Envisioning Health, Interactive Technology and the Patient–Practitioner Dialogue, Medicine Meets Virtual Reality Conference, Newport Beach, California.

Schrof, J. M., & Schultz, S. (1999, June 21). Social anxiety. *U.S. News & World Report,* pp. 50–57.

Schuemie, M. J. (2000). Design of virtual reality exposure therapy systems—Task analysis. *CHI 2000 Extended Abstracts,* pp. 345–346. Retrieved June 8, 2000, from http://is.twi.tudelft.nl/~schuemie/vrpub.html

Schuemie, M. J., Bruynzeel, M., Drost, L., Brinkman, M., de Haan, G., Emmelkamp, P. M. G., & van der Mast, C. A. P. G. (2000). Treatment of acrophobia in VR: A pilot study. In F. Brockx & L. Pauwels (Eds.), *Conference proceedings Euromedia 2000* (pp. 271–275). Antwerp, Belgium: The Society for Computer Simulation International.

Schwartz, M. S., & Associates. (1995). *Biofeedback: A practitioner's guide.* New York: Guilford Press.

Scott, W. (1987). A fear of flying inventory. In P. Kellar & S. Hayman (Eds.), *Innovations of clinical practice* (Vol. 7). Sarasota, FL: Professional Resource Exchange.

Segal, K. R., & Dietz, W. H. (1991). Physiologic responses to playing a video game. *American Journal of Diseases of Children, 145,* 1034–1036.

Seppa, N. (1996, December). Psychologists boost anxiety screening. *The APA Monitor,* p. 31.

Seyrek, S. K., Corah, N. L., & Pace, L. F. (1984). Comparison of three distraction techniques in reducing stress in dental patients. *Journal of the American Dental Association, 108,* 327–329.

Shaw, S. C., Marks, I. M., & Toole, S. (1999, July/August). Lessons from pilot tests of computer self-help for agora/claustrophobia and panic. *MD Computing,* 44–48.

Sheridan, T. B. (1992). Musings on telepresence and virtual presence. *Presence: Teleoperators and Virtual Environments, 1,* 120–125.

Sherman, C. (1997a, May 15). Multiple somatic symptoms may signal anxiety, depression. *Internal Medicine News,* p. 21.

Sherman, C. (1997b, May 15). "Virtual exposure" quells anxiety disorders. *Internal Medicine News,* p. 21.

Shimanuchi, Y. (1999). Children in Japan and multimedia. *Turkish Journal of Pediatrics, 41*(Suppl.), 7–12.

Sieder, J. J. (1996, February 12). The latest head trip: Virtual reality technology may be a cost-effective therapy. *U.S. News & World Report,* p. 55.

Slater, M., Pertaub, D.-P., & Steed, A. (1999). Public speaking in virtual reality: Facing an audience of avatars. *IEEE Computer Graphics and Applications, 19*(2), 6–9.

Slater, M., Usah, M., & Steed, A. (1994). Depth of presence in virtual environments. *Presence: Teleoperators and Virtual Environments, 3,* 130–144.

Slovin, M. (1997). Managing the anxious and phobic dental patient. *New York State Dental Journal, 63,* 36–40.

Smith, K. L., Kirkby, K. C., Montgomery, I. M., & Daniels, B. A. (1997). Computer-delivered modeling of exposure for spider phobia: Relevant versus irrelevant exposure. *Journal of Anxiety Disorders, 11,* 489–497.

Sobel, D., & Ornstein, R. (1997). The cost of anxiety. *Mind/Body Health Newsletter, VI*(1), 7.

Solyom, L., Shugar, R., Bryntwick, S., & Solyom, C. (1973). Treatment of fear of flying. *American Journal of Psychiatry, 130*(4), 423–427.

Spiegel, H., & Spiegel, D. (1987). *Trance and treatment: Clinical uses of hypnosis.* Washington, DC: American Psychiatric Press.

Spielberger, C. (1973). *Manual for the State–Trait Anxiety Inventory for Children.* Palo Alto, CA: Consulting Psychologists Press.

Spielberger, C. D., Gorsuch, R. L., Lushene, R., Vagg, P. R., & Jacobs, G. A. (1983). *Manual for the Stait–Trait Anxiety Inventory.* Palo Alto, CA: Consulting Psychologists Press.

Spitzer, S., Williams, J., Gibbon, M., & First, M. (1992). The structured clinical interview for *DSM–III–R/DSM–IV* (SCID). *Archives of General Psychiatry, 49*(8), 624–629.

Stanley, M. A., & Turner, S. M. (1995). Current status of pharmacological and behavioral treatment in obsessive-compulsive disorder. *Behavior Therapy, 26*, 163–186.

Stanney, K. M. (Ed.) (2002). *Handbook of virtual environments: Design, implementation, and applications (human factors and ergonomics).* Mahwah, NJ: Lawrence Erlbaum Associates, Inc.

Stanney, K. M., & Kennedy, R. S. (1997). The psychometrics of cybersickness. *Communications of the ACM, 40*(8), 67–68.

Stanney, K. M., Mourant, R., & Kennedy, R. S. (1998). Human factors issues in virtual environments: A review of the literature. *Presence: Teleoperators and Virtual Environments, 7*, 327–351.

Stein, M. B., & Uhde, T. W. (1994). The biology of anxiety disorders. In *American Psychiatric Press textbook of psychopharmacology* (pp. 609–628). Washington, DC: American Psychiatric Press.

Steketee, G., Chambless, D. L., Tran, G. Q., Worden, H., & Gillis, M. M. (1996). Behavioral avoidance test for obsessive compulsive disorder. *Behavior Research and Therapy, 34*(1), 73–83.

Stemberger, R. T., Turner, S. M., Beidel, D. C., & Calhoun, K. S. (1995). Social phobia: An analysis of possible developmental factors. *Journal of Abnormal Psychology, 104*, 526–531

Stuart, G. L., Treat, T. A., & Wade, W. A. (2000). Effectiveness of an empirically based treatment for panic disorder delivered in a service clinic setting: 1-year follow-up. *Journal Consulting Clinical Psychology, 68*, 506–512.

Suler, J., & Phillips, W. L. (1998). The bad boys of cyberspace: Deviant behavior in a multimedia chat community. *CyberPsychology & Behavior, 1*, 275–294.

Sutherland, I. (May 1965). The ultimate display. In *Proceedings IFIP Congress* (Vol. 2, pp. 506–508).

Szymanski, J., & O'Donohue, W. (1995). Fear of Spiders Questionnaire. *Journal of Behavioral Therapy and Experimental Psychiatry, 26*, 31–34.

Tanouye, E. (1997, June 30). Easing stage fright could be as simple as swallowing a pill. *The Wall Street Journal,* B1.

Tarnanas, I. (2001, January). *Using virtual reality to teach special populations how to cope in crisis: The case of virtual earthquake.* Proceedings of the Virtual Reality and Mental Health Symposium, Medicine Meets Virtual Reality Conference, Newport Beach, CA.

Taylor, C. B., Fried, L., & Kenardy, J. (1990). The use of a real-time computer diary for data acquisition and processing. *Behavior Research and Therapy, 28*(1), 93–97.

Taylor, J. A. (1953). A personality scale of manifest anxiety. *Journal of Abnormal and Social Psychology, 48*, 285–290.

Tazawa, Y., Soukalo, A. V., Okada, K., & Takada, G. (1997). Excessive playing of home computer games by children presenting unexplained symptoms [Letter]. *Journal of Pediatrics, 130*, 1010–1011.

Travis, D., Watson, T., & Atyeo, M. (1994). Human psychology in virtual environments. In L. MacDonald & J. Vince (Eds.), *Interacting with virtual environments* (pp. 43–59). New York: John Wiley & Sons.

Tellegen, A. (1982). *Brief manual for the Multidimensional Personality Questionnaire.* Unpublished manuscript.

Tellegen, A., & Atkinson, G. (1974). Openness to absorbing and self-altering experiences ("absorption"), a trait related to hypnotic susceptibility. *Journal of Abnormal Psychology, 83,* 268–277.

Turner, J. R., Treiber, F. A., Davis, H., Rectanwald, J., Pipkin, W., & Strong, W. P. (1997). Use of a virtual reality car-driving stressor in cardiovascular reactivity research. *Behavior Research Methods, Instruments, & Computers, 29,* 386–389.

Turner, S. M., Beidel, D. C., & Townsley, R. M. (1992). Social phobia: A comparison of specific and generalized subtypes and avoidant personality disorder. *Journal of Abnormal Psychology, 101,* 326–331.

Uhde, T. W., Boulenger, J. P., Roy-Byrne, P. P., Geraci, M. P., Vittone, B. J., & Post, R. M. (1985). Longitudinal course of panic disorder: Clinical and biological considerations. *Progressive Neuro-Psychopharmacology and Biological Psychiatry, 9,* 39–51.

Uinsworth, N. (1984). Anxiety. *British Dental Journal, 156,* 299.

Ungs, T. J. (1989). Simulator induced syndrome: evidence for long-term aftereffects. *Aviation, Space, & Environmental Medicine, 60*(3), 252–255.

van Vliet, I. M., den Boer, J. A., & Westenberg, H. G. (1994) Psychopharmacological treatment of social phobia; a double blind placebo controlled study with fluvoxamine. *Psychopharmacology* (Berl), *115*(1–2), 128–134.

Vermilyea, J. A., Boice, R., & Barlow, D. H. (1984). Rachman and Hodgson (1974) a decade later: How do desynchronous response systems relate to the treatment of agoraphobia? *Behavior Research and Therapy, 22,* 615–621.

Viirre, E., & Bush, D. (2002). Direct effects of virtual environments on users. In K. M. Stanney (Ed.), *Handbook of virtual environments: Design, implementation, and applications* (pp. 581–588). Mahwah, NJ: Lawrence Erlbaum Associates.

Vince, J. (1995). *Virtual reality systems* (SIGGRAPH Series). Wokingham, England: Addison-Wesley.

Vincelli, F. (1999). From imagination to virtual reality: the future of clinical psychology. *CyberPsychology & Behavior: The Impact of the Internet, Multimedia and Virtual Reality on Behavior and Society, 2*(3), 241–248.

Vincelli, F., Choi, Y. H., Molinari, E., Wiederhold, B. K., & Riva, G. (2000). Experiential cognitive therapy for the treatment of panic disorder with agoraphobia: Definition of a clinical protocol. *CyberPsychology & Behavior: The Impact of the Internet, Multimedia and Virtual Reality on Behavior and Society, 3,* 375–386.

Vincelli, F., & Molinari, E. (1998). Virtual reality and imaginative techniques in clinical psychology. In G. Riva, B. K. Wiederhold, & E. Molinari (Eds.), *Virtual environments in Clinical Psychology and Neuroscience.* Amsterdam: IOS Press.

Vincelli, F., & Riva, G. (2000, January). *Experiential cognitive therapy for the treatment of panic disorders with agoraphobia.* Proceedings of the Virtual Reality and Mental Health Symposium, Medicine Meets Virtual Reality Conference, Newport Beach, CA.

Virtual therapy. (1994, November/December). *Psychology Today,* p. 20.

VR Pain control (chap. 17). Retrieved April 2004, from http://www.hitl.washington.edu/research/burn/

Wald, J. L., Liu, L., & Reil, S. (2000). Concurrent validity of a virtual reality driving assessment for persons with brain injury. *CyberPsychology & Behavior, 3,* 643–654.

Watson, J. P., & Marks, I. M. (1971). Relevant and irrelevant fear and flooding— A crossover study of phobic patients. *Behavior Therapy, 2,* 257–293.

Watts, F. N., & Sharrock, R. (1984). Questionnaire dimensions of spider phobia. *Behaviour Research and Therapy, 22,* 575–580.

Weir, R. O., & Marshall, W. L. (1980). Relaxation and distraction in experimental desensitization. *Journal of Clinical Psychology, 36,* 246–252.

Weissman, M. M., Canino, G. J., Greenwald, S., Joyce, P. R., Karam, E. G., Lee, C. K., et al. (1995). Current rates and symptom profiles of panic disorder in six cross-national studies. *Clinical Neuropharmacology, 18*(Suppl. 2), S1–S6.

Welch, R. B., Blackmon, T. T., Liu, A., Mellers, B. A., & Stark, L. W. (1996). The effects of pictorial realism, delay of visual feedback, and observer interactivity on the subjective sense of presence. *Presence 5*(3), 263–273.

Wells, A. (1997). *Cognitive therapy of anxiety disorders. A practice manual and conceptual guide.* New York: Wiley.

Westra, H. & Stewart, S. H. (1998). Cognitive behavioural therapy and pharmacotherapy: Complimentary or contradictory approaches to the treatment of anxiety? *Clinical Psychology Review, 18,* 307–340.

Westra, H. A., Stewart, S. H., & Conrad, B. E. (2002). Naturalistic manner of benzodiazepine use and cognitive behavioral therapy outcome in panic disorder with agoraphobia. *Journal of Anxiety Disorders, 16,* 233–246.

Westwood, J. D., Hoffman, H. M., Robb, R. A., & Stredney, D. (1999). *Medicine meets virtual reality—The convergence of physical & informational technologies: Options for a new era in healthcare.* Amsterdam: IOS Press.

Whalley, L. J. (1993). Ethical issues in the application of virtual reality to the treatment of mental disorders. In J. Vince (Ed.), *Virtual reality systems* (pp. 273–288). Wokingham, England: Addison-Wesley.

Whang, L. S., Lee, S., & Chang, G. (2003). Internet over-users' psychological profiles: A behavior sampling analysis on Internet addiction. *CyberPsychology & Behavior, 6*(2) 143–150.

Wiederhold, B. K. (1999). A comparison of imaginal exposure and virtual reality exposure for the treatment of fear of flying.(Doctoral dissertation, California School of Professional Psychology, 1999). *Dissertations Abstracts International: Section B: The Sciences and Engineering, 60*(4-B), 1837.

Wiederhold, B. K., Davis, R., & Wiederhold, M. D. (1998). The effects of immersiveness on physiology. In G. Riva, B. K. Wiederhold, & E. Molinari (Eds.), *Virtual environments in clinical psychology and neuroscience: Methods and techniques in advanced patient–therapist interaction* (pp. 52–60). Amsterdam: IOS Press.

Wiederhold, B. K., Gevirtz, R. G., & Spira, J. L. (2001). Virtual reality exposure therapy vs. imagery desensitization therapy in the treatment of flying phobia. In G. Riva & C. Galimberti (Eds.), *Towards cyberpsychology: Mind, cognition, and society in the Internet age* (pp. 253–272). Amsterdam: IOS Press.

Wiederhold, B. K., Gevirtz, R., & Wiederhold, M. D. (1998). Fear of flying: A case report using virtual reality therapy with physiological monitoring. *CyberPsychology & Behavior: The Impact of the Internet, Multimedia and Virtual Reality on Behavior and Society, 1*(2), 97–104.

Wiederhold, B., Gronskya-Palesh, O., Miller, S., del Poso, J., & Wiederhold, M. (2000, January). *Physiological responses to virtual environments.* Proceedings of the Medicine Meets Virtual Reality Conference, Newport Beach, CA.

Wiederhold, B. K., Irvine, J. M., Israel, S. A., & Wiederhold, M. D. (2002, January). *Evaluating reactions to stress in virtual environments.* Proceedings of the VR and Mental Health Symposium, Medicine Meets Virtual Reality Conference, Newport Beach, CA.

Wiederhold, B. K., Jang, D. P., Gervitz, R. G., Kim, S. I., Kim, I. Y., & Wiederhold, M. D. (2002). The treatment of fear of flying: A controlled study of imaginal and virtual reality graded exposure therapy. *IEEE Transactions on Information Technology in Biomedicine, 6*(3), 218–223.

Wiederhold, B. K., Jang, D., Kaneda, M., Cabral, I., Lurie, Y., May, T., et al. (2001). An investigation into physiological responses in virtual environments: An objective measurement of presence. In G. Riva & C. Galimberti (Eds.), *Towards cyberpsychology: Mind, cognition, and society in the Internet age* (pp. 175–184). Amsterdam: IOS Press.

Wiederhold, B. K., Jang, D. P., & Wiederhold, M. D. (2002, January). *Refining the physiometric profile in virtual reality treat-*

ment. Proceedings of the VR and Mental Health Symposium, Medicine Meets Virtual Reality Conference, Newport Beach, CA.

Wiederhold, B. K., Rizzo, A., & Wiederhold, M. D. (1999, March). *An overview of virtual reality in clinical psychology and neuropsychology.* Proceedings of the California Psychological Association Conference, San Diego, CA.

Wiederhold, B. K., & Wiederhold, M. D. (1996). From virtual worlds to the therapist's office: Are virtual reality techniques useful tools in psychotherapy and diagnosis? *IEEE Engineering in Medicine and Biology, 15*(2), 44–46.

Wiederhold, B. K., & Wiederhold, M. D. (1998). A review of virtual reality as a psychotherapeutic tool. *CyberPsychology & Behavior: The Impact of the Internet, Multimedia and Virtual Reality on Behavior and Society, 1,* 45–52.

Wiederhold, B. K., & Wiederhold, M. D. (1999). Clinical observations during virtual reality therapy for specific phobias. *CyberPsychology & Behavior: The Impact of the Internet, Multimedia and Virtual Reality on Behavior and Society, 2,* 161–168.

Wiederhold, B. K., & Wiederhold, M. D. (2000). Lessons learned from 600 virtual reality sessions. *CyberPsychology & Behavior: The Impact of the Internet, Multimedia and Virtual Reality on Behavior and Society, 3,* 393–400.

Wiederhold, B. K., & Wiederhold, M. D. (2001). The use of virtual reality technology in the treatment of anxiety disorders. In M. Akay & A. Marsh (Eds.), *Information technologies in medicine: Vol. 2. Rehabilitation and treatment* (pp. 19–38). New York: John Wiley & Sons.

Wiederhold, B. K., & Wiederhold, M. D. (2003). Three-year follow-up for virtual reality exposure for fear of flying. *CyberPsychology & Behavior: The Impact of the Internet, Multimedia and Virtual Reality on Behavior and Society, 6,* 441–445.

Wiederhold, B. K., Wiederhold, M. D., Jang, D. P., & Kim, S. I. (2000). Use of cellular telephone therapy for fear of driving. *CyberPsychology & Behavior: The Impact of the Internet, Multimedia and Virtual Reality on Behavior and Society, 3,* 1031–1039.

Wiederhold, M. (1999, January). *Medical and psychological issues in VR therapy.* Proceedings from the Medicine Meets Virtual Reality Conference, San Francisco, CA.

Williams, S. L., & Rappoport, J. A. (1983). Cognitive treatment in the natural environment for agoraphobics. *Behavior Therapy, 14,* 299–313.

Winston, S. M. (1996, Fall). Acute stress disorder. *ADAA Reporter,* pp. 2, 19–21.

Witmer, B. G., & Singer, M. J. (1998). Measuring presence in virtual environments: A presence questionnaire. *Presence: Teleoperators and Virtual Environments, 7*(3), 225–240.

Wolpe, J. (1958). *Psychotherapy by reciprocal inhibition.* Palo Alto, CA: Stanford University Press.

Wolpe, J. (1962). Isolation of a conditioning procedure as the crucial psychotherapeutic factor: A case study. *Journal of Nervous and Mental Disease, 134,* 316–329.

Wolpe, J., Brady, J. P., Serber, M., Agras, W. S., & Liberman, R. P. (1973). The current status of systematic desensitization. *American Journal of Psychiatry, 130,* 961–965.

Wolpe, J., & Lang, P. J. (1964). A fear survey schedule for use in behavior therapy. *Behavior Research and Therapy, 2,* 27–30.

Woodbury, M. A. (1998, January). *Cognitive psychiatry: The development of our three-dimensional mode of mental representation and the construction of three-dimensional reality.* Proceedings of the Mental Health Symposium: Medicine Meets Virtual Reality Conference, San Diego, CA.

Index

A

Accident phobias, 117
Acrophobia
    clinical features, 157
    prevalence, 157
    treatment, 158–164
Addiction, 74–75
Adverse effects, 72
Agoraphobia, 27
    aviophobia and, 139
    claustrophobia and, 165
    clinical features, 102–103, 104–105
    computer-simulation treatment, 104
    conventional treatments 97–98
    driving phobia and, 147, 151–153
    panic disorder and, 103
    prevalence, 103
    videoconferencing with patients with, 58
    virtual reality therapy, 103–109
Animation, 50
Anxiety disorders
    assessment and diagnosis, 33, 35–38
    associated medical conditions, 33
    classification, 31
    clinical trials using virtual reality, 27
    concordance and synchrony model, 34–35
    early virtual reality applications in treatment, 13–15
    emotional processing theory, 34
    manifestations, 3, 4, 31, 33
    prevalence, 4
    risk factors, 31–32
    social costs, 4
    treatment methods, 4–5, 191
    See also specific disorder

Arachnophobia, 26
    clinical features, 173
    virtual reality therapy, 173–179
Assessment
    anxiety disorder diagnosis, 33, 35–38
    arousal/reported arousal, 55–57
    behavioral observation, 37–38
    cognitive functioning, 23–24
    contraindications to virtual reality therapy, 63, 69–71
    cybersickness risk, 66, 68–69
    elderly drivers, 154
    ethical practice, 90
    follow-up, 58, 72–74
    intake, 52
    panic disorder, 96
    patient progress, 54–55
    patient selection for virtual reality therapy, 51, 63
    physiological, 35–36, 52, 55–57, 65–66
    post-session observation, 66, 72, 85
    posttraumatic stress disorder, 117, 119, 122
    of presence, 84–86
    questionnaires, 36–37
    signs of dissociation during therapy, 50
    subjective ratings, 37, 53, 54–57
Ataxia, 71
Attention deficit disorder, 24
Augmented reality, 26
Avatar, 26, 89
Aviophobia
    agoraphobia and, 139
    clinical features, 139
    flight simulation software, 145–146
    prevalence, 139–140
    treatment, 140–146

Avoidance behaviors
  assessment, 36–37
  medical care and, 181–182
Avoidant personality disorder, social phobia
  and, 129–130, 136–138

B

Beck Depression Inventory, 36
Behavioral Avoidance Test, 36–37
Behavioral therapies, 5, 40–41
Benzodiazepines, 38–39
Beta-blockers, 38, 130
Biofeedback, 40–41, 174–175
Body dysmorphia, 24–25, 136
Breathing retraining, 40–41
  panic disorder treatment, 101
  in virtual reality therapy, 52
BT Steps, 113
Burn treatment, 185–187

C

Camara, Enrico, 14–15
Cancer treatment, 184–185
Cardiovascular disorders, 64–65, 70, 71
  anxiety disorder-associated, 33
Cardiovascular function
  measures of presence, 85
Carpal tunnel syndrome, 67
Cave Automatic Virtual Environment, 21–
  22, 159, 161–163, 192
Cerebrovascular function, 65, 187
Chemotherapy, 184–185
Children and adolescents, 74
  cancer treatment anxiety, 184
Chronic obstructive pulmonary disease, 70, 71
Claustrophobia, 73–74, 171
  agoraphobia and, 165
  clinical features, 165
  in MRI procedure, 169, 183–184
  precipitating conditions, 165
  prevalence, 165
  virtual reality therapy, 165–171
Clomipramine, 38
Cognitive–behavioral therapy
  anxiety disorder treatment, 191
  aviophobia treatment, 144–145
  glossophobia treatment, 130
  panic disorder treatment, 97–98
  pharmacotherapy and, 39
  phobia treatment, 128
  virtual reality therapy and, 44, 48–49
Cognitive functioning
  assessment, 23–24
  elderly driver assessment, 154
  experiential–cognitive therapy, 98–102
  neurorehabilitation, 187–188

virtual reality therapy techniques, 52–53,
  187–188
Cognitive restructuring, 39, 97
  in experiential–cognitive therapy for
    panic disorder, 101
Cognitive therapy, 39–40
Comfort, 83–84
Competence, therapist, 88, 192
Computers
  evolution of virtual reality technology,
    12–13
  for physiological assessment, 35–36
  in virtual reality technology, 15–16
  in virtual reality therapy, 5–6
Comorbidity, 33, 38, 96, 126, 169
Computer simulations, 104
Concordance, 34–35
Confidentiality, 89, 105
Contraindications to therapy, 63, 65, 69–71
Co-occurrence, 32, 127 See also Comorbidity
Culturally-sensitive practice, 92
  obsessive–compulsive disorder assess-
    ment, 111–112
Cybersickness, 21, 72, 91, 152–153, 155
  characteristics, 66–69
  incidence, 67, 68, 69
  pre-treatment assessment, 66
  strategies for avoiding, 66, 69

D

Data glove, 25–26, 116
Dentophobia, 181–182
Depression
  obsessive–compulsive disorder and, 111
  posttraumatic stress disorder and, 118,
    121
Desensitization, 6, 7, 41
  aviophobia treatment, 140
  in experiential–cognitive therapy, 98
  patient arousal for, 57
  physiological assessment of, 36
  in virtual reality therapy, 42
Digital cameras, 24
Dissociation during therapy, 50
Dissociative Experience Scale, 36, 51
Distraction techniques, 97–98, 185–187
Dizziness, 67, 70, 72
Driver retraining, 147, 153
Driving, fear of
  associated disorders, 147, 150–153
  treatment, 147–150, 151–155

E

Earthquake survivors, 123
Eating disorders, 24, 136
Elderly populations, 154
Electroencephalography, 65, 85

Emotional presence, 80–81
Emotional processing theory, 34, 43–44
Ethical practice, 92
    in assessment, 90
    confidentiality, 89
    in financial arrangements, 90
    informed consent, 91
    multiple relationships, 88–89
    professional guidelines, 87, 92
    research in cyberspace, 89
    therapist competency, 88
Experiential–cognitive therapy, 98–102
Explanation of VR techniques to patient, 53,
        91
Eye Movement Desensitization and
        Reprocessing, 127–128

F
Financial arrangements, 90
First session, 52
Follow-up, 58
    long-term effects of virtual reality expo-
        sure, 72–74
Force-feedback, 26

G
Genetic predisposition to anxiety disorders,
        31–32, 112
Glossophobia, 130–133
Graphics technology, 15–16

H
Hearing problems, 70–71
Heart attack, 33
Heilig, Morton, 11
Helicopter simulation, 119
Hodges, Larry, 15
Homework assignments, 52
    in experiential–cognitive therapy for
        panic disorder, 100
Howlett, Eric, 12
Hypertension, 33, 70, 71
Hyperventilation, 40, 49, 96
    in panic attacks, 101
Hypnosis, 127

I
Identity, 73
Image display, 16, 19
Imaginal exposure, 6–7, 41
    aviophobia treatment, 142–144
    patient capacity for, 128
    phobia treatment, 128
    vs. virtual reality therapy, 42–44, 48
Imipramine, 38
ImmersaDesk®, 22–24, 192
Informed consent, 65–66, 91

Intake, 51, 52
Internet virtual world, 26–27, 58, 89, 133,
        192
Intuition, 78
In vivo exposure, 5, 6, 7, 41
    acrophobia treatment, 159, 161
    arachnophobia treatment, 177–178
    aviophobia treatment, 140, 144
    claustrophobia treatment, 167–168
    panic disorder treatment, 97–98
    phobia treatment, 128
    vs. virtual reality therapy, 42–44, 49–50,
        105
IQ, 118

K
Krueger, Myron, 12, 13–14

L
Lamson, Ralph, 14, 15
Lanier, Jaron, 13
Larijani, L. Casey, 15
Locus of fear, 42
Long-term effects, 72–74

M
Magnetic resonance imaging, 169, 183–184
Maloney, Judith, 11
Manipulation of objects, 79
Medical procedures, 181–188
Memory
    false memory implantation, 74
    during virtual experience, 50
Migraine headaches, 63, 65, 69–70, 91
Monoamine oxidase inhibitors, 39
Motor vehicle accident survivors, 121–122
Musculoskeletal disorders, 70

N
Nausea, 67
Navigational skills in virtual environment, 79
Needle phobia, 182–183
Neurorehabilitation, 187–188
North, Max, 15, 104
North, Sarah, 15

O
Obsessive–compulsive disorder, 26, 73
    clinical features, 111–112
    culture-specific aspects, 111–112
    depression and, 111
    future research, 116
    neurophysiology, 112
    pharmacotherapy, 38
    prevalence, 111
    risk factors, 112–113
    treatment, 113–116

Occupational injury, 122
Olfactory cues, 83, 116

P
Pain management, 26, 48, 185–187
Panic disorder
    agoraphobia and, 103
    behavioral therapies, 40–41
    clinical features, 95, 96
    cognitive model, 101
    conventional treatments, 97–98
    diagnostic criteria, 95
    pharmacotherapy, 38–39
    phobias and, 126, 127
    posttraumatic stress disorder and, 121
    prevalence, 95–96
    risk factors, 32, 96–97
    symptom induction, 102
    virtual reality therapy, 98–102, 110
Patient classification, 55–57
Patient selection, 51
Personality traits
    computer simulation treatment perfor-
        mance and, 104
    social phobia risk, 129
Pharmacotherapy, 5, 38–39
    cybersickness prevention, 69
    glossophobia treatment, 130
    obsessive–compulsive disorder, 113, 116
    panic disorder, 97
    phobia treatment, 127
Phobias
    assessment, 37
    car accident-related, 150–151
    comorbidities, 126, 127
    concordance and synchrony model,
        34–35
    diagnostic criteria, 125
    early virtual reality treatment applica-
        tions, 14–15
    exposure therapies, 6–7, 41
    help-seeking behaviors, 41, 127
    locus of fear, 42
    physiological assessment, 36
    physiological response to virtual reality,
        79
    posttraumatic stress disorder and, 121
    prevalence, 126
    prognosis, 127
    risk factors, 31–32, 126–127
    subtypes, 125–126
    treatment, 6, 127–128
    See also specific phobia
Photic overstimulation, 70
Photographs, 2
Physiological response
    assessing potential for presence, 85

equipment for monitoring, 7, 83–84
    measurement, 193
    monitoring, 7, 58, 72, 193–194
    in obsessive–compulsive disorder, 112
    in patients with posttraumatic stress
        disorder, 120–121, 122
    pre-treatment screening, 65–66, 69–70
    real-time data analysis, 194
    self-reported immersion and, 79
    stress in virtual reality therapy, 64–65
    in virtual reality claustrophobia, 167–168
Posttraumatic stress disorder, 26, 54, 71, 83
    accident phobias and, 117, 147, 150, 151
    assessment, 117, 119, 122
    clinical features, 117
    comorbidities, 118, 121
    exposure therapy, 117
    in motor vehicle accident survivors,
        121–122
    natural disaster-related, 123
    prevalence, 118
    risk factors, 118
    treatment outcomes, 119
    treatment strategies, 119
    in Vietnam veterans, 118–121
    virtual reality therapy, 119–121, 122–124
    work injury-related, 122
Postural instability, 71, 155
Precautions, 71–72
Presence, 18, 193
    in acrophobia treatments, 161
    assessing potential for, 85
    clinical significance, 77, 86
    conceptual models of, 78
    definition, 77–78
    degree of realism in virtual experience
        and, 49–50, 79–80, 82
    in driving simulations, 154
    emotional aspects, 80–81
    in experience of reality, 78
    physiological response and, 79
    quantifying, 84–86
    social interaction and, 78
    strategies for increasing sense of, 82–84
    virtual reality research on, 81–84, 86
Propranolol, 130
Psychodynamic psychotherapy, 5
    virtual reality therapy and, 44
Psychophysiological Stress Profile, 52
Public speaking, fear of, 130–133

Q
Questionnaire on Presence and Realism, 36

R
Rape victims, 123
Rationale refutation, 53

Realism, 49–50, 73, 105, 193
    driving simulators, 149, 153, 154
    presence and, 79–80, 82
    strategies for increasing sense of, in
        virtual reality, 82–84
Relaxation procedures, 40, 41
    aviophobia treatment, 140–141
    claustrophobia treatment, 170
    preparation for virtual reality therapy, 51
Role-playing interventions, 15
    glossophobia treatment, 130–131
Rothbaum, Barbara, 15

S
Schizophrenia, 71, 73
Seizure disorders, 63, 65, 69–70
Self-Evaluation Questionnaire, 36
Serotonin reuptake inhibitors, 38
Setting. *See* Therapy setting
Shyness, 137
Side effects of therapy, 91. See also Cyber-
    sickness, 193
Simulated behavior therapy, 113
Simulator Sickness Questionnaire, 36, 66
Sleepiness, 67
Social anxiety disorder, 24
Social interaction
    concept of presence and, 78
    in internet virtual worlds, 89
    in virtual environments, 195
Social phobia, 26–27, 58, 73, 138
    avoidant personality disorder and, 129–
        130, 136–138
    body dysmorphia and, 136
    clinical features, 128
    fear of public speaking, 130–133
    generalized, 129–130
    prevalence, 129, 130
    risk factors, 129
    social skills training for, 134–136
    test anxiety, 134
    virtual reality therapy, 130–133, 134–136
Social skills training, 15, 134–136
Software, 15–16, 192
    costs, 19
    flight simulations, 145–146
    system compatibility issues, 19–21
    vendors, 20
Somatoform disorders, 136
Sopite syndrome, 67
Sound, 83
Special education, 194–195
State–Trait Anxiety Inventory, 36
Substance use, 65, 73
    posttraumatic stress disorder and, 118
    social phobia and, 128
Suicidal behavior/ideation, 128

Sutherland, Ivan, 12
Synchrony, 34–35, 54, 84

T
Tactile experience, 25–26, 59, 82–83
Tart, Charles, 14
Tele-presence, 16
Tellegen Absorption Scale, 36, 51
Temperature, 83
Test anxiety, 134
Therapeutic relationship
    multiple relationships, 88–89
    in virtual reality therapy, 44–45, 57, 58
Therapy setting, 24
    virtual reality rooms, 59–62
Thought stopping, 52–53
Tourette's syndrome, 112–113
Tracking device, 16
Treatment
    current approaches, 4–5, 38–41
    current virtual reality system applications,
        21–26, 27
    evolution of virtual reality technology for,
        12, 13–15, 27
    exposure techniques, 6–7, 40, 41
    See also Virtual reality therapy
Tricyclic antidepressants, 38

V
Vection, 67
Vertigo, 70
Vestibular disorders, 70
Videoconferencing, 58
Video games, 195
Vietnam veterans, 118–121
Virtual Reality Medical Center, 47–48, 51,
    54, 55, 66
Virtual reality technology, 11–13
    Cave Automatic Virtual Environment,
        21–22
    compatibility of systems, 19–21
    costs, 18, 19, 22, 191–192
    future prospects, 26–27
    ImmersaDesk® system, 22–24
    PC-based systems, 18–21
    presence, 18
    terminology, 15–16
    vendors, 20
Virtual reality therapy, 7–9
    acrophobia treatment, 158–164
    advantages, 5, 7, 42–44, 49, 75, 105, 110,
        191
    agoraphobia treatment, 103–109
    applications, 6, 48, 63, 71, 191, 193, 194–
        195, 196
    applications in medical procedures,
        181–188

Virtual reality therapy, *continued*
  arachnophobia treatment, 173–179
  assessment in, 35–38, 63
  aviophobia treatment, 141–146
  body dysmorphic disorder treatment, 136
  claustrophobia treatment, 165–171
  clinical context, 195–196
  clinical trends, 6, 196
  computer technology in, 5–6, 19
  contraindications, 63, 65, 69–71
  course of, 52–55
  dedicated rooms for, 59–62
  dissociation during, 50
  efficacy, 191
  equipment costs, 7, 191–192
  ethical practice, 87–92
  evolution of mental health applications,
    12, 13–15
  evolution of technology for, 11–13
  evolution of VRMC approach, 47–48
  explanation of techniques to patient, 53,
    91
  fear of driving interventions, 147–150,
    151–155
  fidelity to realism in, 49–50
  first session, 52
  follow-up, 58
  future prospects, 192–193, 194–196
  glossophobia treatment, 130–133
  inconveniences associated with, 192
  intake, 51, 52
  long-term effects, 72–74
  for neurorehabilitation, 187–188
  obsessive–compulsive disorder treatment,
    114–116
  panic disorder treatment, 98–102, 110
  patient classification for, 55–57
  patient control in, 91
  patient presence in, 50, 77
  patient selection for, 51
  personality factors in, 104
  physiological feedback in, 58
  physiological stress in, 64–65
  possible negative effects, 64
  post-session, 72, 85
  posttraumatic stress disorder treatment,
    119–121, 122–124
  precautions, 71–72, 75
  psychodynamic psychotherapy and, 44
  resources, 196
  side effects, 91, 193
  social phobia treatment, 130–131
  social skills training, 134–136
  test anxiety intervention, 134
  therapeutic relationship in, 44–45, 57, 58
  therapist competency for, 88, 192
  videoconferencing in, 58
  See also Virtual reality technology
Vision problems, 67, 70–71
VRMC. *See* Virtual Reality Medical Center

W
Wound care, 185–187

About the Authors

Brenda K. Wiederhold, MBA, PhD, BCIA, serves as Executive Director of the Virtual Reality Medical Center (VRMC), a professional medical corporation with offices in San Diego, Los Angeles, and Palo Alto, California, and as Chief Executive Officer of the Interactive Media Institute, a nonprofit organization dedicated to furthering the application of advanced technologies for patient care and training. She is also a professor in the Department of Psychiatry at the University of California at San Diego and a licensed clinical psychologist with national certification in both biofeedback and neurofeedback.

Mark D. Wiederhold, MD, PhD, FACP, serves as President of the Virtual Reality Medical Center (VRMC). He received a PhD in 1982 from the University of Illinois Medical Center in Pathology and completed his MD from Rush Medical College in 1987. He completed training in internal medicine and critical care medicine at the Scripps Clinic in La Jolla, California. He is editor-in-chief of the *CyberPsychology & Behavior Journal* and has over 200 publications.